An Arab - Syrian
Gentleman and Warrior

In the Period of the Crusades

Memoirs of Usamah ibn-Munqidh
(Kitab Al 'Itibar)

Translated By
Philip K. Hitti
Princeton University

Qadeem Press

Qadeem Press

Qadeem Press Edition
Breathing Life into Forgotten Pages
www.qadeempress.com

Originally Published by Columbia University Press in 1929
Reprinted by Qadeem Press in 2025

Find our titles on your favourite online bookstore using the keyword 'Qadeem Press'

Courtesy of Dr. T. Salloum, Hamah, Syria

A TOWER OF THE CASTLE OF SHAYZAR

One of the best preserved towers of the castle, as seen from the northeast.

PREFACE

THE initiative for the production of this work was taken by Professor Dana C. Munro, a lifelong friend of Usāmah, at whose suggestion the Editor of the "Records of Civilization" asked the writer to undertake a fresh study of the life and memoirs of Usāmah. A comparison of the photographic reproduction of folio 36 of the original manuscript, appearing at the end of Hartwig Derenbourg's *Texte arabe de l'autobiographie d'Ousāma* (Paris, 1886) with the corresponding pages 37–38 of the book convinced me of the suspect character of the published text and of the necessity of going back of it to the original copy of the manuscript. Through the good offices of the American Embassy at Madrid a photostatic reproduction of the original unique manuscript in the Escurial was procured. It is this copy that forms the basis of this work.

The thanks of the writer are due to many friends whose aid he solicited and received in reading the original text as well as in comprehending it and rendering it into English. Among these, special mention should be made of Amin Bey Kisbany, former secretary of King Feisal, whose intimate and first-hand knowledge of things Arabic served to illuminate many an obscure passage, Dr. Stephen J. Herben, of Princeton University, who generously advised me on terminology used in medieval warfare and armory, Professor Henry L. Savage, who helped in disentangling many verbal and technical knots in connection with falconry and the hunt, and, in particular, Professor Munro and the Editor of the series, who read the work through and offered a number of valuable criticisms.

Acknowledgment should also be made of the services of my wife, who read the proofs, sketched the map and prepared the index.

PHILIP K. HITTI

PRINCETON, NEW JERSEY
March, 1929

CONTENTS

PAGE

INTRODUCTION 3

SECTION I

WARS, TRAVELS AND OTHER EXPERIENCES

1. FIGHTING AGAINST THE FRANKS 25

Zanki's victory near Qinnasrīn, 25 The Byzantines and Franks besiege Shayzar, 25

2. USĀMAH'S FIRST SOJOURN IN DAMASCUS, 1138–1144 A.D. 28

3. USĀMAH IN EGYPT, 1144–1154 A.D. 30

Mutiny in the Egyptian army, 30 Ibn-al-Sallār's successful revolt against al-Ẓāfir, 31 Ibn-Masāl, the rival of ibn-al-Sallār, defeated, 32 The Fātimite caliph conspires to kill his vizier, 33 Usāmah saves a fugitive negro, 33 A forger beheaded, 34 The cooperation of Nūr-al-Dīn is sought against the Franks, 34 A curious Arab tribe at al-Jafr, 35 Lost in the desert, 37 The treasure bag lost, 38 Usāmah's interview with Nūr-al-Dīn, 39 The cleft at Petra Mosque, 39 An encounter with the Franks at 'Asqalān, 40. Another encounter on the way back from Bayt-Jibrīl, 41 An assault on Yubna, 42 Usāmah's brother killed, 42 Al-'Ādil murdered, 42 'Abbās becomes vizier, 44 The caliph instigates ibn-'Abbās against his father, 44 The caliph assassinated by his vizier, 45

Al-Ẓāfir's son proclaimed caliph, 46 Other members of the royal family put to death, 47 The watchman dies performing his duty, 47 'Abbās subdues the rebels, 47 'Abbās resolves to depart for Syria, 48 'Abbās prepares for the trip, 49 A conspiracy is hatched, 50 Usāmah wounded, 52 'Abbās killed by the Franks, 53 Perils at Petra, 53 Arrival in Damascus, 54 The story of a rich saddle belonging to Usāmah, 54 The unheeded example of al-Afḍal, 55 Usāmah on a mission to al-Afḍal, 56 Riḍwān imprisoned in Egypt, 58. Riḍwān killed by one of his own men, 58. Bloodletting saves the life of a wounded soldier, 59

4. USĀMAH'S SECOND SOJOURN IN DAMASCUS, 1154–1164 A.D. . 60

Usāmah's family pillaged by Franks on way from Egypt, 60.

5. BATTLES AGAINST FRANKS AND MOSLEMS 63

The cavalier's sense of honor Jum'ah avenges his honor, 63 A duel between two Moslem champions, 64 Fāris's miraculous escape from a deadly blow, 65 Usāmah's first experience in warfare against the Franks, 67. A Moslem cavalier survives a Frankish thrust which cuts his heart vein, 70.

PAGE

An artisan dies from a needle prick, 70 The exploits of al-Zamarrakal, the brigand, 70. Horse stealing, 73. The atābek appropriates for himself Usāmah's horse, 73 Fatal blows in unusual parts of the body In the throat, 74. In the chest of a mare, 74. In the bone of the lower arm, 75. Noteworthy lance thrusts One cuts ribs and elbow, 76 One cuts coat of mail, 76 One transpierces a Frankish knight, 77 One kills two horsemen at once, 78 One kills two horsemen and two horses, 78

Usāmah's father A warrior, 79 A Koran copier, 81 An exemplary attendant of Usāmah's uncle, 81 Usāmah's uncle stabbed in eyelid, 83 Acts of bravery by Usāmah's uncle and father, 84 A Frankish ruse on Shayzar foiled, 85 Usāmah and Jum'ah rout eight knights but are themselves routed by one footman, 86 The battle of Kafartāb Unexpected cures, 87 Narrow escape of Usāmah's cousin, 88. An unusual way of curing dropsy, 88 A falcon's eye cured in a strange way, 89 In flight before the Franks of Antioch, 90 Even Jum'ah flees, 91 Usāmah strikes the wrong man, 91 Jum'ah saves a farmer and his cow, 92 The high position enjoyed by the Frankish knights, 93 Tancred's guarantee of safety proves worthless, 94 Badrhawa the knight routs four Moslem cavaliers, 96.

Single-handed feats One knight charges a Moslem army, 97 One man carries away booty from eight men, 99 One Frank captures a cavern, 99 Usāmah's uncle ransoms a woman, 100 A maiden's ingenuity saves the day, 100 Other single-handed feats, 101 A stratagem by the governor of Aleppo, 105 Numayr storms a cavern in which Franks were hiding, 106 One man routs many near Rafaniyyah, 107 One man captures a whole castle, 107 Superiority among men in zeal A native Christian muleteer, 108. The fidelity of a Bedouin, 109 Usāmah ransoms captives, 110 Cases of miraculous escape An unsuccessful attempt at Āmid, 112 Delivered from the jaws of the lion, 113 Reason and warfare Think first, then act, 114 The consequences of ignorance An attempt to burn the Frankish camp, 115 A deacon inadvertently sets his church on fire, 115 Presence of mind when attacked by a lion, 116

Wise administrations The case of Usāmah's uncle, 117 The case of the lord of Diyār-Bakr, 117 The case of the lord of Badlīs, 118 The case of the lord of Ja'bar, 119 Courage of no avail in the case of destiny The case of ibn-Sarāya, 120 Usāmah's cousin saved by him, 121 Under Allah's protection An ascetic overlooked by the Franks, 121 The case of a Moslem captive ransomed by an unknown man, 122 An angel comes to the succor of Usāmah, 123 The Prophet comes to the rescue of a prisoner, 123 Fighting for heavenly reward A jurisconsult and an ascetic, 124 Fighting because of loyalty Fāris the Kurd, 124

Stories of horses An enduring horse, 126 A horse with its heart cut carries its rider, 127 Another feels normal with three wounds, 127 Usāmah's horse fails him on account of a little scratch, 127 Ṭirād's horse does not give up with its entrails out, 128 Always prepared for battle Usāmah's case, 129. Testing Usāmah's presence of mind, 130

6. Adventures with Lions and Other Wild Animals . 133

A glimpse into Usāmah's breeding, 133 How men differ A weak Turkoman, 134 A hornet's sting proves fatal to a miller, 135 A slave singled out by a lion, 135 Usāmah's experience with a fearless lion, 136 A lion flees before a sheep, 137 A dog saves its master from a lion, 137 All animals fear the lion, 138 Kills a lion but is killed by a scorpion, 138 The habits of the lion as studied by Usāmah, 139 Usāmah and his companions riddle a leopard, 139. A leopard jumps from a church window and kills a

PAGE

Frank, 140. Distinction between a leopard and a cheetah, 141. A leopard turned loose in a lord's sitting room, 141. An adventure with a tiger, 141.

7. OTHER WAR EXPERIENCES 143

Byzantine mangonels at the siege of Shayzar, 143. The unlucky march of the Franks against Damascus, 144 A Kurd carries his brother's head as a trophy, 145 Blows of sharp swords: One breaks an Ismā'īlite skull, 146 Usāmah's blow cuts a blade and a forearm, 146 Usāmah's father cuts his groom's outfit and arm with a sheathed sword, 147 Two blows kill two men, 147 Heroic deeds by women, 148 Baldwin succeeds Roger in Antioch, 148 Ṭughdakīn beheads Robert, 149 Baldwin exempts Usāmah's uncle from payment of an indemnity, 150 Baldwin cedes Antioch to Bohemond's son, 150 Bohemond II in battle against Usāmah's people, 150. An encounter with the son of Bohemond, 151 The story of Buraykah, 152. A woman warrior in Shayzar, 153 Usāmah's mother as a warrior, 154. An aged maid also fights, 154 Usāmah's grandmother gives him wise advice, 154 The piety of Usāmah's grandmother, 156 'Ali, the far-sighted, is killed by his wife for his betrayal of the Moslem cause, 156 A Frankish woman inflicts a wound on a Moslem with her jar, 158. A Shayzar woman captures three Franks, 158 Prefers to be a Frankish shoemaker's wife to life in a Moslem castle, 159 A Frank and his children revert to Christianity, 160

8. AN APPRECIATION OF THE FRANKISH CHARACTER . . . 161

Their lack of sense, 161 Their curious medication, 162 Newly arrived Franks are especially rough· One insists that Usāmah should pray eastward, 163 Another wants to show to a Moslem God as a child, 164 Franks lack jealousy in sex affairs, 164 Another curious case of medication, 166 A funny race between two aged women, 167 Their judicial trials A duel, 167 Ordeal by water, 168 A Frank domesticated in Syria abstains from eating pork, 169

9. SUNDRY EXPERIENCES AND OBSERVATIONS 171

Unusual forms of weakness. Usāmah's uncle scared by a mouse, 171. A hero scared by a snake, 171 Trifles may lead to serious results Loose reins, 172 No stirrup, 172 Usāmah hurt more by a hyena than by lions, 173 One man faints at the sight of gushing blood, 174 Another would faint at the sight of bloodletting, 175 Strong spirits A negro saws his own leg, 175 One afflicted with dropsy is cured by slashing his abdomen, 176. Frankish knights take a part of Shayzar unawares, but are repulsed, 177. A Moslem captive drowns herself, 179 The value of stratagem in warfare. A ruse against the army of Damascus, 180 Usāmah tries a ruse against the army of Kafartāb, 181 Disadvantages of excessive audacity Usāmah recovers stolen calico, 182. Usāmah's party loses some of its members through inexperience, 183 Ambition as the cause of heroic adventure· The case of al-Sawr, 185 The case of al-Bāri'ah, 186 The ferocity of Ṣalāḥ-al-Dīn Muḥammad He cuts one of his men in two, 186. Another is halved, 187. He cuts the beard of an old man, 188 He takes captive people of the covenant, 189 The Ismā'īlites in Shayzar, 190. Reflections by Usāmah on old age, 190. The duration of life is predetermined The case of a Shayzar man cut by an Ismā'īlite, 192. Another survives a deep gash in his face, 193 The burden of old age, 194. A eulogy of Saladin, 195.

SECTION II

RARE ANECDOTES

PAGE

1. Stories of Holy Men 202

Al-Basri's clairvoyance, 202. A man in Kūfah hears a voice from Ḥamāh, 202 The wish of a dying sheikh granted, 203 A man at Ma'arrah is conscious of the death of one at Mecca, 204 Dreams come true 'Ali removes a tumor from a custodian of one of his mosques, 205 The Prophet sends a poor man to Malik-Shāh, 206 The Prophet sends a father of three daughters to the caliph's vizier, 207 A paralyzed man miraculously healed by 'Ali, 208. Prayer answered. A reward for honesty, 210.

2. Noteworthy Cures 213

A carbuncle removed by supping a raw egg, 213. Hernia cured by eating ravens, 213 Dropsy cured by vipers in vinegar, 214 Marvelous cures by ibn-Butlān, 215 Usāmah's cold cured by Indian melon, 217 Colic cured by a dream, 217

SECTION III

USĀMAH'S HUNTING EXPERIENCES

1. Hunting in Syria, Mesopotamia and Egypt . 222

Usāmah's father as a hunter, 222 Hunting with Zanki, 222 Hunting in Damascus, 224 Chase in Egypt, 224 Hunting in 'Akka, 226 Hunting in Ḥiṣn-Kayfa, 226. The hunt with Nūr-al-Dīn, 226

2. Usāmah's Father as a Hunter 228

Al-Yaḥshūr, 232 A remarkable cheetah, 236 The red-eyed falcon, 238 A Frankish falcon, 239 A young shahin, 240 Hunting dogs, 241 A hunting trip interrupted by the return of the Franks, 243 An Arab mare contrasted with a hackney, 243 A teacher's scruples against killing birds, 244 Hunting hares, 244 A starling caught by a falcon, 245 Hunting geese and bustards, 245 The '*aymah*, 246 A lion scared by a falcon, 246 Watching the fishermen, 247 Ghanā'im, the falconer, 247 Hunting wild asses, 248 Someone afraid the falcon would drown, 249 Birds have their fates, too, 250 Hunting the wild boar, 251 An indefatigable mameluke, 252 Playing chess on a bitch, 253 Hunting according to a system, 253. Hunting gazelles and francolins, 253 Epilogue, 254.

The End of the Book 255

Index 259

ILLUSTRATIONS

A Tower of the Castle of Shayzar . . . . . *Frontispiece*

Facsimiles of Folios 37a and 37b of the Manuscript 22, 23

The Castle of Shayzar 178

Map of Places Visited by Usāmah 257

INTRODUCTION

INTRODUCTION[1]

Usāmah was a warrior, a hunter, a gentleman, a poet and a man of letters. His life was an epitome of Arab civilization as it flourished during the early crusading period on Syrian soil. He was a flower of the Arab-Syrian chivalry which found its full bloom later in his patron and friend, the great Saladin.

The *Memoirs* of Usāmah are a unique piece of Arabic literature. They open before our eyes a wide and new vista into medieval times and constitute an invaluable contribution to our knowledge of Arabic culture, in itself as well as in its relation to Western thought and practice.

Three months before Urban II delivered his speech at Clermont, judged by its memorable consequences one of the most effective speeches in all history, a boy was born, Sunday, Jumāda II 27, 488 (July 4, 1095), in Shayzar, northern Syria, to one of the Munqidhite amīrs, the lords of the castle on the Orontes. This boy was destined to take a prominent part in the future defense of the castle against the Franks and to become himself the most illustrious member of a distinguished family, many of whose members attained national and even international reputation. This boy was Usāmah, the hero of our story.

About fifteen miles north of Ḥamāh (Epiphania), on the north end of the rocky slope by which the valley of the Orontes is bounded on the east, stands the picturesque and strategic Castle of Shayzar.

[1] The following is a partial bibliography for this Introduction Ibn-al-Athīr, *al-Kāmil fi al-Ta'rīkh*, ed Tornberg (Leyden and Upsala, 1851–74, 13 vols), vols II, VII, VIII, IX, X, XI, XII, and in *Recueil des historiens des croisades historiens orientaux* (Paris, 1872–1906, 5 vols), vols I–III, abu-Shāmah, *Kitāb al-Rawḍatayn fi Akhbār al-Dawlatayn* (Cairo, 1287 A H , 2 vols), and in *Recueil des historiens des croisades historiens orientaux*, vols IV, V; ibn-'Asākir, *al-Ta'rīkh al-Kabīr* (Damascus, 1329–32 A H , 5 vols), vol II, ibn-Khallikān, *Ta'rīkh* (Cairo, 1299 A H , 3 vols), vols I, II = de Slane, *Ibn-Khallikān's Biographical Dictionary* (Paris, 1842–71, 4 vols), Ṣāliḥ ibn-Yaḥya, *Ta'rīkh Bayrūt*, ed Cheikho (Beirūt, 1902); Yāqūt, *Mu'jam al-Buldān*, ed Wüstenfeld (Leipzig, 1866–70, 6 vols), vol III, 'Imād-al-Dīn al-Kātib, *Kharīdah al-Qaṣr*, extract by Hartwig Derenbourg (Paris, 1887), al-Dhahabi, *Ta'rīkh al-Islām*, extract by Derenbourg (Paris, 1887), Derenbourg, *Anthologie de textes arabes inédits par Ousāma et sur Ousāma* (Paris, 1893), and the same appended to Derenbourg, *Ousāma Ibn Mounkidh . vie d'Ousāma* (Paris, 1889), pp 499–605

The steep ridge on which it stands is described by Arab authors as *'urf al-dīk*, "the cock's crest." The Orontes (al-'Āṣi) issues here from a rocky, narrow gorge, and, after skirting the contour of the hill on almost three sides, it continues its way in an attempt to regain its normal northward course.

Shayzar is one of the most ancient towns of that ancient land, Syria. It figures under the names *Senzar* and *Sezar* in the inscriptions of Thutmose III and Amenhotep II [2] and in the Tell-el-Amarna letters. It is the *Sidzara* of the ancient Greeks and the *Sezer* of the Byzantines. Some of the Western historians of the Crusades, including William of Tyre, refer to it as *Caesarea*, or *Caesarea ad Orontem* ("Caesarea-on-the-Orontes"), to distinguish it from other Caesareas. In the latter part of the fourth century before our era, Seleucus I settled colonists in it from Larissa in Thessaly and rechristened it after the name of that town, but the old name reasserted itself in Arabic *Shayzar*. In this form it occurs in a widely quoted verse by the pre-Islamic poet Imru'-al-Qays. Sayjar is the colloquial form of the name of the present-day village which lies wholly inside of the walls of the historic castle, still crowning a hill precipitously rising above the Orontes on its western bank.

An invading army entering Syria from the north would find before it two routes to follow. It could take the route of the maritime plain southward via al-Lādhiqiyyah (Laodicea) and the Phoenician littoral, as Alexander and some of the early Assyrian conquerors did; or, if it took the inland route, it would soon find itself following the Orontes valley and hemmed in on the west by the Nuṣayriyyah mountains, of which the western range of Lebanon is but a southern continuation. In the latter case, access to the sea could be effected only at the pass separating the Nuṣayriyyah from the Lebanon Mountain, or, further south, at the termination of the Lebanon; and the army following this inland route southward, as many of the crusading armies did, would find its passage obstructed by Afāmiyah (Apamea) and its southern sister, the Castle of Shayzar. Likewise an invading army from the south, as in the case of the Egyptian armies of Thutmose and Ramses, could not attempt the conquest of the inland without passing by and

[2] James Henry Breasted, *Ancient Records of Egypt* (University of Chicago Press, 1906), vol. II, §§ 584, 314.

subduing Shayzar. Hence the strategic importance of the position of that castle.

In the year 17 A.H. (638 A.D.) abu-'Ubaydah, the conqueror of Syria for the Moslem Arabs, received the capitulation of Shayzar, whose people "went out to meet him, bowing before him and accompanied by players on the tambourines and singers,"[3] but the town for many centuries after that passed, like a football, from Arab to Byzantine and from Byzantine to Arab hands. In the year 999 Basil II (976–1025) subdued it, and for the next eighty-one years it remained in Byzantine possession.

About 1025 Ṣāliḥ al-Mirdāsi, the governor of Aleppo, granted the Munqidhites, of the tribe of banu-Kinānah, the feudal land around Shayzar. In 1041 we find a Munqidhite, Muqallad, ruling over Kafarṭāb. Later his successor, abu-al-Mutawwaj Muqallad ibn-Naṣr, extended his territory down to the Orontes and probably built the Citadel of the Bridge (Ḥiṣn al-Jisr) at the bridgehead below Shayzar; but the town itself, Shayzar, remained in the hands of the Byzantines until December 19, 1081, when 'Izz-al-Dawlah Sadīd-al-Mulk (the grandfather of Usāmah) succeeded in acquiring it from the Emperor Alexius Comnenus. This Sadīd-al-Mulk was therefore the real founder of the Munqidhite dynasty in Shayzar. Upon his death in the following year, he was succeeded by his pious son, 'Izz-al-Dawlah abu-al-Murhaf Naṣr, a peaceful and art-loving prince, under whom the territory of Shayzar included for a time Afāmiyah, Kafartāb and al-Lādhiqiyyah by the sea. Even at that time the Byzantines had not ceased to cast a covetous eye on Shayzar; for we find them during his rule besieging the castle more than once, but always unsuccessfully.

Abu-al-Murhaf died childless in 1098 and the lordship of the castle passed to his younger brother, Majd-al-Dīn abu-Salāmah Murshid (1068–1137), the father of Usāmah. But this pious man, who was more interested in the hunt and calligraphy than in politics and government, declined in favor of his youngest brother, 'Izz-al-Dīn abu-al-'Asākir Sulṭān, with a remark which gives us a clue to his whole character: "I shall not, by Allah, accept the lordship, as I would rather make my exit from this world in the same

[3] Al-Balādhuri, in Philip K. Hitti, *Origins of the Islamic State* (Columbia University Press, 1916), pp. 201–2.

condition as I made my entrance into it." [4] It is this Sulṭān, now the lord of the castle and the head of the family, who figures prominently in the early life of our Usāmah.

During Sulṭān's amīrate, Shayzar was the object of frequent raids by the banu-Kilāb of Aleppo, the Franks, the Ismā'īlites and other enemies, all of whom failed to reduce the stronghold. After laying siege to it from April 20 to May 21, 1138, and bombarding it for ten days in succession, Emperor John Comnenus had to withdraw. Its position rendered it impregnable to such attacks. It stood on a steep ridge, with the river enveloping it on the north and east and with the site of the castle cut off by a deep moat from the high plateau which formed its continuation. In addition the only passage across the river was the stone bridge, the Jisr bani-Munqidh, which was now defended by a citadel.

Usāmah was an eyewitness to many of these events. In his account the upper town (al-Balad = the *praesidium, oppidum, pars superior civitatis* of European sources) lay within the Qal'ah (the Castle), the fortifications of which were evidently strongest on the north and south sides, as these are the sides best preserved to our day. It had only three gates, one of which, leading to the Jisr (the Bridge), formed the only entrance to the castle. The Jisr, the *Gistrum* of European sources, was guarded by a citadel (Ḥiṣn al-Jisr) and around it grew the lower town (al-Madīnah = *suburbium, pars inferior civitatis*). Sulṭān's period of rule furnishes the background for most of the interesting events in Usāmah's *Memoirs*, and it is that period which the *Memoirs* immortalize.

Sulṭān died in, or a little before, 1154 and was succeeded by his son, Tāj-al-Dawlah Nāṣir-al-Dīn Muḥammad, the last of the Munqidhites. Tāj-al-Dawlah perished with almost all the members of his family in a terrific earthquake which overtook them in the midst of a festival and which almost destroyed Shayzar, Afāmiyah, Kafarṭāb and their environs. His wife, who was pulled out from the ruins in which she was buried, was evidently the only Munqidhite to survive the tragedy. This earthquake took place in 552/1157 and was known as the Earthquake of Ḥamāh. Ibn-al-Athīr [5] tells us that a school-teacher in Ḥamāh, who happened to be outside

[4] *Al-Rawḍatayn*, vol I, pp 111–12.

[5] In *Recueil: historiens orientaux*, vol. I, pp. 503–6, and vol. II, pt. II, p. 200.

the school building when the trembling took place, received no inquiry whatever from any parent regarding the fate of any child. Not one parent and not one child survived.

The destruction of Tāj-al-Dawlah and his children closed the last page in the Munqidhite chapter of the history of Shayzar. The stronghold, however, was in the same year repaired and taken possession of by Nūr-al-Dīn of Damascus.

To return to Sulṭān and young Usāmah. As long as Sultān had no male children he took keen interest in Usāmah and presided over his military education, singling him out from among his three brothers, one of whom was older than Usāmah. He often gave him advice regarding the conduct of warfare, intrusted to his care important missions (see *infra*, p. 177) and made attempts to probe his presence of mind during combat (*infra*, p. 130). But when Sulṭān was blessed with male heirs his attitude towards his young protégé changed, and his jealousy led Usāmah in 1129 to leave Shayzar for a time. He later returned, but the death of his father, the brother of Sulṭān, on May 30, 1137, resulted in his definitive departure the following year.

Next to Sultān's influence, the paternal influence of the father was apparently the strongest single force in Usāmah's life. The picture Usāmah has left us in his *Memoirs* of his father is that of a devout Moslem who "employed all his time reading the Koran, fasting and hunting during the day, and copying the Book of Allah at night" (*infra*, p. 228. Cf. p. 242). His chief diversions were falconry and the chase, in which he excelled. Usāmah knew nobody comparable to his father in this respect (*infra*, p. 228). And withal he was no coward or weakling. "It is in my horoscope," once he declared to his son, "that I should feel no fear" (*infra*, p. 85). One of the very rare seemingly incredible stories told by Usāmah relates how his father in a fit of anger struck his groom with a sheathed sword, with such force that the sword cut through "the outfit, the silver sandal, a mantle and a woolen shawl which the groom had on, and then cut through the bone of the elbow" (*infra*, p. 147). His physical strength was apparently commensurate with his moral courage.

Of special interest to us are the remarks which throw light on Usāmah's training by his father. The young boy once climbed the wall of their courtyard and, under the very eyes of the father, cut off with a knife the head of a serpent which had suddenly made its appearance on the wall (*infra*, p. 133). When only ten years old he killed a servant of his father without seeming to bring forth any special discipline from his father (*infra*, p. 174). "I never saw my father . . . forbid my taking part in a combat or facing a danger" (*infra*, p. 133), is the way Usāmah sums it up, citing only one exception: a hazardous onslaught on a lion (*infra*, p. 134). When certain Frankish and Armenian hostages held in Shayzar were on their way back home and were waylaid by some Moslem horsemen, the father's instructions to the son were especially significant: "Pursue the ambuscade with thy men, hurl yourselves on them and deliver your hostages" (*infra*, p. 133). The words "hurl yourselves" especially impressed Usāmah.

Usāmah seems to have been bound to his father by strong bonds of filial affection and regard. He touchingly remarks, after making an excursus relating to his father's interest in copying the Koran, "My book does not require the mention of this fact. But I did mention it in order to appeal to those who read my book to solicit Allah's mercy upon my father" (*infra*, p. 81).

Usāmah's mother was made of the stuff of which "mothers of men" are made (*infra*, p. 156). One instance opens before us a window through which we can look into her character and life. In an emergency, and when the male members of the family were away, she got hold of her son's weapons, distributed them among those who could fight, put her daughter (an elder sister of Usāmah) at the balcony of the castle and herself sat at the entrance to the balcony ready to throw her daughter over rather than to see her in the hands of the Ismā'īlites, "the peasants and ravishers" (*infra*, p. 154).

Such was the spiritual environment in which the soul of Usāmah unfolded itself.

Inured to hardihood and struggle and nurtured in the best atmosphere of Syrian chivalry, Usāmah, with his passion for adventure, adaptability and many-sidedness, grew up to a robust and military manhood. The land around his native town, unlike the Northern Syria of today, contained many lions, panthers, hyenas and other ferocious animals. The period in which he lived bristled with problems, difficulties and struggles with the Franks, Ismā'īlites, Bāṭinites and other Arabs, keeping the scene lively and busy. Even when they went out of Shayzar for the hunt, they went out armed, for they "never felt secure on account of the Franks whose territory was adjacent" to theirs (*infra*, p. 230). Thus Usāmah's name has become associated in Arabic annals with war and heroism. Al-Dhahabi calls him "a veritable hero of Islam."[6] Ibn-al-Athīr attributes to him "a degree of valor to which there is no limit."[7] When still a tyro he fought valiantly and successfully against the Franks (*infra*, p. 68). In and around Shayzar and Ḥamāh of Northern Syria, in 'Asqalān and Bayt-Jibrīl of Palestine, in the Sinaitic peninsula and Egypt, in al-Mawṣil and Diyār-Bakr he took part in battles against Franks and Arabs, Christians and Moslems. "How many sword cuts and lance thrusts have I received! How many wounds with darts and arbalest stones have been inflicted on me!" (*infra*, p. 194) exclaims Usāmah in his old age, and this was probably no mere rhetorical exclamation; for he lived in one of the most turbulent periods in the history of that land in which more military history has probably been enacted than in any other land of equal size. Even in his old age he laments his passive life and covets action:

> But now I have become like an idle maid who lies
> On stuffed cushions behind screens and curtains.
> I have almost become rotten from lying still so long, just as
> The sword of Indian steel becomes rusty when kept long in its sheath.
> (*Infra*, p 191.)

And through it all, Usāmah took his defeat, as he took his victory, with no sense of individual pride or personal resentment but with utter resignation and as an unavoidable execution of the divine will. To him, as to all true Moslems, it is Allah who giveth victory or defeat to whomsoever he willeth, and who predetermineth the lengths of ages (*infra*, pp. 177, 192). The reaction of such a philosophy of life on his own behavior can hardly be overestimated.

And in his dealings with his adversaries, Usāmah astounds us with his sense of chivalry and fairness. "This is not fair," was his terse and uncompromising reply to his companion, who evidently

[6] *Duwal al-Islām* (Ḥayderābād, 1337 A H.), vol II, p 71.
[7] *Atābeks* in *Recueil. historiens orientaux*, vol. II, pt. II, p. 207.

suggested resort to a stratagem, as they sighted at a distance a band of eight Frankish knights. "We should rather make an open assault on them, both thou and I" (*infra*, p. 86). And no sooner does he conclude recounting this experience, in which he and his companion routed eight knights, to his credit, than he starts the narration of another one, on the debit side, in which he and his companion were routed by one footman.

When not engaged in fighting human adversaries, Usāmah had animals and wild beasts to fight. "I have battled against beasts of prey on occasions so numerous that I cannot count them all" (*infra*, p. 139), he tells us about himself. On another occasion he informs us that he was engaged in the hunt during a period of about "seventy years" (*infra*, p 254). Referring to Usāmah, the Fāṭimite Caliph al-Ḥāfiẓ once remarked, "And what other business has this man but to fight and to hunt?" (*infra*, p. 225).

This long record as a hunter offered Usāmah an excellent opportunity to study the habits of birds and other animals. His powers of observation, his keen interest in things animate and inanimate, and his sense of curiosity found here an ample field for exercise and development. At the end of his *Memoirs* he devotes a whole chapter (*infra*, Section III, pp. 219 *seq.*) to the hunt in which he shows first-hand familiarity with the hunting practices of Syria, Mesopotamia and Egypt. He felt equally at home with the waterfowl of the Nile, the fish of the Euphrates and the wild animals on the banks of the Orontes. By his own experience he discovered that a leopard, on account of its swiftness and long leaps, is really more dangerous than a lion, that a lion tends to go back to a thicket by the same route it took out of it, and that "it becomes the real lion it is" when wounded (*infra*, p. 139). When a Frank in Ḥaifa offered to sell him a "cheetah," which was in reality a leopard, he could tell the difference right away from the shape of the head and the color of the eyes (*infra*, p. 141).

At last it was his intrepidity, as manifested in a hunting experience, that brought him into trouble with his ruling uncle and aroused the latter's jealousy, resulting in Usāmah's enforced and lifelong exile from his native place, Shayzar. His departure in 1138 was the beginning of a series of sojourns that carried him into the capitals of the Moslem world — Damascus, Jerusalem, Cairo, al-Mawṣil, Mecca — and that did not end until he was an octogenarian. As young Usāmah one evening entered the town carrying as trophy the head of a huge lion which he bagged, his grandmother [8] met him and warned him against his uncle, assuring him that such a thing would alienate him from his uncle, instead of endearing him to his heart (*infra*, p. 156). This episode proved "the last straw" and tolled the death-knell of Usāmah's life in Shayzar.

With all that, Usāmah shows a remarkable degree of self-restraint and hardly has an unkind word against his uncle in all his narrative. And when finally in the year 552/1157, Shayzar was destroyed by the earthquake, and his cousin, Sulṭān's son, perished with his family, Usāmah's heart was evidently deeply moved with sorrow and sympathy. He wrote a touching elegy in verse in which he said:

> The blood of my uncle's children, like that of my father's children, is my blood,
> Notwithstanding the hostility and hatred they showed me.[9]

That Usāmah was brought up in a wholesome atmosphere of gallant and aristocratic behavior — in spite of the aforementioned episode — is evinced by various other instances. His grandfather and uncles are often referred to by the Arab chronicles as "the Kings of Shayzar." One uncle was a high official in the Fāṭimite court of Egypt (*infra*, p. 239). Usāmah's own son, Murhaf, became later "one of the amīrs" of Egypt and a table companion and comrade-at-arms of the illustrious Saladin. It was evidently this Murhaf who pleaded the case of his octogenarian and forsaken father before Saladin, who consequently summoned Usāmah, in the year 1174, from Ḥiṣn-Kayfa and installed him in a palace in Damascus. Ṣāliḥ ibn-Yaḥya [10] tells us that Usāmah was "one of those treated as great [*min al-mu'aẓẓamīn*] by the Sultan [Saladin] who put no one above him in matters of counsel and advice." Saladin appointed him governor of Beirūt, which he soon after delivered into the hands of the Franks without offering resistance. A nephew of Usāmah, Shams-al-Dawlah, was sent by Saladin in 1190 as his ambassador extraordinary to the court of the Almohades

[8] "His mother" according to ibn-al-Athīr, *Atābeks* in *Recueil historiens orientaux*, vol II, pt II, pp 199–200, quoted by *al-Rawḍatayn*, vol I, p 112

[9] *Al-Rawḍatayn*, vol I, p. 106.

[10] *Ta'rīkh*, pp. 35–36.

(al-Muwaḥḥidūn) in Morocco, to solicit the aid of their fleet to intercept the maritime communications of the Franks.

Usāmah's sense of chivalry is attested by other incidents of his life. When a woman who was foisted on Usāmah's uncle, Sulṭān, and was divorced by him because she turned out to be dumb and deaf, fell captive into the hands of the Franks, Sulṭān did not hesitate to ransom her, for he could not tolerate the idea of a woman remaining in the hands of the Franks after uncovering before him (*infra*, p. 100). The Christian hostages released from Shayzar and waylaid by Moslems from Ḥamāh had to be rescued at all costs (*infra*, p. 133).

Amidst the court intrigues of the Fāṭimites in Egypt (and no royal court was perhaps more rife with intrigues, feuds and jealousies than that court), of Nūr-al-Dīn in Damascus and of Zanki in al-Mawṣil, Usāmah seems to have kept his hands more or less unsoiled Ibn-al-Athīr [11] charges him with duplicity in his dealings and with instigating the murder of al-'Ādil ibn-al-Sallār, the vizier of al-Ẓāfir, but in the *Memoirs*, Usāmah's influence seems on the whole to be on the side of what is right and honorable. When the ferocity of Ṣalāḥ-al-Dīn Muḥammad leads him to order the cutting in two of an innocent man, Usāmah is not afraid to plead the cause of the poor victim (*infra*, p. 187). Nor does he hesitate to intercede in behalf of a captive from Māsurra who was condemned to undergo the same punishment in the holy month of Ramaḍān (*infra*, p. 188). An aged slave, who had brought him up, Usāmah addresses as "mother" and devotes an apartment in his home to her exclusive use (*infra*, p. 218). In our own day, students at the American University of Beirūt, and even professors, always refer to the aged gatekeeper, who has been for many years in the service of the institution, as 'Ammi (uncle) As'ad.

Usāmah's liberal education consisted of some ten years of study under private tutors whose curriculum comprised grammar, calligraphy, poetry and the Koran (*infra*, pp. 237–8). Poetry formed an essential part of the mental equipment of an educated Arabian aristocrat, and to this rule Usāmah was no exception. He is quoted by al-Dhahabi [12] as having said that he knew by heart "over

[11] *Al-Kāmil*, vol XI, p 122.
[12] Extract appended to Derenbourg, *Vie d'Ousāma*, p. 595.

twenty thousand verses of pre-Islamic poetry." It is not likely that so many verses of pre-Islamic poetry had survived to the time of Usāmah, but the writer simply wanted to convey the impression that Usāmah knew a great many of them.

Nor was Usāmah a mere *rāwi*, a memorizer and reproducer of poems. He was a composer himself. In fact, to many of his biographers he is known primarily through his *Dīwān* (anthologies). Ibn-'Asākir, the historian of Damascus who knew Usāmah personally, calls him "the poet of the age" and describes his verse as "sweeter than honey and more to be relished than slumber after a prolonged period of vigilance."[13] Yāqūt in his *Mu'jam*[14] quotes his poetry. Ṣāliḥ ibn-Yaḥya[15] boasts of possessing a copy of Usāmah's *Dīwān* in the latter's own handwriting. "Especially fond of his poetry" was Saladin, who esteemed it so highly as to have kept with him a copy of Usāmah's *Dīwān*.[16]

Among the most quoted verses of Usāmah are those he composed and inscribed on the wall of a mosque in Aleppo[17] on the occasion of his return from a pilgrimage to the holy cities of Mecca and Medīnah, and those he composed on the occasion of pulling out his tooth and in which he showed some originality:

O what a rare companion I had whose company never brought ennui
to me,
Who suffered in my service and struggled with assiduity!
Whilst we were together I never saw him, but the moment he made
his appearance
Before my eyes, we parted forever.[18]

Usāmah "had a white hand in literature, in prose as well as in poetry" to use a phrase of his student, ibn-'Asākir.[19] His fondness for books is indicated by the lifelong "heartsore" (*infra*, p. 61) which the loss of his four thousand volumes en route from Egypt left in him

His quiet stay during his old age at Ḥiṣn-Kayfa afforded him an opportunity to compose many of the books he wrote and of

[13] *Al-Ta'rīkh*, vol II, p 401. [14] *Op. cit*, vol II, p 417. [15] *Ta'rīkh*, p 36
[16] *Al-Rawḍatayn*, vol I, p 247
[17] Ibn-al-Athīr, *Atābeks* in *Recueil historiens orientaux*, vol. II, pt. II, p 208; *al-Kāmil*, vol XI, p 188
[18] Ibn-'Asākir, vol II, p. 402, ibn-Khallikān, *op. cit.*, vol. I, p. 112, *al-Rawḍatayn*, vol I, p 264, 'Imād-al-Dīn, *op cit*, p 123.
[19] *Al-Ta'rīkh*, vol. II, pp. 400–401.

which Derenbourg[20] enumerates eleven. Some of these are listed in Ḥāji Khalfah, *Kashf al-Ẓunūn*. A twelfth book, *Lubāb al-Ādāb* (*The Pith of Literature*), has since been discovered in manuscript form and reported in *al-Muqtaṭaf* (Cairo, 1908), vol. XXXIII, pp. 308 *seq.*

When finally established under Saladin's ægis in Damascus, Usāmah, as we can easily imagine, soon became the center of attraction and respect for a host of admirers and well-wishers, and his home became a sort of literary salon for the intelligentsia of the famous capital. He was appointed lecturer at the Ḥanafiyyah academy, and tutored in rhetoric. Saladin restored to him a fief which he was supposed to have once possessed in Ma'arrah-al-Nu'mān. Something, however, we do not exactly know what, made him fall from grace in the eyes of his patron. Could it have been some secret sympathy with the Shī'ah cause, of which the orthodox Saladin was a champion opponent and with which Usāmah may have been inoculated during his sojourn in Fāṭimite Egypt? That Usāmah had cherished such sympathies may be inferred from a passage in al-Dhahabi.[21] It was at that time and under these conditions that Usāmah produced his memorable work *Kitāb al-I'tibār*.

Among all the works of Usāmah, this *Kitāb al-I'tibār*, containing his reminiscences, stands undoubtedly supreme. But that is not all. Ancient Arabic literature has preserved for us other biographies, memoirs and reminiscences by many great men, but there is hardly anything superior to this one in its simplicity of narrative, dignity and wealth of contents and general human interest. It gives us a glimpse into Syrian methods of warfare, hawking and medication, and ushers us into the intimacies of Moslem court life as well as private home life. But its chief value consists in the fact that it deals with a point of military and cultural contact between the East and the West during a period about which our information from other sources is especially meager.

Usāmah wrote this book, more probably dictated it, when he was climbing the hill of the age of ninety (*infra*, p. 190). His hand was then "too feeble to carry a pen, after it had been strong enough to break a lance in a lion's breast" (*infra*, p. 194). Ripe

[20] *Vie d'Ousâma*, pp. 330–38. [21] Appended to Derenbourg, *Vie d'Ousâma*, p. 602.

with years and mellowed with varied experiences of adversity and success, this patriarch of early Moslem days stands at the vantage point of his ninetieth lunar year, to review before us his past life as one parade of thrilling adventures and remarkable feats, with one procession following another.

If any book is the man, *Kitāb al-I'tibār* is certainly Usāmah. Shaken by years, amiably rambling in his talk and reminiscences, our nonagenarian spins one anecdote after another, slipping into his story bits of his philosophy of life couched in such homely and poignant, often naïve, phrases as to be remembered. More delectable stories can be had nowhere else in Arabic literature. The author appears as a consummate story-teller who might qualify for a competitive prize in a modern school of journalism. His masterpiece is perhaps the story of the necklace found by a pilgrim in Mecca (*infra*, p. 210). His rare insight into human nature, his keen powers of observation and analysis, his unfailing sense of humor, coupled with his sincerity, fairness and high standard of veracity make his book one of the great books of the Arabic language.

The author intends his book to be didactic. Hence the title *al-I'tibār*, i.e., learning by example. The favorite theme is that the duration of the life of man is predetermined, that its end can neither be retarded nor advanced (*infra*, p. 192) by anything man might or might not do. In season and out of season he preaches his sermon, of which he does not seem to tire. Exposure to perils and dangers does not affect in the least the allotted term of life on this earth, and no one should "assume for a moment that the hour of death is advanced by exposing one's self to danger, or retarded by overcautiousness" (*infra*, p. 194). "Victory in warfare is from Allah (blessed and exalted is he!) and is not due to organization and planning" (*infra*, p. 177).

His passage from the telling of one tale to another is determined by the association of ideas. One happening suggests to his memory another happening because of similarity or dissimilarity, comparison or contrast. After seemingly exhausting a subject and starting on another he may digress and revert to the former. Logic and scientific classification of data were no idols to him, any more than they were to other writers of his time. Even the most gullible of readers may find here and there an anecdote hard to believe, or a detail forced by the desire to tell a good story. In his stories regarding holy men (*infra*, Section II, pp. 202 *seq.*) Usāmah did not rise above the level of the credulity of his generation, nor in his stories relating to dreams and their interpretation. How could he? And yet through it all there is no feeling on the part of the reader of conscious fabrication by the author. The simplicity of the narrative forbids it. But what is more, there is a decided feeling that the author is desirous to keep his mind open and his judgment fair and accurate. Consider his retrospective remark after extolling the virtues and hunting ability of his father: "I know not whether this was due to the fact that I was viewing him with the eye of love . . . or whether my opinion of him was based on reality" (*infra*, p. 228). No sooner does he conclude one anecdote proving the curious and primitive methods of Frankish medication than he starts another showing its efficacy (*infra*, pp. 162 *seq.*).

His observations on the Franks, while not as full and deep as we should like them to be, yet are perhaps as valuable as any left us by ibn-Jubayr, ibn-al-Athīr and other travelers and chroniclers. They are first-hand and frank, and reflect the prevalent Moslem public opinion. To a conservative Moslem, as he was, the apparently free sex relations among the Franks must have seemed loose and shocking. To him "the Franks lack jealousy in sex affairs" and "are void of all zeal and jealousy" (*infra*, p. 164). Their methods of ordeal by water and duel (*infra*, pp. 167–8) especially come up for censure, for they impressed him as far inferior to the Moslem judicial procedure then in vogue. Their system of medication (*infra*, pp. 162 *seq.*) appeared odd and primitive compared with the more highly developed system of the Arabs. The desire of one of them to show to a Moslem "God as a child" (*infra*, p. 164) in a church at Jerusalem was as shocking as it was amusing. Again and again Usāmah draws a distinction between the "acclimatized" Franks in Moslem lands and the outlandish, rude "recent comers" (*infra*, pp. 163, 169). But through it all he does not seem especially obtrusive, bitter or unfair.

Following the perfunctory verbal usage of his time, he does not fail to refer to *al-Ifranj* (the Franks) as "devils" and "infidels" and to add a curse or an imprecation after the mention of their name. But in almost the same breath he refers to the Templars in Jerusalem as "my friends" (*infra*, p. 164), and does not hesitate to inform us that "a Frankish reverend knight" used to call him "my brother" (*infra*, p. 161). His account of the impressions he gained from his enemies, the Franks, gives us probably the best index to his judicious character as a writer.

And now for the manuscript itself. The *Kitāb al-I'tibār* of the Escurial is a unique manuscript of 134 folios, exclusive of the first twenty-one folios, which are missing. It is written in black ink in the style of Syrian calligraphy belonging to the thirteenth or early fourteenth century and bears in the colophon the following:

At the end of the book the following words occurred:

"I have read this book from beginning to end in a number of sessions under the direction of my lord . . . 'Aḍud-al-Dīn, the companion of kings and sultans . . . And I have asked him to give me a certificate authorizing me to transmit the contents of this book to others, which he did, inscribing the certificate with his own noble hand. And that was on Thursday, the thirteenth of Safar, in the year 610."

(*Infra*, p 255.)

Ṣafar 13, 610 (July 4, 1213) I take to be the date of the writing of the mother of our copy and not of our copy itself as Derenbourg[22] seems to think. The opening words of the colophon make that clear. Our copy, therefore, is undated, but is taken from an earlier one written twenty-six lunar years after the death of the author and bearing a certificate of identification signed by his favorite son, Murhaf. The colloquialisms used and the mistakes in grammar and spelling committed leave no doubt that a copyist's hand had played havoc with the original. Usāmah may have dictated his book in a more or less conversational style, but the author of a *Dīwān* which was considered a classic and of a book on *al-Badī'* (rhetoric) could not have been guilty of such inelegant phrases as are common in the extant manuscript.

Many of the weaknesses common to Arabic transcription and orthography characterize our copy — paucity of diacritical marks, rarity of vowel points, absence of punctuation marks (including those denoting the completion of a full sentence and those setting off quoted matter) and lack of any system to indicate proper nouns.

Besides, there are other difficulties inherent in the task of

[22] *Ousāma Ibn Mounḳidh, texte arabe* (Paris, 1886), Avertissement, p. x.

accurately understanding a document produced some seven hundred years ago, when certain passages and words might have connoted shades of meaning different from those that they would connote to us today, and in faithfully dressing up the meaning in such alien garb as is the English with respect to the Arabic. As the translator was puzzling over the exact implications of certain passages in the manuscript before him, he found no small measure of solace and comfort in the fact that millions of his fellow countrymen were equally puzzling over the exact implication of the formula, "I do not choose to run," employed by a contemporaneous and high dignitary.

Some of the above-mentioned weaknesses will be appreciated only by those who know Arabic. For the benefit of others, let me now give a few illustrations. Twenty-two out of the twenty-eight characters which constitute the Arabic alphabet are distinguished by the presence or absence of one or more dots above or below those characters. But our manuscript quite often ignores those dots altogether. A case in English would be parallel if there were in the English alphabet over twenty letters similar to *i* and *t*, distinguished by dots and crosses, and some writer should choose to ignore them. In the case of one proper noun which occurs in our manuscript, this complication gives us seven possible different readings: *Jarrār*, *Jazzār*, *Khazzār*, *Khazzāz*, *Ḥarrāz*, *Kharrāz*, *Ḥarāz* (*infra*, p. 153, n. 29), all of which are *bona fide* Arabic names, from which you can make your choice. In another case the difference of a couple of dots makes Derenbourg read a certain word *tasbaquhum*,[23] which he properly translates *en les précédant*[24] and makes me read *yashnuqūhum*, meaning "to hang them" (*infra*, p. 101). Between the two readings there is just a difference of a couple of diacritical marks, but between "going ahead" of a person and "hanging" him is all the difference in the world.

Disagreement in supplying the necessary vowel points which were lacking made Derenbourg name a person whose name was "Waththāb" (*infra*, p. 135), "Withāb."[25] The difference in the supposed position of one vowel point led Derenbourg to read a certain word *'adl*[26] and translate *demandant justice* and *la séance*,[27]

[23] *Texte arabe*, p 54
[24] *Autobiographie d'Ousāma Ibn Mounkidh* (Paris, 1895), p. 73.
[25] *Autobiographie*, p. 104. [26] *Texte arabe*, p 83. [27] *Autobiographie*, p. 110.

although the word is *'idl*, meaning "sack," and refers to the sack in which the leopard was brought before a lord (*infra*, p. 141).

The lack of any system of capitalization inherent in Arabic orthography often results in the confusion of proper and common nouns. "Al-'Alāh" (*infra*, pp 78, 236), the name of a place in Northern Syria, is treated by Derenbourg as a common noun and translated *de la ville haute;*[28] *qaryah kharibah*, on the other hand, which means "a village in ruins" (*infra*, p. 110), is treated as a proper noun;[29] "al-Ṣāliḥ" (*infra*, p. 122), which is a proper noun, is considered a common one and translated *un saint homme.*[30]

Referring the pronoun to its proper antecedent is often a source of worry in Arabic composition. This difficulty made Derenbourg in one instance cause the wrong man to fly off his saddle,[31] in another to fall unconscious,[32] and in a third to cut off the leg of a patient.[33] In another case the quoted words are put in the mouth of the wrong speaker.[34]

The fact that in Arabic there is no mechanical device to indicate the end of a direct quotation caused the discrepancy in translating the last part of Usāmah's speech to the footmen at 'Asqalān.[35]

Our author knew no foreign languages but, nevertheless, used in his work a number of Persian and Turkish words which were evidently floating in the Arabic world of his time. Most of the Arabic names of weapons are of Persian origin, just as in English they are of French origin. In one place he uses a Turkish word *jawbān* (Turkish pronunciation *chobān*), meaning "herdsman," which Derenbourg[36] mistakes for a proper name of a person In that interesting story illustrating Frankish medication, he speaks of a woman afflicted with *nishāf*, which has all the earmarks of an Arabic word (connected with a stem *nashafa*, "to dry up"), and which Derenbourg[37] translates *consomption* but which is in reality a Persian word meaning "imbecility" (*infra*, p. 162). The *barjam*,[38] which the beard of the watchman cut off by Ṣalāḥ-al-Dīn resembled, is Persian *parcham*, meaning "the tail of the sea-cow" (*infra*, p. 189),

28 *Ibid*, p 50 Cf p. 198. 29 *Ibid*, p 81. 30 *Ibid*, p 93
31 Cf *Autobiographie*, p 63, with *infra*, p 92
32 Cf *ibid*, p 142, with *infra*, p 175 33 Cf *ibid*, p 142, with *infra*, p 175.
34 Cf *ibid*, p. 61, l 22, with *infra*, p 89
35 Cf. *ibid*, p. 14, with *infra*, p. 40. 36 Cf. *ibid.*, p 105, with *infra*, p. 136.
37 *Autobiographie*, p 129.
38 *Texte arabe*, p. 118.

and is not to be confused with Arabic *barājim*, meaning *articulations de doigts*.[39]

Fortunately a number of the colloquial phrases used in the book are still in current use in Syria, otherwise it would have been impossible for us to ascertain their exact significance. This explains, for instance, the difference between translating *wa-tammu yaṭridūna-hum*[40] into "and pursued them for a long distance" (*infra*, p. 79) and translating it *et les contraignirent à abandonner jusqu'au dernier le champ de bataille*.[41]

On the whole, however, it must be said that Derenbourg did a very creditable and honest piece of work, considering the handicaps under which he labored.

The work of Georg Schumann, *Usāma Ibn Munkidh, Memoiren* (Innsbruck, 1905), follows almost slavishly the French translation, rather than the Arabic original, and shares its weaknesses. The degree of dependence is demonstrated by the fact that in one place Derenbourg[42] inadvertently omits the first name of the preacher of Is'ird, "Sirāj-al-Dīn," and so does Schumann;[43] in another place Derenbourg[44] adds to the name of Nāṣir-al-Dīn ibn-'Abbās a middle name, "Naṣr," which does not occur in the original text (*infra*, pp. 52, 53), and Schumann[45] follows suit; in a third place Derenbourg[46] forgets to translate the word *thamāni* = "eight" (or he may have misread it for *thaman* = "price"), and makes the rent of the mill *cent dīnārs* instead of eight hundred dīnārs (*infra*, p 135), and Schumann forgets also, fixing the rent as *hundert Denaren*[47]

The system of transliteration used in this volume is with one or two slight modifications the same as that approved by the International Oriental Congress. Certain geographical names long domesticated in the English language are used in their anglicized forms: "Syria" for *al-Shām*, "Damascus" for *Dimashq* and "Mecca" for *Makkah*. For the same reason such words as "sheikh" (instead of *shaykh*) and "mameluke" (instead of *mamlūk*) are reluctantly accepted and reproduced in their corrupt English forms. And since the work is meant not only for orientalists but for medievalists as well, most of whom are not acquainted with the

[39] *Autobiographie*, p. 156 [40] *Texte arabe*, p 37 [41] *Autobiographie*, p 51.
[42] *Autobiographie*, p. 165 [43] *Memoiren*, p 229
[44] *Autobiographie*, p 26, ll 14, 37 [45] *Memoiren*, pp 50, 51
[46] *Autobiographie*, p. 104, ll. 19, 28. [47] *Memoiren*, p. 154, ll. 15–16, 24.

Arabic language, an attempt has been made to include among the references books in their translations into European languages.

The attention of the reader is here called to the fact that the division of the text into sections, subsections and paragraphs, with one exception indicated in its proper place, is the work of the translator. He is also responsible for all headings of these divisions and for the figures in square brackets which indicate his pagination of the manuscript.

On Monday, the 23d of Ramaḍān, of the year 584 (November 16, 1188), the year after the conquest of Jerusalem by Saladin, Usāmah passed away in Damascus at the age of 96 lunar (93 solar) years and was interred on the second day at the east side of Mt Qāsiyūn, considered by Moslem tradition "sacred and most venerated"[48] and associated with the names of Adam, Abel, Abraham and many other prophets and martyrs. His tomb was visited a few decades later by the Damascene biographer, ibn-Khallikān, who writes: "I entered his mausoleum, which lies on the northern bank of the Yazīd River,[49] and recited an extract from the Koran over his grave, imploring Allah's mercy upon him."

[48] Yāqūt, *op cit*, vol IV, p 13

[49] A branch of the Barada. For this quotation see *Ta'rīkh*, vol I, p 112 = *Biographical Dictionary*, vol. I, pp. 179–80.

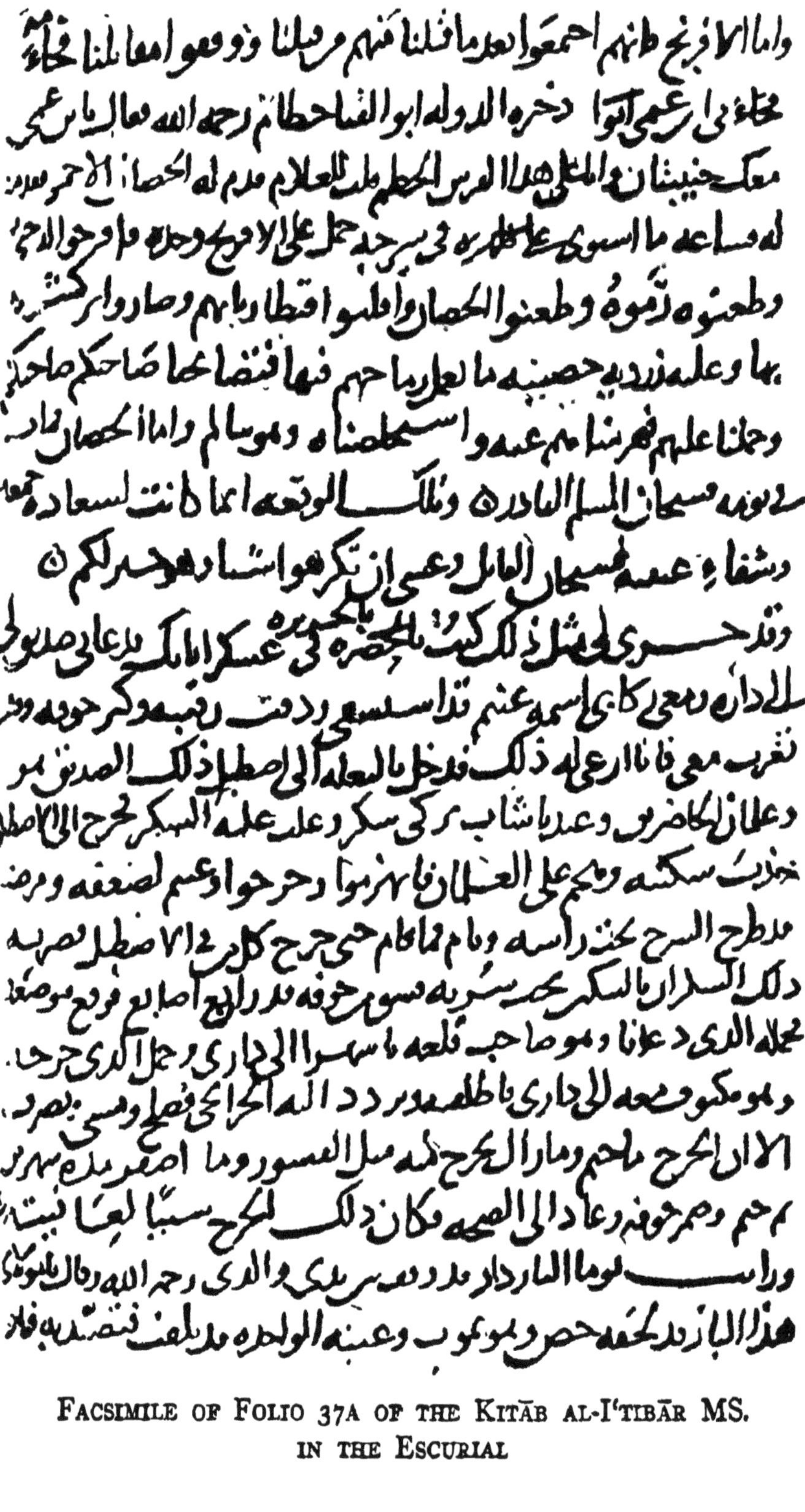

FACSIMILE OF FOLIO 37A OF THE KITĀB AL-I'TIBĀR MS.
IN THE ESCURIAL

FACSIMILE OF FOLIO 37B OF THE KITĀB AL-I'TIBĀR MS.
IN THE ESCURIAL

SECTION I

WARS, TRAVELS AND OTHER EXPERIENCES

SECTION I

WARS, TRAVELS AND OTHER EXPERIENCES

1. FIGHTING AGAINST THE FRANKS[1]

Zanki's victory near Qinnasrīn.[2] — . . . . [1][3] In the course of that combat the massacre was not great in the ranks of the Moslems.

Before the battle there had arrived ibn-Bishr,[4] an envoy from the Imām[5] al-Rāshid ibn-al-Mustarshid (may Allah's mercy rest upon their two souls![6]), in order to summon the atābek[7] to appear before him [the caliph]. Bishr took part in that battle clad in a gilden byrnie [*jawshan*]. A Frankish knight, named ibn-al-Daqīq,[8] smote and pierced him in the chest with a lance, making the lance come out of his back (may Allah's mercy rest upon his soul!). The slaughter was rather great in the lines of the Franks.

The atābek (may Allah's mercy rest upon his soul!) gave orders according to which their heads were assembled in a field opposite the castle, and they turned out to be about three thousand.

The Byzantines and Franks besiege Shayzar. — Later on in the

[1] This and all other headings for sections, subsections and paragraphs are not in the original but are added by the translator. The word "Chapter," without a number, at the beginning of Section II is in the original.

[2] A reference to this battle by Usāmah is preserved in al-Dhahabi, *Ta'rīkh al-Islām*, a section of which is appended to H. Derenbourg, *Vie d'Ousāma* (Paris, 1889), pp. 594–605, and indicates (pp. 601–2) that Usāmah himself took part in the fight. Qinnasrīn, ancient Chalcis, lies southwest of Aleppo (Ḥalab) in northern Syria.

[3] The first pages of the manuscript, forty-two in all, are missing.

[4] Abu-Bakr Bishr ibn-Karīm ibn-Bishr, mentioned by Kamāl-al-Dīn, *Ta'rīkh Ḥalab* in *Recueil des historiens des croisades: historiens orientaux* (Paris, 1884), vol. III, p. 670, and referred to by ibn-al-Athīr, *al-Kāmil*, *ibid.*, vol. I, p. 405.

[5] That is, the caliph. Al-Rāshid was a 'Abbāsid caliph who ruled in Baghdād September 7, 1135–August 8, 1136 A.D.

[6] The souls of al-Rāshid and his father al-Mustarshid. This formula is used by Arab authors after the name of one already deceased.

[7] A Turco-Persian title (*ata* = "father," plus *bek* = "prince" or "lord") meaning "the lord father" and given originally to the guardian and tutor of Turkish princes during the Seljūq period, but applied later to regents and other powerful amīrs. The reference here is to 'Imād-al-Dīn Zanki of al-Mawsil, modern Mūṣul, who ruled September, 1127–September, 1147.

[8] Literally "the son of flour" or "the son of the slender one," and possibly a corruption of *Benedictus*, pronounced in the French of those days *Benedeit*. See H. Derenbourg, *Ousāma Ibn Mounkidh un émir syrien au premier siècle des croisades, première partie, vie d'Ousāma* (Paris, 1889), p. 152, n. 3, and p. 472, n. 4.

year 532,[9] the emperor of the Byzantines [10] once more set out against the land of Syria and made an alliance with the Franks (may Allah render them helpless! [11]) to go conjointly against Shayzar and attack it. Ṣalāḥ-al-Dīn thereupon said to me, "Dost thou not see what this timorous fellow has done?" referring to his own son Shihāb-al-Dīn Aḥmad. "And what has he done?" said I. "He sent me word," replied Ṣalāḥ-al-Dīn, "saying, 'Find someone else to take charge of thy town.'" "And what didst thou do then?" asked I. "Well," replied Ṣalāḥ-al-Dīn, "I sent word to the atābek, saying, 'Take back thy place.'" I then remarked, "What an awful thing thou hast done! Will not now the atābek say to thee, 'When it was meat he ate it, but now that it has become bone he threw it away to me.'" [12] "What shall I do then?" asked he. To this I replied, "I shall establish myself in it [Shayzar]. If Allah (exalted is he!) vouchsafes its safety, it will be to thy future welfare and will redound to thy glory [13] with thy lord. If, on the other hand, the town is taken and we are killed, that will be our fate and thou wilt not be to blame." To this he replied, "No other man has ever said such a thing to me!"

Believing that he would act accordingly, I brought together sheep, a large quantity of flour, butter and other provisions needed during a siege. But as I was in my home at sunset time, his messenger came to me, saying, "Ṣalāḥ-al-Dīn wants thee to know that the day after tomorrow we shall be on the march to al-Mawṣil. Prepare thyself, therefore, for the march." This filled my heart with great anxiety and I said, "Shall I leave my children, my brothers and my women folk under siege and proceed to al-Mawṣil?"

Early the second morning, I went on horseback to Ṣalāḥ-al-Dīn, who was still in his tent, and asked his permission to go to Shayzar and bring back such supplies and money as I should need on the way. This permission he granted, adding, "Lose no time there." [14]

[9] September 19, 1137–September 8, 1138 A D

[10] Arabic *al-rūm* = Romans, i.e , East Romans. The emperor referred to is John Comnenus, 1118–43

[11] *khadhalahum allāh* used by the author where a modern English-speaking person would say "confound them!"

[12] A widely used Arabic adage

[13] Literally, "it will render thy face white"

[14] The writing of this sentence is blurred in the manuscript H. Derenbourg, *Ousāma Ibn Mounḳidh, texte arabe* (Paris, 1886), p. 3, reconstructs this sentence and the preceding phrase differently. Cf. his translation, *Autobiographie d'Ousāma Ibn Mounḳidh* (Paris, 1895), p. 2.

Accordingly, I rode my mount and proceeded to Shayzar. The sight I saw there saddened my heart. The enemy had defeated my son [15] and fought their way as far as my home, from which they carried away all the tents, weapons and furniture that were therein, captured my beloved ones and put to flight my comrades.[16] Thus the calamity was great and terrible.

[15] 'Aḍud-al-Dawlah abu-al-Fawāris Murhaf, the favorite son of Usāmah

[16] A number of words in this passage are illegible Derenbourg, *Texte arabe*, p. 3 = *Autobiographie*, p 3, reads and translates differently.

2. USĀMAH'S FIRST SOJOURN IN DAMASCUS 1138–1144 A.D.

Conditions now made it necessary for me to start for Damascus. The emissaries of the atābek were coming one after the other to the lord of Damascus, asking him to send me to the atābek. I spent in that city eight years,[1] and its lord (may Allah have mercy upon his soul!) bestowed great gifts and fiefs bountifully on me. He distinguished me by putting me in a position close to him and by other special honors. All that was in addition to the marks of favor from al-Amīr Muʻīn-al-Dīn[2] (may Allah's mercy rest upon his soul!), his constant company [2] and his taking my interests under his patronage.

Certain causes, however, made it necessary for me to depart for Egypt. This resulted in the loss of such pieces of my home furniture and weapons as I could not carry along. In this another calamity befell me in my possessions; and al-Amīr Muʻīn-al-Dīn (may Allah's mercy rest upon his soul!), although benevolent, deeply sympathetic with me and greatly afflicted with sorrow for my departure, acknowledged his inability to redeem the situation for me. He even went so far as to send me his secretary, al-Ḥājib [chamberlain] Maḥmūd al-Mustarshid (may Allah's mercy rest upon his soul!), through whom he said:

> By Allah, if one half of the people were on my side, I would risk hurling them against the other half; even if one third were on my side, I would risk hurling them against the two thirds rather than risk parting with thee! But as it is, all the people have coalesced against me, and I have become powerless. But wherever thou mayest be, the friendship between us shall ever remain at its best.

This was the occasion for my composing the following verses:

O Muʻīn-al-Dīn, how numerous are thy necklaces of bounty
On my neck, irremovable as the rings around the pigeon's throat!

[1] In the year 532 A.H., when John Comnenus laid siege to Shayzar, Usāmah was still at home. In the year 539 A.H. we find him in Egypt. He could not therefore have spent more than seven years in Damascus.

[2] Muʻīn-al-Dīn Anar, the trusted vizier of Shihāb-al-Dīn Maḥmūd and the patron of Usāmah, died August 3, 1149.

Thy benevolence has made me indeed thy voluntary bondsman,
For to the noble, benevolence is his fetters.
So much so that I have now begun to trace my genealogy to thy friendship,
Though I belong to the noble class by both pedigree and personal achievements.
Dost thou not know that it was because of my close relationship to thee
That from all sides shafts have been hurled at me?
Had it not been for thy sake, my refractory nature would not have been appeased,
In the face of harsh treatment by others, without effectively applying the sword.
But because I was afraid for thine own safety from the fires of the enemy,
I played the rôle of one who quenches the flame.

3. USĀMAH IN EGYPT
1144–1154 A.D.

Mutiny in the Egyptian army. — My arrival in Cairo [1] fell on Thursday, the second of Jumāda II, year 539.[2] As soon as I arrived there, al-Ḥāfiẓ li-Dīn-Allāh [3] assigned me a place to live, had me invested with a robe of honor in his presence, bestowed on me a full wardrobe together with one hundred dīnārs, authorized [4] me to use his baths and assigned for my residence one of the mansions of al-Afḍal, son of the Amīr-al-Juyūsh,[5] which was extremely magnificent, fully equipped with carpets, furniture and a complete outfit of brass utensils. All that was put at my disposal with the understanding that nothing of it would be reclaimed. Here I settled for a long period [6] of time as the recipient of honor, respect and uninterrupted favors, besides a revenue easy to collect from a special fief.

There now developed a great dispute and quarrel among the Sūdānese (who were very numerous), more particularly between the Rayḥāniyyah on the one hand, who were loyal slaves of al-Ḥāfiẓ, and the Juyūshiyyah,[7] the Alexandrians and the Faraḥiyyah on the other hand. The Rayḥāniyyah stood alone on one side; while all the others stood on the other side allied together against the Rayḥāniyyah. A group of the special guard [8] joined hands with the Juyūshiyyah. Both parties were assembled in great numbers. Al-Ḥāfiẓ was then absent. His emissaries went back and forth, as he was anxious to see reconciliation effected between the two sides, but the response was not favorable. The Rayḥāniyyah and the inhabitants of the town were siding with him.[9]

Early in the morning,[10] the encounter took place in Cairo. The

[1] Arabic *miṣr*, used for both Cairo and Egypt [2] November 30, 1144 A D
[3] The eleventh Fātimite caliph, died October, 1149
[4] Original illegible, reconstructed by conjecture
[5] "Commander of the armies" A title borne at this time by the powerful vizier Badr al-Jamāli, an Armenian. [6] 1144–54 A D
[7] So called after a past vizier, Amīr-al-Juyūsh Badr al-Jamāli, who organized this corps See al-Qalqashandi, *Ṣubh al-A'sha* (Cairo, 1916–25), vol III, p 482
[8] *ṣibyān al-khāṣṣ*, who numbered some five hundred Qalqashandi, *op. cit.*, vol. III, p. 481. [9] Original not clear [10] September 23, 1149.

Juyūshiyyah and their allies won the victory over the Rayḥāniyyah, of whom were killed in the Suwayqah [3] Amīr-al-Juyūsh [11] one thousand men, whose corpses blocked the passage in the Suwayqah. As for us, we remained under arms by night and day for fear that they might in turn attack us, as they had done prior to my arrival in Egypt.

When the Rayhāniyyah were thus slaughtered, people thought that al-Ḥāfiẓ would denounce the act and would destroy their murderers. But al-Ḥāfiẓ was lying sick on the verge of death, and two days later the end came (may Allah's mercy rest upon his soul!). Not even two goats locked horns on account of the massacre [12]

Ibn-al-Sallār's successful revolt against al-Ẓāfir. — His youngest son, al-Ẓāfir bi-Amr-Allāh, succeeded him and chose for vizier Najm-al-Dīn ibn-Maṣāl, who was already an aged man. Al-Amīr Sayf-al-Dīn abu-al-Ḥasan 'Ali ibn-al-Sallār,[13] who was then in his province,[14] recruited some troops, brought them together, marched against Cairo and sent word to his house. Al-Ẓāfir bi-Amr-Allāh immediately called a convocation of amīrs in the Vizierate Palace and dispatched to us the major-domo of the palace,[15] who said to us, "Know ye amīrs that this Najm-al-Dīn is my vizier and representative. Let him, therefore, who obeys me obey him and comply with his orders." The amīrs replied, "We are the slaves of our master, obedient and loyal." The prefect carried back this response.

Thereupon an aged amīr, named Lakrūn, said, "O amīrs, shall we leave 'Ali ibn-al-Sallār to be killed?" To this they replied, "No, by Allah!" "Rise up, therefore," said he. Accordingly they all rushed out from the palace, saddled their horses and mules and hastened to the succor of Sayf-al-Dīn ibn-al-Sallār. Seeing that, and finding himself unable to resist him, al-Ḥāfiẓ put at the disposal of Najm-al-Dīn ibn-Maṣāl a large sum of money and said, "Go out to al-Ḥawf,[16] recruit and assemble an army, distribute money among them and repulse ibn-al-Sallār."

Ibn-Maṣāl set out to execute these orders. In the meantime,

[11] The market place named after the "commander of the armies"

[12] A well-known Arabic proverb signifying that perfect peace and tranquillity prevailed

[13] Spelled "Salār" in *Encyclopaedia of Islam*, art "al-'Ādil"

[14] Alexandria and Buḥayrah.

[15] *zimām al-quṣūr*, "chief prefect" See Qalqashandi, vol III, p. 485.

[16] A district in the eastern part of the Delta.

ibn-al-Sallār had entered Cairo and made his way into the Vizierate Palace. The entire army agreed to be loyal to him, and he treated them bountifully. As for me, he gave instructions that I, together with my companions, should spend the night in his own mansion, a part of which he reserved for my exclusive use.

In al-Ḥawf, ibn-Maṣāl amassed a large body of men, consisting of Lawātah,[17] Egyptian troops, Sūdānese and Bedouins. Rukn-al-Dīn 'Abbās, a stepson of 'Ali ibn-al-Sallār, had in the meantime gone out of the town and pitched his tents in the suburb of Cairo. Early the second morning a Lawātah band under the command of a relative of ibn-Maṣāl made their way into the camp of 'Abbās. A group of Egyptian men in the army of 'Abbās forsook him and took to flight. But he stood firm, together with his attendants and those of his troops who remained faithful to him, during all the night, foiling the enemy.

Ibn-al-Sallār, having heard the news, summoned me in the nighttime — I was with him in his own home — and said, "Those dogs (referring to the Egyptian troops) occupied the attention of the amīr (meaning 'Abbās) with insignificant things until a Lawātah band crossed over, swimming, to his camp early in the morning. They then forsook him and took to flight. Some of them have even entered their homes in Cairo. But the amīr is still taking a stand against the enemy." "My lord," I replied, "at dawn we shall ride against them, and by the time the sun is up we shall have been done with them — if it be Allah's will, exalted is he!" "Right," said he. "Start early on thy ride."

Early the second morning we set out against them, and none escaped except those whose horses swam with them across the Nile. The relative of ibn-Maṣāl was taken prisoner and his head was cut off.

Ibn-Maṣāl, the rival of ibn-al-Sallār, defeated. — [4] The army was then reunited under 'Abbās, who led it against ibn-Maṣāl, whom he encountered near Dalāṣ.[18] He routed the enemy, killed ibn-Maṣāl and put to the sword seventeen thousand Sūdānese and others. The head of ibn-Maṣāl was carried to Cairo. None remained after this to oppose Sayf-al-Dīn or contend against him.

[17] A Berber tribe scattered all over northern Africa

[18] A city and a district in Upper Egypt. Yāqūt, *Mu'jam al-Buldān*, ed. Wüstenfeld (Leipzig, 1866–73), vol. II, p. 581.

Al-Ẓāfir then invested him [Sayf-al-Dīn ibn-al-Sallār] with the robes of the vizierate, giving him the title al-Malik al-'Ādil [the equitable ruler]. Ibn-al-Sallār had full charge of affairs. Nevertheless, al-Ẓāfir cherished aversion and repugnance toward him and secretly entertained evil toward him.

The Fāṭimite caliph conspires to kill his vizier. — Al-Ẓāfir now planned to put al-'Ādil to death. He concerted with a group of young men from his special bodyguard, together with others whom he won over to the scheme by distributing money among them, that they attack al-'Ādil in his home and put him to death. This was in the month of Ramaḍān.[19] The conspirators convened in a house adjoining that of al-'Ādil, waiting for midnight and the dispersion of his companions. That night I was staying with him.

When his guests were done with the supper and dispersed, al-'Ādil, having been informed of the conspiracy by someone who had taken part in it, summoned two of his attendants and ordered that an attack be made immediately upon the conspirators in the house where they were assembled. This house, since it was Allah's will that some be spared, had two doors: one near the home of al-'Ādil, and the other far off. One of the detachments made the assault from the near-by door before the other detachment had arrived at the second door. The conspirators were put to flight and escaped through that door. Of those who escaped, some ten men belonging to the special guard [of al-Ḥāfiẓ], being friends of my attendants, came to me seeking refuge. The town awoke the second morning to find itself the scene of a thorough search for the fugitives — every one of them who was caught was executed.

Usāmah saves a fugitive negro. — One of the amazing things which I witnessed that day was the case of a Sūdānese who had been a party to the conspiracy and who sought refuge at the top of my house, pursued by a few men with swords in their hands. He looked down from that considerable elevation to the courtyard where was a huge lote tree, jumped from the roof to that tree and perched on it. Then he descended and entered through an adjacent passage into the sitting room. As he entered, he tripped over a brass candlestick and broke it, but kept on until he got

[19] January, 1150 A.D.

behind a load of baggage[20] in the sitting room, where he hid himself. As the pursuers looked down from above, I yelled at them and ordered my attendants to climb to them which they did, driving them back. I then sought the negro, who immediately took off a cloak he had on him and said, "Take it for thyself." I replied, "May Allah increase thy bounty![21] I have no need for the cloak." I then let him out, accompanied by a band of my attendants. Thus he escaped.

A forger beheaded. — Then I sat down on a stone bench in the vestibule of my home, when all of a sudden a young man entered into my presence and, after greeting me, sat down. I found him interesting in conversation and clever in discussion. But as he was conversing, there came a man and called him. So he joined him and went away. I dispatched one of my attendants behind him in order to find out why he was called. I was then close by the palace of al-'Ādil. The moment that young man presented himself before al-'Ādil, the latter ordered that his head be cut off. So he was immediately put to death. My attendant returned after having inquired about his guilt and having been told that he used to counterfeit official signatures. Worthy of admiration,[22] therefore, is he who determines the length of life and fixes the hour of death!

The cooperation of Nūr-al-Dīn is sought against the Franks. — [5] Al-Malik al-'Ādil [the vizier] (may Allah's mercy rest upon his soul!) then instructed me to get ready to proceed to al-Malik al-'Ādil Nūr-al-Dīn[23] (may Allah's mercy rest with his soul!), saying, "Thou shalt take with thee money and present thyself before him with a view to having him attack Tiberias [Ṭabarayyah] and divert the attention of the Franks from us so that we may be able to set out from there and devastate Ghazzah." The Franks (may Allah render them helpless!) had just begun the reconstruction of Ghazzah[24] in order to be in a position to blockade 'Asqalān [Ascalon].

[20] *rihl* = "load of baggage," but one diacritical point will make it *rajul* = "man." Since the manuscript is deficient in diacritical marks, it is not possible to tell with certainty which of the two readings is meant here

[21] The ordinary formula corresponding to "thank you"

[22] By this formula, *subhān*, which is very common in the Arabic language, the author means to bring out the contrast between the case of this young man and the case of the negro reported immediately before him, and to explain it on the basis of the almighty power of Allah

[23] Son of the Atābek Zanki, and his successor in 1146.

[24] Gaza The reference is to the attempt made by Baldwin III, king of Jerusalem, in 1149 or 1150.

I replied, "O my lord, in case he offers excuses or has some business which would hinder him from carrying out this plan, what are then thy instructions to me?" To this he replied:

If he sets out against Tiberias, give him the money which thou hast, but if there is anything to prevent him, then enlist thou as many soldiers as thou canst, go up to 'Asqalān, and establish thyself in it for combat against the Franks. As soon as thou arrivest there, write me and I shall send thee instructions as to what to do next.

He then put at my disposal six thousand Egyptian dīnārs, a camel load of Dabīqi [25] clothes, of ciclatoun, of squirrel-furred gowns, of Dimyāti [26] brocade, and of turbans. He also arranged for a group of Arab guides to accompany me. Thus I proceeded, after he had removed every difficulty in the way of my departure by supplying me with everything I needed, whether great or small.

A curious Arab tribe at al-Jafr. — As we approached al-Jafr,[27] my guides said to me, "Here is a place which is rarely free from Franks." Acting upon my order, two guides riding on Mahri [28] camels preceded us to al-Jafr. No sooner, however, had they departed than they returned, with their camels almost flying under them, and said, "The Franks are at al-Jafr." I immediately halted, assembled the camels which carried my luggage, and certain members of the caravan who were in my company, and turned back toward the west. Choosing then six horsemen from among my mamelukes,[29] I said to them, "Go ahead of us and I shall follow right after you." They dashed off at a gallop and I dashed behind them. One of them returned to me, saying, "Not a single one at al-Jafr! Perhaps what the guides saw was nomadic Arabs." [30] An argument ensued between him and the guides. I dispatched someone who immediately turned the camels back, and continued my way

[25] Fabricated in Dabīq (perhaps modern Dabīj), a town which lay in the district of Dimyāt, Lower Egypt The cloth was woven of linen, occasionally interwoven with gold and silk

[26] Dimyāt (Damietta), colloquially Dumyāt, famed throughout the Moslem world, especially during the Fāṭimite period, for its textiles, manufactured mostly of white linen or silk with an admixture of gold threads

[27] An oasis in the desert between Egypt and Palestine

[28] A breed of dromedaries, so called after an Arab tribe of that name

[29] *mamlūk*, literally "possessed" or "owned," used by Arabic writers for slaves when not black.

[30] *'urbān.* Since the manuscript ignores the diacritical marks, the word may be *ghirbān* = "ravens."

When I arrived at al-Jafr, which is rich in water, grass and trees, behold, there emerged from among the grass a man dressed in a black garment. We immediately captured him. My companions thereupon scattered around and seized another man, two women and some young folks. One of the women hurried to me, held my garments and said, "O sheikh! I am at thy mercy!" To which I replied, "Thou art safe. Now, what is the matter with thee?" "Thy companions," she replied, "have taken away from me a garment, a braying one, a barking one, and a bead." I said to my attendants, "Let him who has taken anything whatsoever return it." One of them produced a piece of clothing, perhaps two cubits [31] in length, and she said, "This is the garment." Another produced a piece of sandarach; and she said, "This is the bead." "What about the donkey and the dog?" asked I. To this they replied that they had bound the fore and hind legs of the donkey and thrown it upon the grass. As for the dog, it was free, running from place to place.

As I brought the prisoners together, I found them afflicted with a great affliction: their dry skins had stuck to their bones.[32] "What are ye?" asked I. "We belong to the [6] banu-Ubayy tribe," they replied. Now the banu-Ubayy are a clan of the Arab tribe called Ṭayy. They eat nothing but dead animals,[33] and yet they say, "We are the best of all Arabs. None of us suffers from elephantiasis, leprosy, any chronic disease or blindness." Whenever a guest visits them, they slay for him an animal and feed him other than their food. I asked them, "What brought you here?" "We have in Ḥisma," [34] they replied, "heaps of broom corn [35] buried in the ground. So we came in order to take it." "How long have ye been here?" I asked. "Since the last feast of Ramaḍān," they replied, "we have been here, without seeing food with our eyes." "What do ye live on, then?" I inquired. "On carrion," they

[31] *dhirā'*, originally, the part of the arm from the elbow to the end of the middle finger; later, a measure of distance

[32] A figurative way of saying "very lean and thin," corresponding to English "skin and bone"

[33] *maytah*, the eating of which is prohibited by the Koran V 4

[34] Or *Ḥismā'*. Name given to an extensive region covering the central part of the southern Syrian desert (east of Sinai) and northern Ḥijāz Yāqūt, *op cit*, vol. II, p. 267.

[35] *dhurah*, from the seed of which a coarse bread is made See George E. Post, *Flora of Syria, Palestine and Sinai* (Beirūt, 1896), p 854

replied, meaning decayed bones which are cast away, "which we crush and boil with water and orach leaves (a plant quite common to that region). And we subsist on that." "How about your dogs and donkeys?" I then asked. "The dogs," they replied, "we feed on our own food; but the donkeys eat grass." "Why," asked I, "did ye not enter Damascus?" "We were afraid of the pest," they replied. But in truth, there could be no pest worse than the one with which they were already afflicted. This event took place after the Greater Bairam.[36]

I stopped there until our camels arrived, and distributed among them some of the provisions which we had. A napkin which I had on my head, I cut in two and gave to the two women. They all almost lost their wits with joy on account of the food. And I said to them, "Stay not here lest the Franks should take you as captives."

Lost in the desert. — One of the strange things that happened to me on the way was the following.

I dismounted one evening to recite the sunset and dusk prayers abridged and combined.[37] The camels kept on their way. I then stood over an elevation of land and said to my attendants, "Disband in search of the camels, and come back to me. I shall not move from this spot where I am." Accordingly, they disbanded and ran in this direction and in that direction, but they did not sight them. So they all came back to me and said, "We found them not, nor do we know how they went." Then said I, "Depending upon Allah's help, we shall march guided by the setting of the stars." So we started, confronted with a difficult situation by being separated from our camels in a desert.

But there was among the guides one called Jazziyyah, full of vigilance and sagacity. Reckoning our tardiness, he realized that we had gone astray. So while riding on a camel he took a piece of steel and began to strike it against a flint stone, causing the sparks to fly in this and in that direction. Seeing him at a distance, we made the fire our objective until we caught up with the rest of the

[36] *'Īd al-aḍḥa*, the sacrificial feast concluding the ceremonies of the annual pilgrimage at Mecca This tribe must therefore have been over two months in that region

[37] *qaṣran wa-jam'an*, meaning he abridged the prayer by making two genuflexions instead of four, and he combined the two prayers of sunset and dusk into one.

party. Had it not been for Allah's kindness, and the inspiration which that man had, we should have perished.

The treasure bag lost. — It also happened to me on that same trip that al-Malik al-'Ādil [the vizier] (may Allah's mercy rest upon his soul!) had said to me, "Let not the guides accompanying thee know that thou hast the money." Accordingly, I deposited four thousand dīnārs in a bag on a saddle mule led by the halter by my side and put it under the charge of an attendant. The other two thousand dīnārs, together with my own expense money, a gold bridle [38] and some Maghribi dīnārs, I deposited in another bag upon another horse led by my side and put under the charge of another attendant. Whenever I wanted to make a stop, I would put the bags in [7] the center of a rug, fold its ends around them, spread another rug on top and sleep over the bags. At the time of departure, I would wake up before my companions, deliver the two bags to the two attendants in charge, and after they had tied the bags on the animals beside mine, I would mount and arouse my companions. We were then ready for the start.

One night we made our stop in the Desert of the Children of Israel.[39] When I arose to depart, the attendant in charge of the extra mule led by my side took the bag and threw it on the two hips of the mule and then turned behind the mule in order to fasten it with the belt to the saddle. The mule slipped and went galloping with the bag on its back. I immediately mounted my horse, which my groom had brought me, and saying to my attendants, "Mount! Mount!" I galloped in pursuit of the mule, but failed to catch up with it, as it was going like an onager. My horse was already exhausted, because of the long distance covered, when my attendant caught up with me. I then said to him, "Pursue the mule in this direction." He did so and then returned, saying, "By Allah, O my lord, I have not seen the mule, but I have found this bag which I picked up." "It was exactly the bag which I was seeking," I replied. "As for the mule, its loss is much easier for me." I then returned to the camp, and behold, the mule came back galloping

[38] *sarfasār* from Persian *sar-afsār* = "head of the reins," i e , the part held in the hand

[39] *tīh bani-isrā'īl* = the desert of Mt Sinai, through which passed the main caravan route between Egypt and Palestine, leading north to Syria See Alois Musil, *The Northern Ḥeǧâz* (New York, 1926), pp 273, 316.

and made its way into the horses' picket line [40] and took its place there as though it had no other object [in the flight] but the loss of the four thousand dīnārs.

Usāmah's interview with Nūr-al-Dīn. — On our way we stopped in Buṣra,[41] where we learned that al-Malik al-'Ādil Nūr-al-Dīn (may Allah's mercy rest upon his soul!) was camping against Damascus. There had arrived in Buṣra, al-Amīr Asad-al-Dīn Shīrkūh[42] (may Allah's mercy rest upon his soul!). So I joined him and went to the army, where we arrived the evening preceding Monday. Early the next morning, I held an interview with Nūr-al-Dīn on the subject of my mission. He said, "O, so and so,[43] the people of Damascus are our enemies, and the Franks are our enemies, too. I trust neither these nor those in case I go in between them." I therefore asked him, "Wilt thou then authorize me to enlist troops from among those who were rejected from service in the regular army? These I shall take and go back, but thou shalt dispatch with me one of thine own men at the head of thirty horsemen, so that the campaign may be considered as having been carried out in thy name." Nūr-al-Dīn replied, "Go ahead and do it." Accordingly, I recruited until the following Monday eight hundred and sixty horsemen. These I took with me, marching in the heart of the Frankish territory, making our stops at the call of the bugle and starting again at the call of the bugle. Nūr-al-Dīn dispatched in my company 'Ayn-al-Dawlah al-Yārūqi [44] at the head of thirty horsemen.

The cleft at Petra Mosque. — On my way back I passed through al-Kahf and al-Raqīm[45] and made a stop there. I entered the mosque [46] and prayed in it; but the cleft in it I did not go through. One of the Turkish amīrs, however, who were in my company, named Barshak, came with the intention of entering through that narrow cleft. I said to him, "What art thou doing there? Pray outside of it." "There is no god but Allah," he replied. "I must

[40] *ṭuwālah* = a rope by which horses are tied to graze, or around a box of fodder in the open air The word is also applied to the horses themselves so tied

[41] Eski-Shām, once the capital of the Ḥawrān region, south of Damascus

[42] Uncle of Saladin

[43] *fulān*, meaning in this case Usāmah

[44] A Turk who was previous to this in the service of Zanki

[45] Petra south of the Dead Sea, identified by some with al-Raqīm, mentioned in the Koran XVIII 8, as the place of the Seven Sleepers

[46] Identified by some with the mosque referred to in the Koran XVIII 20, as rising over the spot where the Seven Sleepers had their experience.

then be a bastard if I cannot enter through that narrow cleft!" "What is this that thou art saying?" I asked. "This is a place," he replied, [8] "through which no son of adultery can enter. He cannot possibly enter therein." This statement made me rise and enter in that place. I prayed in it and came out without, as Allah knows, believing what he had said. Most of the troops, thereupon, came, went in and recited their prayers. But one of my officers, Barāq al-Zubaydi, had a black slave, devout and assiduous in prayer. The same, though one of the leanest and tallest of men, came in turn to that place, exerted every effort to get in, but could not do it. The poor fellow came back crying, moaning and sighing for having failed to get in through the cleft.

An encounter with the Franks at 'Asqalān.—We arrived in 'Asqalān at dawn and had just finished unloading our baggage and putting it by the public place of prayer when, with the rising sun, the sight of the Franks greeted our eyes. Presently, Nāṣir-al-Dīn Yāqūt, the governor of 'Asqalān, hurried towards us saying, "Lift away, lift away, your loads!" "Art thou afraid," said I, "lest [47] the Franks should wrest them from us?" "Yes," said he. "Well," I replied, "fear not. They have been sighting us in the desert and following a route opposite ours until we got to 'Asqalān, and we had no fear of them. Shall we now then have fear of them while we are here by a town that belongs to us?"

After remaining quietly at some distance from us for a little while, the Franks returned to their territory, mustered more men and came against us with their cavalry, infantry and tents, bent upon the attack of 'Asqalān. We went out to meet them and found that the foot soldiers of 'Asqalān had also made a sortie against them. So I made a tour around this band of foot soldiers and said to them, "Friends! Go back behind your wall and leave us alone with them. If we win the victory over them, then ye shall join us; but if they win the victory over us, then ye shall be safe behind your wall." But they refused to return. So I left them alone and went against the Franks, who had just unloaded their tents in order to pitch them. We surrounded them and pressed them so hard that they had no time to fold their tents. So they threw them away, spread as they were, and hastily retreated.

[47] The manuscript has *la*, which should probably be corrected to read *li'alla*.

As the Franks were at some distance from the town, they were pursued by a number of unworthy meddlers [48] incapable of resistance and devoid of capacity. The Franks turned once more against them, attacked them and slew a few of their number. So the foot soldiers, whom I had asked to keep back but who refused to do so, were routed and threw down their shields. We then made another encounter with the Franks, repulsed them and made them return to their own territory, which was close to 'Asqalān. Those of the foot soldiers who were put to rout came back blaming each other and saying, "Ibn-Munqidh certainly knew more than we did. He advised us to return, but we refused, which resulted in our rout and disgrace"

Another encounter on the way back from Bayt-Jibrīl. — Among those who had come in my company from Damascus to 'Asqalān were my brother 'Izz-al-Dawlah abu-al-Ḥasan 'Ali [49] (may Allah's mercy rest upon his soul!) and his followers He (may Allah's mercy rest upon his soul!) was one of the distinguished cavaliers of the Moslems — one who fought for the sake of religion and not for the sake of this world. One day we went out together from 'Asqalān for an incursion against Bayt-Jibrīl [50] and for an attack upon its inhabitants. After we arrived there and fought them, [9] I saw, as we were returning to our town, heaps of grain. I immediately ordered my companions to halt, and we began to strike sparks of fire and apply them to the threshing floors, following this course from one place to another while the main body of the army had preceded me. The Franks (may Allah's curse be upon them!) [51] assembled from all their fortresses, which were near each other teeming with cavalry ever in readiness for an attack upon 'Asqalān by day or by night, and came out against our comrades.

A horseman from our men came to me galloping and said, "The Franks are here!" So I hastened towards them as the vanguard of the Franks had come into contact with them. The Franks

[48] The word, possibly *al-fuḍūliyyīn*, is blurred in the original.

[49] An elder brother of Usāmah, died in Ghazzah, A D 1152

[50] Or Bayt-Jibrīn, a fortified place about halfway between Ghazzah and Jerusalem. Yāqūt, *op cit*, vol I, p 776

[51] This is a literal translation of an Arabic phrase, *la'anahum allāh*, used rather conventionally by Usāmah whenever the name of the Franks is mentioned as an imprecation of evil and in opposition to the invocation of blessing, mercy or favor used after the names of prominent Moslems and the Prophet.

(may Allah's curse be upon them!), who of all men are the most cautious in warfare, climbed to the top of a small hill where they made their stand, and we climbed to the top of another hill, opposite them. Between the two hills stretched an open place in which our isolated comrades and those leading the extra horses were passing, right beneath the Franks, without having a horseman [52] descend to them for fear of some ambush or stratagem of war, although if they had descended they would have succeeded in capturing them to the last man. Thus we stood facing them on that hill in spite of the inferior number of our force and the fact that the main part of our army had gone ahead of us in flight.

The Franks kept their post on top of the hill until the passage of our comrades had ceased. They then marched towards us and we immediately retreated before them, fighting the while. They made no effort to follow after us; but any one of us who stopped his horse they slew, and any one whose horse fell they took as prisoner. Finally the Franks turned back from us. Thus Allah (worthy of admiration is he!) had decreed our safety through their overcautiousness. Had we been as numerous as they were and had won the victory over them as they had won over us, we would have exterminated them.

An assault on Yubna. — In 'Asqalān I spent four months with the object of fighting the Franks. In the course of this time, we made an attack on Yubna [53] in which we killed about a hundred persons and carried away some prisoners.

Usāmah's brother killed. — At the expiration of this period a letter was received from al-Malik al-'Ādil (may Allah's mercy rest upon his soul!) summoning me to his presence. Consequently I proceeded to Egypt, while my brother, 'Izz-al-Dawlah abu-al-Ḥasan 'Ali (may Allah's mercy rest upon his soul!), remained in 'Asqalān. The army of 'Asqalān set out for an attack on Ghazzah in the course of which my brother (may Allah's mercy rest upon his soul!) fell martyr. He was one of the distinguished savants, cavaliers and devout men among the Moslems.

Al-'Ādil murdered. — As for the rebellion in which al-Malik

[52] Ar *fāris* is equally used for "horseman" and "knight" It is therefore difficult to know in each case how to render it exactly in English

[53] An ancient seaport in Palestine, mentioned in Jos. XV : 11 and II Chron. XXVI : 6.

al-'Ādil ibn-al-Sallār was killed (may Allah's mercy rest upon his soul!) its story is as follows:

Ibn-al-Sallār had equipped for the conquest of Bilbīs [54] an army commanded by the son of his wife Rukn-al-Dīn 'Abbās ibn-abi-al-Futūḥ ibn-Tamīm ibn-Badīs. Its object was to keep the land free from the Franks. In the company of 'Abbās was his son, Nāṣir-al-Dīn Naṣr ibn-'Abbās (may Allah's mercy rest upon his soul!), who, after staying with his father in the army for a few days, entered Cairo without permission or authorization from al-'Ādil. Al-'Ādil disapproved of his action and ordered him to rejoin the army, acting under the assumption that the young man had gone to Cairo for the sake of amusement and curiosity [10] and on account of having been bored with life in a soldiers' camp

But ibn-'Abbās had in the meantime worked out a plan with al-Ẓāfir according to which he arranged that a group of al-Ẓāfir's attendants should, under his leadership, assault al-'Ādil in his own residence after he had entered into the harem apartment in the evening to bathe and to sleep, and should thus put him to death. Ibn-'Abbās had also arranged with one of the prefects [55] of al-'Ādil to have him notify ibn-'Abbās as soon as al-'Ādil was asleep. Since the mistress of the house, the wife of al-'Ādil, was the grandmother of ibn-'Abbās, the latter could be admitted without special permission.

When al-'Ādil had gone to sleep, that prefect notified ibn-'Abbās, who, with six of his attendants, made an assault upon him in the house in which he was sleeping and killed him (may Allah's mercy rest upon his soul!). Ibn-'Abbās cut off his head and carried it to al-Ẓāfir. That took place on Thursday, the sixth of Muḥarram, in the year 548.[56]

In the palace of al-'Ādil were about a thousand men, including his mamelukes and the sentry on duty. But all these were in his reception palace [57] while he was killed in his harem's palace. These men now rushed from the palace and a battle raged between them

[54] Colloquially "Bilbays," a city lying northeast of Cairo on the main caravan route to Syria.

[55] *min ustādhi al-dār* = *ostadar*, one of the eunuchs in the service of the palace. See Qalqashandi, *op cit*, vol III, pp 484–85

[56] April 3, 1153

[57] *dār al-salām*, Turkish *salāmlik*, that part of the house where callers are received Moslem houses are built in two sections, one for men callers on the master and the other, private for the harem

and the followers of al-Ẓāfir and ibn-'Abbās until the head of al-'Ādil was raised on the point of a lance. As soon as they saw that, they split up into two groups, one of which went out through the Cairo Gate [*bāb-al-qāhirah*] to where 'Abbās was, offering him their services and loyalty, and the other group laid down their arms and presented themselves before Naṣr ibn-'Abbās, kissing the ground before him and holding themselves ready for his service.

'Abbās becomes vizier. — In the morning his father, 'Abbās, entered Cairo and installed himself in the Vizierate Palace. Al-Ẓāfir invested him with the robe of honor and intrusted to him the whole administration. As for Naṣr himself he became the constant companion and associate of the caliph to the great dislike of his father, 'Abbās, who distrusted his son because he ['Abbās] was cognizant of the common practice by which one party was usually instigated against another, until both parties were exterminated and all their possessions were then appropriated by the instigator.

As they were one evening in seclusion engaging in mutual recrimination, 'Abbās and his son called me to their presence. 'Abbās was reiterating one reproach after another in the hearing of his son, whose head was bowed down, as if he were a leopard, and who was refuting his charges word by word, which made 'Abbās rage more and more with anger and redouble his blame and reprimand. Hearing that, I said to 'Abbās:

O my lord al-Afḍal,[58] how much wilt thou blame my lord Nāsir-al-Dīn and rebuke him while he is silent? Rather direct thy blame against me, for I am his associate in everything he does, and cannot absolve myself from the wrong or right thing he accomplishes. Now what is his guilt? He did not maltreat any of thy followers, did not squander any of thy money and did not adversely criticize thy administration. He has rather risked his life to the end that thou mayest acquire this high position. There is nothing, therefore, which he has done to deserve thy blame.

Hearing that, his father desisted, and the son took favorable note of my attitude.

The caliph instigates ibn-'Abbās against his father. — Al-Ẓāfir now took steps to induce ibn-'Abbās to kill his own father, promising to install him in the vizierate as his successor. To this end he began

[58] A title of 'Abbās See abu-Shāmah, *Kitāb al-Rawḍatayn fi Akhbār al-Dawlatayn* (Cairo, 1287–88 A.H), vol I, p. 98

to bestow rich gifts on him. I was one day present in the company of Naṣr when he received twenty trays of silver holding twenty thousand dīnārs. After neglecting him for a few days, the caliph sent him an assortment of clothing of all kinds, [11] the like of which I never saw before in one collection. After neglecting him again for a few more days, he sent him this time fifty trays of silver holding fifty thousand dīnārs. Again he neglected him for a few days, and then sent him thirty saddle mules and forty camels, all fully provided with their outfits, bags and ropes. The man who acted as a medium between the caliph and Naṣr was one named Murtafa' ibn-Faḥl. All that took place while I was in the constant company of ibn-'Abbās, who would not allow me to be absent by night or by day. I used to sleep with my head at the end of his pillow.

One night as I was staying with him in the Shābūrah Palace, behold, there came Murtafa' ibn-Faḥl and carried on a conversation with him during the first third of the night, while I kept away by myself. When Murtafa' departed, Naṣr called me and said, "Where art thou?" "By the window," I replied, "reading the Koran; for all day long I have had no time to read it." He then began to disclose to me something of what they were discussing, in order to learn my sentiments, desiring me at the same time to fortify him in the evil resolution which al-Ẓāfir was inducing him to carry out. I said to him, "O my lord, let not the devil cause thee to stumble, and be not deceived by him who wishes to delude thee! To murder thy father is not the same as to murder al-'Ādil. Undertake to do nothing, therefore, for which thou shalt be accursed till judgment day." Naṣr bent his head down and cut short the conversation. We then both went to sleep.

The caliph assassinated by his vizier. — Finally, he disclosed the scheme[59] to his father, who cajoled him, won him over to his side and, in turn, concerted with him the murder of al-Ẓāfir. The caliph and Naṣr were in the habit of going out by night disguised, as they were comrades and of the same age. So one day Nasr invited the caliph to come to his residence, which was situated in Sūq al-Suyūfiyyīn,[60] after having installed a band of his followers on one side of

[59] The Arabic construction is such that it may mean that the scheme was disclosed to the father by someone else.

[60] The sword-makers' street.

the house. As soon as the caliph was seated, the band rushed upon him and killed him. This took place during the night preceding Thursday, the last day of Muḥarram, year 549.[61] Naṣr threw the body in a deep pit under his home. The caliph was accompanied by a black servant named Sa'īd-al-Dawlah, who never left his company. He also was killed.

The next morning 'Abbās proceeded to the palace, as he was wont to do, in order to present his greetings, the day being Thursday. He took his berth in the vizierate assembly room as if he was expecting the arrival of al-Ẓāfir to receive the usual morning homage. When the time in which al-Ẓāfir was accustomed to give audience had passed, 'Abbās called the major-domo of the palace and said to him, "What is the matter with our lord that he has not yet taken his seat in order to receive our homage?" The major-domo hesitated, not knowing what to answer. 'Abbās then yelled at him, saying, "Why dost thou not answer me?" "My master," he replied, "we know not where our lord is." 'Abbās then said, "Can the like of our lord be lost? Hasten back and find out what the matter is." The major-domo departed and returned, saying, "We have not found our lord." 'Abbās thereupon said, "The Moslem community cannot stay without a caliph. Go in, therefore, to where the amīrs, his brothers, are, so that one of them may come out and we shall swear allegiance to him as the new caliph." He departed and then returned saying, "The amīrs say to thee, 'We have nothing whatsoever to do in the matter. Al-Ẓāfir's father has disinherited us all from authority and invested it in al-Ẓāfir. After him, authority belongs to his son.'" "Bring him out," said 'Abbās, "so that we may swear allegiance to him."

Al-Ẓāfir's son proclaimed caliph.—'Abbās, having put al-Ẓāfir to death, proposed now [12] to claim that it was his own brothers who had killed him, and then to punish them for the crime by putting them to death. The son of al-Ẓāfir, who was still an infant, appeared before the people, carried on the shoulder of one of the prefects. 'Abbās took the boy and carried him in his arms. The people wept. Then 'Abbās, still carrying the child, entered the audience chamber of al-Ẓāfir, in which were gathered the sons

[61] April 15, 1154.

of al-Ḥāfiẓ, al-Amīr Yūsuf and al-Amīr Jibrīl, together with the son of their brother, al-Amīr abu-al-Baqa.[62]

Other members of the royal family put to death. — As we were sitting in the portico, with about a thousand of the Egyptian troops in the palace, we were startled with the rushing out of a band from the audience chamber towards the hall, while the clatter of the swords on the body of a victim could be heard. I then said to an Armenian attendant who was in my company, "Find out who this is that they are killing." He immediately went and returned, saying, "These people cannot be Moslems! It is my lord abu-al-Amānah (referring to al-Amīr Jibrīl) whom they have killed. One of them has cut open his abdomen and is pulling out his intestines." Then 'Abbās came out, dragging the Amīr Yūsuf by tucking under his armpit Yūsuf's uncovered head streaming with blood from a sword slash administered by him. Abu-al-Baqa, the son of the brother of al-Ẓāfir, followed, conducted by Naṣr ibn-'Abbās. They were both taken inside of an inner chamber in the palace and killed. All this took place while inside the palace were a thousand swords all unsheathed.

That day was one of the most distressing days I have passed in my life, on account of the abhorrent injustice committed in it, which is condemned by Allah (exalted is he!) and by all his creatures.

The watchman dies performing his duty. — An extraordinary incident that happened that day was the following:

When 'Abbās wanted to enter the audience room, he found that its door had been locked from the inside. The man in charge of opening and locking the audience room was an old watchman named Amīn-al-Mulk. They managed after several attempts to force the door open, and as they went in, they found that watchman behind the door dead with the key still in his hand.

'Abbās subdues the rebels. — As for the rebellion which broke out in Cairo and resulted in the victory of 'Abbās over the Egyptian army, it took place as follows:

When 'Abbās did with the children of al-Ḥāfiẓ (may Allah's mercy rest upon his soul!) what he did, all the people's hearts were hardened against him and harbored in them hostility and hatred. Those daughters of al-Ḥāfiẓ who had remained in the palace now

[62] *Al-Rawḍatayn*, vol. I, p 98. "abu-al-Baqā'."

entered into correspondence with the leading champion of the Moslems, abu-al-Ghārāt Ṭalā'i' ibn-Ruzzīk (may Allah's mercy rest upon his soul!), appealing to him for aid. He set out from the province [63] over which he ruled and marched towards Cairo. 'Abbās issued his orders, and the fleet was immediately put in repair and provided with the necessary provisions, weapons and coffers. He then ordered his troops to mount and march with him. This took place on Thursday, the tenth of Ṣafar, in the year 49.[64] He ordered his son, Nāṣir-al-Dīn, to remain in Cairo and said to me, "Thou shalt remain with him"

As 'Abbās left his home to meet ibn-Ruzzīk, the army hatched a plot against him and closed the gates of Cairo. The battle raged between them and us in the streets and in the alleys, their cavalry fighting us in the streets, their infantry showering us [13] with arrows and stones from the roofs, and their women and children hurling stones at us from the windows. The fighting between us lasted from early morning till late afternoon, resulting in the victory of 'Abbās. The rebels opened the gates of Cairo and took to flight. 'Abbās chased them into the interior of the land of Egypt, and having killed whom he could of their number, he returned to his home and reëstablished himself in his position of issuing orders and prohibitions. He issued orders for the destruction of al-Barqiyyah [65] quarter by fire, because the homes of the soldiers were all grouped in it, but I sought gently to cool him down on this matter by saying to him, "O my lord, in case the fire is started it will consume what thou pleasest and what thou dost not please, and thou wouldst not know how to extinguish it." Thus I succeeded in changing his idea regarding this. I also succeeded in securing from him a guarantee of safety in behalf of al-Amīr al-Mu'taman ibn-abi-Ramādah after he had ordered his execution. I offered an apology for him, and 'Abbās pardoned his guilt.

'Abbās resolves to depart for Syria. — The rebellion now subsided, but 'Abbās was greatly alarmed on account of it, because it demonstrated beyond doubt to him the hostility of the army and amīrs, and convinced him that he could no more live among them. He made up his mind to depart from Egypt and go to Syria to

[63] Munyah bani-Khasīb, in Upper Egypt.
[64] That is, 549 = April 26, 1154.
[65] A quarter of Cairo in the eastern part of the city, so called after the regiment from Barqah (Barca).

al-Malik al-'Ādil Nūr-al-Dīn (may Allah's mercy rest upon his soul!) in order to implore his assistance. In the meantime, the messengers between those who were in the palaces [66] and ibn-Ruzzīk were going back and forth. With the latter (may Allah's mercy rest upon his soul!) I was bound by ties of amity and fellowship ever since I entered the land of Egypt. He now dispatched a messenger to me, saying:

'Abbās will not be able to stay in Egypt; he is rather departing from it to Syria I shall then rule over the land, and thou knowest what exists between me and thee. Depart not therefore with him; though he, in his need for thee in Syria, shall encourage thee to accompany him. I conjure thee by Allah to join him not, for thou art my partner in everything good that I may attain.

It must have been the devils who whispered all this into the ears of 'Abbās, or perhaps he suspected it because he was cognizant of the bond of friendship between me and ibn-Ruzzīk.

'Abbās prepares for the trip. — As for the conspiracy which resulted in the departure of 'Abbās from Egypt and his death at the hands of the Franks, its story is as follows:

When he suspected what he suspected regarding the accord between ibn-Ruzzīk and myself, or when he was informed about it, he called me to his presence and made me take the most solemn oaths, from which there is no escape, that I should depart with him and keep his constant company. Even that did not satisfy him until he sent in the nighttime the chief prefect of his palace, who had permission to enter into his harem apartment, and made him take my wife,[67] my mother and my children into his palace, and said to me, "I shall defray for thee all expenses connected with their travel and shall transport them with the mother of Nāṣir-al-Dīn." 'Abbās made ready for the voyage his horses, camels and mules, which numbered two hundred horses and mares led by ropes attached to the hands of footmen, according to the custom of Egypt, two hundred saddle mules, and four hundred camels for carrying the baggage.

'Abbās was devoted to the study of the stars, and under the influence of a favorable horoscope he had fixed Saturday, the

[66] That is, between the members of the royal family.
[67] *ahl*, which may also mean "wives."

fifteenth of Rabī' I [68] of that year as the day of departure. I was in his presence when an attendant, called 'Antar [69] al-Kabīr ["the great"], who was in charge of all his affairs, big and small, entered and said:

O my lord, what thing is there to hope for from our departure to Syria? Rather take thy treasure, family, servants and those who [14] wish to follow thee and take us to Alexandria, where we can recruit and muster new troops and then return to fight ibn-Ruzzīk and his partisans If we win the victory, thou shalt reestablish thyself in thy home and in thy kingdom, but if we fail, we shall return to Alexandria, to a town where we can fortify ourselves and which our enemy will find impossible to reduce.

'Abbās rebuked him and declared his counsel wrong, although it was the right one.

The second day, Friday, 'Abbās summoned me early in the morning; and when I presented myself before him, I said to him, "O my lord, if I am going to be in thy company from dawn till night, when am I then to make the necessary preparation for the voyage?"

"We have with us some messengers from Damascus," said he. "Thou shalt see them off and then go and attend to thy business."

A conspiracy is hatched. — Previous to this, he had brought before him certain amīrs from whom he exacted an oath that they would not betray him nor enter into a conspiracy against him. He had also brought before him a group of the chiefs of certain Arab tribes, including Darmā', Zurayq, Judhām, Sinbis, Ṭalḥah, Ja'far and Lawātah,[70] and made them take an oath by the Koran and by divorce, for the same object. But as I was in his company early Friday morning, we were startled to see the people in full armor marching against us, headed by the same amīrs whose oaths he had exacted the day before.

'Abbās immediately ordered that his mounts be all saddled. Accordingly they were saddled and brought to halt before the door of his residence, thus forming a barrier between us and the Egyptians, which prevented the Egyptians from reaching us on account

[68] May 30, 1154

[69] Or 'Anbar, as his name occurs in Usāmah's *Dīwān* and in *al-Rawḍatayn*, vol. I, p 98

[70] This is a Berber and not an Arab tribe.

of the crowding of the beasts in the way. Then his attendant, 'Antar al-Kabīr, who had offered 'Abbās that counsel, appeared before the other attendants, whose major he was, howling at them and cursing them, saying, "Go to your homes!" Accordingly they let the beasts alone; the grooms, the muleteers, and the camel-drivers all dispersed, and the beasts were left by themselves. Plunder was carried on without obstacle among them.

'Abbās then said to me, "Go out and bring here the Turks who are stationed near Bāb-al-Naṣr,[71] and the secretaries shall pay them liberally." As soon as I came to them and summoned them, they all mounted their horses, they being about eight hundred horsemen, and went out through the Cairo Gate, turning their backs in flight against the battle scene. The mamelukes, who were even more numerous than the Turks, also made their way out through Bāb-al-Naṣr. And I returned to 'Abbās and gave him all the information. I then busied myself in taking out my family, whom he had transported into his residence. I succeeded in taking them out, and in taking out also the family of 'Abbās. And when the way was clear and all the beasts were plundered to the last one, the Egyptian troops reached us and turned us out of our place, we being only few in number and they a great host.

When we had passed out of Bāb-al-Naṣr, they went around all the gates of the city, closed them up and turned back to our homes, which they plundered. From the hall of my home they carried away forty huge camel bags all sewn up and containing great quantities of silver, gold and clothing, and from my stable they marched away thirty-six horses and female saddle mules with their saddles and full equipment, together with twenty-five camels. From my fief in Kūm-Ashfīn they took away two hundred head of cattle from the tenants, a thousand sheep and a granary-full of wheat.

As we got a short distance away from Bāb-al-Naṣr, the same Arab tribes from whom 'Abbās had exacted an oath assembled and fought against us from Friday [15] early in the morning until Thursday, the twentieth of Rabī' I [72] They would fight us all day long, and when the night fell and we dismounted, they would let

[71] The gate of victory. Al-Maqrīzī, *al-Khiṭaṭ*, ed. Gaston Wiet (Cairo, 1913), vol. II, pp 92, 174

[72] May 29 to June 4, 1154.

us alone until we slept, and then they would send a hundred horsemen who would mount and hurl their horses at the sides of our camp, yelling with loud voices. Such of our horses as were startled and ran in their direction they would immediately seize.

Usāmah wounded. — One day I found myself separated from my companions, with a white horse under me which was the worst of all my horses. The groom had saddled it without knowing what was going to happen. I had no weapon except my sword. The Arabs made an assault on me, but I found nothing with which to repulse them, my horse was incapable of carrying me outside of their reach, and their lances were already reaching me. I said to myself, "I shall jump down from my horse, draw my sword and repulse them." As I collected myself in order to jump, my horse stumbled and I fell upon stones and rough ground. A piece of skin was cut from my head, and I became so dizzy that I knew not where I was. As I sat there stunned, with my head covered and my sheathed sword thrown off, some of the Arabs stood by me. One of them struck me twice with the sword, saying, "Deliver the money!" But I knew not what he said. They then made off with my horse and my sword.

Seeing me, the Turks hurried back to me. Nāsir-al-Dīn ibn-'Abbās dispatched to me a horse and a sword. And I started without having even a bandage to dress my wounds. Worthy of admiration is he whose kingdom lasts forever!

We all set out with none of us having a handful of provisions. When I wanted to drink, I would dismount and drink from the palm of my hand, while the night before I started, as I was sitting on a chair in one of the hallways of my home, somebody had offered me sixteen camels for carrying water,[73] with as many as Allah the praiseworthy wanted of water and food bags.

Finding myself unable to transfer my family, I made them go back from Bilbīs to al-Malik al-Ṣāliḥ abu-al-Ghārāt Ṭalā'i' ibn-Ruzzīk (may Allah's mercy rest upon his soul!) who treated them with favor, assigned to them a dwelling place and fixed a stipend to pay for their needs.

When the Arabs who were fighting us wanted to desist and go

[73] *jamal rawāya.* It may, however, read *ḥamlah rawāya*, which would make it "skin water bags."

back, they came to us demanding a guaranty of safety for the period after our return.[74]

'Abbās killed by the Franks. — We continued our march until Sunday, the 23d of Rabī' I,[75] on the morning of which the Franks suddenly encountered us *en masse* at al-Muwayliḥ.[76] They killed 'Abbās and his son Ḥusām-al-Mulk and captured his other son Nāṣir-al-Dīn.[77] They took the treasures of 'Abbās and his harem, and put to death all those [of the troops] who fell into their hands. They also took my brother Najm-al-Dawlah abu-'Abdallāh Muḥammad (may Allah's mercy rest upon his soul!) captive. They finally turned away from us after we had fortified ourselves against them in the mountains.

Perils at Petra. — Then we made our way in the territory of the Franks in a state worse than death, with no provisions for the men and no fodder for the horses until we arrived in [16] the mountains of the banu-Fuhayd (may Allah's curse be upon them!) in Wādi-Mūsa.[78] Our climb was effected through narrow rough roads leading into a vast plain and among men who were accursed devils. Any one of us they found isolated from the rest, they put to death.

That region is never free from some Rabī'ah amīrs of the banu-Ṭayy. So I asked, "Who is here now of the banu-Rabī'ah amīrs?" And I was answered, "Manṣūr ibn-Ghidafl." Now this man was my friend. So I paid someone two dīnārs and said, "Go to Manṣūr and tell him, 'Thy friend, ibn-Munqidh, presents his salaams and asks thee to come to him early in the morning.'" That night we spent ill for fear of them.

When the morning light dawned, they came fully equipped and stationed themselves at the spring and said, "We shall not let you drink our water and let ourselves die of thirst." They said this, in spite of the fact that the spring had sufficient water for both Rabī'ah and Muḍar,[79] and that they had many other springs like it in their lands. Their object was simply to provoke trouble between them and us and then to capture us.

[74] *Al-Rawḍatayn*, vol I, p 98 [75] June 7, 1154

[76] A station on the route between Egypt and Palestine, lying in the mountain of the same name separating the Sinaitic Peninsula from Arabia Petraea.

[77] His sad fate is described by ibn-Khallikān, *Ta'rīkh* (Cairo), vol II, p 123 = *Biographical Dictionary*, translated by de Slane (Paris, 1842–71), vol. II, p. 427.

[78] The valley in which Petra is located This name it still bears.

[79] The two main groups into which the north Arabs are divided by Arab writers. The meaning here is that there was enough water for all the Arabs put together.

As we were in this juncture, lo, Manṣūr ibn-Ghidafl arrived, howled at them and cursed them. So they dispersed. Then he said, "Mount!" So we rode and descended, following a road even narrower and rougher than the one which I had followed going up. We arrived at the bottom of the valley safe and sound after coming very near losing our lives. I then made a collection of a thousand Egyptian dīnārs for al-Amīr Manṣūr and paid it to him. He then returned.

Arrival in Damascus. — We continued our march with those of us who escaped the massacre of the Franks and banu-Fuhayd until we arrived in Damascus on Friday, the fifth of Rabīʻ I, of the same year.[80] Our safety on such a journey was one of the manifest signs of the almightiness of Allah (powerful and majestic is he!) and of his magnificent protection.

The story of a rich saddle belonging to Usāmah. — One of the amazing things that happened to me during that conflict was the following:

Al-Ẓāfir had once sent to ibn-ʻAbbās a young graceful ambler of Frankish breed. One day I went to a village which belonged to me, while my son abu-al-Fawāris Murhaf was in the company of ibn-ʻAbbās. The latter said, "We wish to secure for this ambler an elegant saddle, one of those made in Ghazzah." My son replied, "I know one, my lord, which is above desire." "Where is it?" he asked. "It is in the home of thy servant, my father," replied my son. "He has a Ghazzi saddle which is elegant." Ibn-ʻAbbās said, "Send someone to fetch it." So he sent a messenger to my home and took the saddle. Ibn-ʻAbbās admired the saddle and fixed it on the ambler. This saddle was brought with me from Syria on one of the extra horses led by my side. It was quilted, had a black border and was of extraordinarily beautiful effect. It weighed one hundred thirty *mithqāls*.[81]

On my return from my fief, Nāṣir-al-Dīn said to me, "Taking advantage of our friendship, we felt bold to take this saddle from thy house." To this I replied, "O my lord, how happy I am to be of service to thee!"

Now when the Franks made the attack on us at al-Muwayliḥ,

[80] June 19, 1154

[81] A *mithqāl* is ordinarily three to four grams This would make the saddle entirely too light.

I had with me five of my mamelukes riding on camels, the Arabs having taken their horses. When the Franks attacked and defeated us, some horses were left riderless and my attendants dismounted from [17] their camels, intercepted the course of the horses and took of them such as they required to ride. And, behold, on one of the horses which they took was that same saddle of gold which ibn-'Abbās had appropriated for himself.

Among those who survived from our party were Ḥusām-al-Mulk, a cousin of 'Abbās, and a brother [82] of 'Abbās ibn-al-'Ādil.[83] Ḥusām-al-Mulk, who had heard the story of the saddle, said in my hearing, "Everything that this poor fellow (referring to ibn-'Abbās) possessed has been pillaged, some by the Franks and some by his own companions." I said to him, "Perhaps thou art alluding to the saddle of gold." "Yes," said he. So I ordered that the saddle be brought and said to him, "Read what is on it. Is it 'Abbās' name and his son's, or is it my name? And who else in the days of al-Ḥāfiẓ could ride in Egypt on a gold saddle but I?" My name was written in black around the border of the saddle, the center of which was quilted. Having read what was on it, he apologized and kept his silence.

The unheeded example of al-Afḍal. — Had it not been for the unavoidable execution of the divine will on 'Abbās and his son and for the consequences of injustice and ingratitude, 'Abbās would certainly have learned a lesson from what had happened before him to al-Afḍal Riḍwān ibn-al-Walakhshi (may Allah's mercy rest upon his soul!). The latter was a vizier when the troops, at the instigation of al-Ḥāfiẓ, rose against him just as they rose against 'Abbās, and he departed from Egypt for Syria. His home and his harem were pillaged to such an extent that a man known by the name of al-Qā'id [84] Muqbil saw with the Sūdānese a maid whom he bought from them and sent to his own home. Muqbil had a virtuous wife who took the maid up to a chamber in the uppermost part of the house. There she heard the maid say, "May Allah enable us to triumph over those who have dealt so unjustly with us and abjured our benefactions to them!" So she asked her, "Who art thou?" And the maid replied, "I am Qatr-al-Nada,[85] daughter of

[82] In fact, a half brother [83] This al-'Ādil was the vizier ibn-al-Sallār

[84] Commander of a hundred, al-Tabari, *Ta'rikh* (Leyden, 1883–84), vol. III, p. 1799. [85] "Dewdrop."

Riḍwān." The wife immediately sent word to her husband, al-Qā'id Muqbil, who was on duty at the door of the [royal] palace, made him come home and acquainted him with the condition of the young girl. So he wrote a report to al-Ḥāfiẓ and acquainted him with the facts. Al-Ḥāfiẓ dispatched certain servants to the palace, who took her from the Muqbil's home and brought her back to the palace.

Usāmah on a mission to al-Afḍal. — After that, Riḍwān arrived in Ṣalkhad [86] where was Amīr-al-Dawlah Ṭughdakīn [87] Atābek (may Allah's mercy rest upon his soul!). The latter received Riḍwān with special honor, offered him a dwelling place and put his services at his disposal. At this time, the Malik-al-Umarā' [88] Atābek Zanki ibn-Āqsunqur (may Allah's mercy rest upon his soul!) was camping outside of Ba'labakk besieging it. So he communicated with Riḍwān and it was agreed that the latter would join him. Riḍwān was a perfect man, generous, courageous, good in writing and learned; the troops felt special inclination toward him on account of his generosity. Therefore al-Amīr Mu'īn-al-Dīn [89] (may Allah's favor be upon him!) said to me, "If this man should join the atābek, a great deal of disadvantage will ensue to us on account of him." "What dost thou propose, then?" asked I. "Thou shalt go to him," said he, "and perhaps thou shalt succeed in changing his mind regarding joining the atābek. Let him go to Damascus. Thou shalt use in carrying out this project thine own judgment and discretion."

Accordingly I made my way to Riḍwān in Ṣalkhad, where I met with him and with his brother, al-Awḥad, and held an interview with them. Al-Afḍal Riḍwān said to me, "This matter has now passed out of my hand. I have already given my promise to [18] this sultan that I shall join him. The fulfillment of my promise is now binding upon me." "May Allah have nothing but good awaiting thee!" said I. "As for me, I shall return to my master, for I know that he can never do without me; but he counted on me to disclose to thee what is in my heart." "Disclose it!" said he.

[86] One of the towns still standing in Ḥawrān

[87] This is probably a scribal error for "Kumushtakīn," since Ṭughdakīn was already dead by this time.

[88] "The king of princes," a title of 'Imād-al-Dīn Zanki.

[89] Mu'īn-al-Dīn Anar, vizier of Damascus.

"When thou joinest the atābek," said I, "would he have enough troops to divide into two halves, send one half with thee to Egypt and leave the other half to blockade us?" "No," he replied. "Well then," asked I, "when he camps outside of Damascus, lays siege to it and captures it, after a long period, would he then be able — with his troops depleted, their provisions exhausted and their march prolonged — to proceed with thee to Egypt before he replenishes his animal transport and strengthens his army?" "No," he replied. I said:

By that time he will say to thee, "We shall proceed to Aleppo in order to renovate our travel equipment." When ye arrive in Aleppo, he will say, "We shall advance to the Euphrates [90] in order to recruit the Turkomans." Once ye camp on the banks of the Euphrates he will say, "Unless we cross the Euphrates, we shall not be able to enlist the Turkomans." And when ye have crossed the Euphrates, he will send thee before him and boast over the sultans of the Orient, saying, "Behold! this is the ruler of Egypt,[91] who is now in my service!" It is then that thou wouldst wish to see one of the stones of Syria, but thou shalt not be able to do so. Thou shalt at that time recall my word and say, "He has given me good advice, but I did not accept it."

Riḍwān bent down his head, thinking, and not knowing what to say. He then turned his head towards me and said, "What can I do so long as thou desirest to return?" I replied, "If in my stay here I can further our interest, I shall stay." "Do so," said he.

Accordingly I stayed. The interviews between him and me were repeated until it was agreed that he would go to Damascus on condition that he should receive thirty thousand dīnārs, one half of which would be in cash and the other half in fief; that he should have, besides, the al-'Aqīqi Mansion [*dār*]; and that his companions should have special stipends. Riḍwān, who was an excellent writer, wrote with his own hand these conditions and said, "If thou wilt, I shall accompany thee." "No," said I, "I shall rather depart and take with me the pigeons from here. After I get there, vacate the mansion for thee and fix everything properly; I shall then let the pigeons fly to thee. At the same time I shall

[90] *al-furāt*, miscopied here in the manuscript to read *al-qurāt*, but spelled properly in the following lines

[91] *'azīz miṣr* a title borne by the Fāṭimite caliphs after the sixth one, 'Azīz (975–96), and also by the modern Khedives of Egypt

set out, so that I may meet thee midway, and thus enter Damascus in thy company." This was agreed upon. So I took leave of him and departed.

Riḍwān imprisoned in Egypt. — Amīn-al-Dawlah, on his part, was anxious that Riḍwān should return to Egypt, in view of the promises he had made in his behalf and the ambitions he had aroused in him. So he mustered the men whom he could and sent them out with him after I had left him. As soon as Riḍwān had crossed the frontiers of Egypt,[92] the Turkish troops who were with him betrayed him and pillaged his baggage. He himself took refuge in one of the Arab camps and opened correspondence with al-Ḥāfiẓ and asked him for a safe-conduct. He entered Cairo,[93] and the moment he arrived there both he and his son, on the orders of al-Ḥāfiẓ, were put in prison.

When I returned to Cairo[94] it happened that he was still in prison in a building on one side of the palace. By means of an iron nail he later dug a hole fourteen cubits [*dhirā'*] long and escaped the night preceding Thursday. He had among the amīrs a relative who was cognizant of his plans and who waited for him by the palace, together with a protégé of his belonging to the Lawātah tribe. The three walked to the Nile and crossed over into al-Jīzah.[95] Cairo was all in commotion [19] on account of his flight. The second morning found him in a belvedere in al-Jīzah, people rallied around him while the Egyptian army was getting ready for the combat against him. Early in the morning of Friday he recrossed into Cairo while the Egyptian army under the leadership of Qaymāz[96] Ṣāḥib-al-Bāb,[97] clad in their coats of mail, were all ready for the encounter. As soon as Riḍwān met them, he put them to flight and entered Cairo.

Riḍwān killed by one of his own men. — Riding on my horse, with my companions I had started towards the palace door before Riḍwān had made his entrance into the city. But I found the doors of the palace closed, with nobody standing by. So I turned back

92 September, 1139.
93 *miṣr*, which may as well mean Egypt.
94 November, 1144
95 Pronounced "al-Gīzah" by the modern Egyptians; ancient Memphis.
96 Tāj-al-Mulūk Qaymāz was his full name
97 "Master of the gate," a title given to an under-vizier. Qalqashandi, *op. cit.*, vol. III, p 483.

and entered my own home. Riḍwān established himself in al-Aqmar Mosque.[98]

The amīrs came to him *en masse* bringing to him food and money. In the meantime, al-Ḥāfiẓ had assembled a group of Sūdānese in his palace, who drank to the point of intoxication. He then opened for them the door of the palace and they rushed in seeking Riḍwān. When the screams were heard, all the amīrs who were with Riḍwān mounted their horses and dispersed. In his turn, Riḍwān went out of the mosque only to find that his horse had been taken away by the groom, who had disappeared.

A young man of the bodyguard saw Riḍwān standing by the door of the mosque and said to him, "O my lord, dost thou not want to ride my horse?" "Surely," replied Riḍwān. So the young man came at a gallop towards him with his sword in his hand. He then moved his arm as though he were bending to dismount and struck him with the sword. Riḍwān fell to the ground. The Sūdānese rushed and put him to death. The people of Egypt parceled out his flesh among them and ate it in order to acquire bravery.

His case was an object lesson, for learning by example,[99] and a warning — but the divine will must be executed.

Bloodletting saves the life of a wounded soldier. — On that battle day, one of our Syrian comrades received a number of wounds. His brother came to me and said, "My brother is in desperate plight. He has received so many wounds from swords and other weapons, and he is now unconscious and does not come to his senses." "Go back," said I, "and bleed him." He replied, "He has already lost twenty rotls [100] of blood!" "Go back," I repeated, "and bleed him! I have had more experience with wounds than thou. There is no other remedy for him but bloodletting." He went away, absented himself for two hours and then returned with his face showing signs of gratification, and said, "I have bled him and he regained his senses, sat up, ate and drank. All ill has departed from him." "Praise be to Allah!" said I. "Had I not tried this on my own self a number of times, I would not have prescribed it to thee."

[98] Built by the Fāṭimite Caliph al-Āmir in 1125

[99] *mu'tabar*, related to *i'tibār*, which is the name of this book

[100] An Oriental way of saying that he had already lost a great deal of blood. The Egyptian rotl today is equal to one pound avoirdupois

4. USĀMAH'S SECOND SOJOURN IN DAMASCUS 1154–1164 A.D.

After that I attached myself to the service of al-Malik al-'Ādil Nūr-al-Dīn (may Allah's mercy rest upon his soul!). He entered into correspondence with al-Malik al-Ṣāliḥ [1] with a view to letting my wife and children, who had lingered in Egypt and had been treated with benevolence, start on their journey. Al-Ṣāliḥ sent back the messenger and gave as excuse the fact that he feared for their safety from the Franks. He also wrote to me, saying:

Thou shalt return to Egypt, and thou knowest well what is between me and thee. If thou dost feel that the personnel of the palace cherish ill feeling towards thee, then proceed to Mecca, where I shall deliver to thee a communication granting thee the governorship of the city of Uswān.[2] I shall, moreover, reenforce thee with whatever is necessary for thee to wage successful warfare against the Abyssinians (Uswān being one of the border fortifications of the Moslem territory). I shall then let go to thee thy wives and thy children.

I consulted al-Malik al-'Ādil and sought his opinion and he said:

O Usāmah,[3] thou wert so glad to get rid of Egypt with its rebellions that thou didst hardly believe the day when it came, and now thou wantest to return to it! Life is too short for that. I [20] shall communicate with the king of the Franks [4] in order to secure a safe-conduct for thy family, and I shall then send someone to bring them hither.

Accordingly Nūr-al-Dīn (may Allah's mercy rest upon his soul!) dispatched a messenger and secured the safe-conduct of the king, with the cross on it,[5] good for both land and sea.

Usāmah's family pillaged by Franks on way from Egypt. — This safe-conduct I sent with one of my servants, who carried also a letter from al-Malik al-'Ādil and my letter to al-Malik al-Ṣāliḥ. Al-Ṣāliḥ transported my family on one of his private boats to

[1] Ibn-Ruzzīk [2] Present day Aswān, in Upper Egypt.
[3] *fulān*, used in place of any proper noun
[4] King Baldwin III of Jerusalem (1142–62)
[5] *waṣalībahu*, which may be read *waṣṣalanīhi* = "which was delivered to me."

Dimyāṭ, provided them with all the money and provisions they needed and gave them the proper recommendation. From Dimyāṭ they sailed in a Frankish vessel. As they approached 'Akka [Acre] where the king (may Allah's mercy not rest upon his soul!) was, he sent, in a small boat, a few men who broke the vessel with their axes under the very eyes of my people. The king mounted his horse, stood by the coast and pillaged everything that was there.

One of my retainers came swimming to the king, taking the safe-conduct with him, and said, "O my lord the king, is this not thy safe-conduct?" "Sure enough," replied the king. "But this is the usage for the Moslems. Whenever one of their vessels is wrecked near a town, the people of that town pillage it." "Art thou going, then, to take us captive?" inquired my retainer. "No," replied the king. The king (may Allah's curse be upon him!) then put them in a house, had the women searched and took everything they all possessed. In the vessel were jewelry, which had been intrusted to the women, clothes, gems, swords, weapons and gold and silver amounting to about thirty thousand dīnārs. The king took it all. He then sent my people five hundred dīnārs and said, "This will see you home," though they were no less than fifty persons, men and women.

At that time I was in the company of al-Malik al-'Ādil in the land of King Mas'ūd [6] in Ra'bān and Kaysūn. The safety of my children, my brother's children, and our harem made the loss of money which we suffered a comparatively easy matter to endure — with the exception of the books, which were four thousand volumes, all of the most valuable kind. Their loss has left a heartsore that will stay with me to the last day of my life.

Verily these are calamities which shake mountains and annihilate riches! But may Allah (worthy of admiration is he!) recompense [us] with his mercy and bring things to a good end by his kindness and forgiveness! Those were great happenings which I have experienced in addition to the calamities with which I was afflicted and out of which my person came safe, until the hour of fate should strike, but they left me ruined in my fortune.

Between those happenings were intervals in which I took part in innumerable battles against unbelievers as well as Moslems.

[6] Sultan of Iconium.

And now I shall proceed to recount what my memory has retained of the marvels I witnessed and experienced in warfare; for oblivion is not to be considered a cause for blame in the case of one by whom has passed a long series of years. Oblivion is rather a heritage of the children of Adam from their first father (may Allah's blessing and peace be upon him!).

5. BATTLES AGAINST FRANKS AND MOSLEMS

The cavalier's sense of honor: Jum'ah avenges his honor.— Among those marvels is what I witnessed of the horsemen's sense of honor and their intrepidity in facing dangers as illustrated in the following:

There was an encounter between us and Shihāb-al-Dīn Mahmūd ibn-Qarāja, the lord of Ḥamāh at that time.[1] The contest between us [21] continued without respite, the detachments being always ready and the swift riders[2] ever on the chase. There came to me one of our most distinguished soldiers and horsemen, named Jum'ah of the banu-Numayr, in tears. I asked him, "What is the matter with thee, O abu-Maḥmūd? Is this the time for crying?" "I have been pierced by a lance," he replied, "from the hand of Sarhank[3] ibn-abi-Manṣūr." "And suppose thou didst receive a wound from Sarhank," I asked, "what of it?" "Nothing at all," he replied, "except the idea that one like Sarhank should stab me! By Allah, death would have been easier for me than to have been wounded by him! But he took me by surprise and unaware." I then began to calm him and make matters look easy for him; but he turned the head of his horse and started back. "Where goest thou, O abu-Maḥmūd?" I asked. "To Sarhank," he replied. "By Allah, I shall either smite him or die in the attempt!" He absented himself for a short period, while I was busy with those [of the enemy] who were facing me. Then he came back laughing. I asked him, "What hast thou done?" And he replied, "I did stab him, by Allah! And had I not stabbed him, my soul would have surely departed from me"[4] What he did was to make an attack upon him while the latter was in the midst of his comrades, smite him and come right back.

[1] About 1123

[2] *mutasarri'ah*, which may be taken to mean "champion knights of duel," "leaders"

[3] Persian *sar-hang* = "combatant," "champion," "chief"

[4] He means to say that he would have died of regret for having failed to wound his adversary

The following verses were composed as if with reference to Sarhank and Jum'ah:

Hast thou considered, by Allah, how grand is the deed of one
Thirsty for vengeance, unforgetful of wrong!
Thou hast awakened him, then thou hast gone to sleep thyself; but he did not sleep,
On account of his rage against thee. And how can one so vigilant slumber?
If the vicissitudes of time shall yield him a chance — and perhaps they will
Some day — then will he mete out to thee an overflowing measure.

This Sarhank was one of the most noteworthy horsemen, a chief among the Kurds. But he was a young man, while Jum'ah was middle-aged, having the distinction of seniority of age as well as experience in acts of courage.

A duel between two Moslem champions. — In connection with this case of Sarhank I am reminded of what Mālik ibn-al-Ḥārith al-Ashtar (may Allah's mercy rest upon his soul!) did with abu-Musaykah al-Iyādi. It happened when the Arabs apostatized from Islam in the days of abu-Bakr al-Ṣiddīq (may Allah's high favor rest upon him!) and Allah (worthy of admiration is he!) made him resolve to fight them. He mustered his troops and set them against the apostate Arabs. Abu-Musaykah al-Iyādi was on the side of banu-Ḥanīfah, who were the most powerful of the Arabs, while Mālik al-Ashtar was at the head of the army of abu-Bakr. As the armies stood in battle array, Mālik stepped forward between the two ranks and shouted, "O abu-Musaykah!" In response, the latter stepped forward. Mālik then said to him, "Woe unto thee, O abu-Musaykah! After thy Islam and thy being one of the readers of the Koran, thou hast gone back to unbelief!" Abu-Musaykah replied, "Away from me, O Mālik! Moslems forbid the use of wine, and I cannot do without it." Mālik said, "I challenge thee to a duel with me." "I accept," replied abu-Musaykah. So the two had an encounter with the lances, and another encounter with the swords, in the course of which abu-Musaykah struck Mālik, split his head and inverted his eyelids. [22] On account of that blow, he was nicknamed al-Ashtar.[5] Mālik then retreated to his tent, hugging the neck of his horse. A group

[5] The man with the inverted eyelids.

of his relatives and friends gathered around him crying. So he said to one of them, "Put thy hand in my mouth." The man put his finger inside of Mālik's mouth and the latter bit it. The man twisted with pain. "Well," said Mālik, "nothing wrong with your man. For it is said that as long as the teeth are safe the head is safe. Stuff it (referring to the wound) with fine flour and bandage it with a turban." As soon as they had it stuffed and bandaged, he said, "Fetch my mare." "Whereto?" asked they. "To abu-Musaykah," he replied. Presently he issued between the two ranks and shouted, "O abu-Musaykah!" Abu-Musaykah sallied forth towards him like an arrow. Mālik struck him with the sword on his shoulder, which he split as far down as the saddle, and killed him. Mālik returned to his camp, where he remained forty days unable to move. After that he recovered and was healed from his wound.

Fāris's miraculous escape from a deadly blow. — Another illustration of the recovery of a stabbed person after it was thought that he was sure to die is the following case which I witnessed:

We had an encounter with the advance cavalry of Shihāb-al-Dīn Maḥmūd ibn-Qarāja,[6] who had invaded our territory and laid for us an ambuscade. After our forces and his had stood in battle array, our cavalry disbanded. One of our horsemen, named 'Ali ibn-Salām, a Numayrite, came to me and said, "Our horsemen have spread out. If the enemy should now attack them, they will annihilate them." I said to him, "Hold back from me my brothers and cousins so that I may bring those horsemen back." So he shouted, "O amīrs, let him bring back our men and follow him not. Otherwise the enemy will attack them and dislodge them." "Let him go," they replied. Accordingly I set out, trotting my horse until I brought them back, the enemy having kept away from them in order to draw them away as far as possible and then be able to overpower them. Seeing that I was bringing them back, the enemy attacked us; and those of them who lay in ambush came out, as I was at some distance from my comrades. I immediately turned back to oppose them, desiring thereby to defend the rear of my comrades, and found that my cousin, Layth-al-Dawlah Yaḥya (may Allah's mercy rest upon his soul!), had already turned around

[6] Lord of Ḥamāh.

from the rear of my comrades on the south side of the road while I was on the north side of it. So we both made a joint assault on them.

One of their horsemen, Fāris ibn-Zimām by name, a well-known Arab horseman, hurriedly passed us desiring to exercise his lance on our comrades. My cousin got to him before I did and smote him with his lance. Both he and his horse fell. The lance broke with such a crack that I and the others could hear it.

My father (may Allah's mercy rest upon his soul!) had previous to this sent a messenger to Shihāb-al-Dīn who brought the messenger along with him when he set out to fight against us. Now when Fāris ibn-Zimām was stabbed and Shihāb-al-Dīn failed in his plan against us, he sent back that same messenger from where he was, carrying a reply to the message he had brought him, and returned to Ḥamāh.

I asked the messenger, "Did Fāris ibn-Zimām die?" "No," he replied, "By Allah, there isn't even a wound in him." To this he added:

Layth-al-Dawlah smote him with the lance, while I was looking at him. He threw him and his horse down. I myself heard the crack of the lance when it broke. When Layth-al-Dawlah enveloped him from the left, Fāris turned his right side, holding in his hand his lance, upon which his horse fell, [23] while the lance fell under it into a ditch and broke. Layth-al-Dawlah turned behind his adversary to smite him with the lance, but the lance fell from his hand. What thou hast heard therefore was the crack of the lance of Fāris ibn-Zimām. As for the lance of Layth-al-Dawlah, it was brought before Shihāb-al-Dīn in my presence, and it was intact — not a break in it. And Fāris had not the least wound on him. I was amazed at his safety. That thrust was just as effective as the "stab of a consummate master of combat" mentioned by 'Antar:

> The horses and the horsemen know that I have
> Dispersed their assembly with the stab of a consummate master.

The whole army, including those who lay in ambush, returned without accomplishing what they had started out to do.

The verse quoted above is from a poem by 'Antarah ibn-Shaddād, in which he says:

Verily I am a man of whom one part belongs to the noble lineage of 'Abs,
But the other part I protect with my own sword.[7]

[7] 'Antarah's mother was a slave, so what he means to say here is that he is on one side of noble Arab descent but on the other self-made.

At the time in which the forces halt their advance and look askance,
I am found better than he who takes pride in his paternal and maternal
uncles.
If there was a way of representing death, it should certainly be presented
In my form — when they find themselves in a tight place.
The horses and the horsemen know that I have
Dispersed their assembly with the stab of a consummate master.
And as they challenged me to fight on horseback,
I was the first to enter the arena
For why should I ride a horse unless I am going to fight on its back?

Usāmah's first experience in warfare against the Franks.— Something similar to that happened to me during an attack on Afāmiyah.[8] It happened that Najm-al-Dīn Īlghāzi[9] ibn-Urtuq (may Allah's mercy rest upon his soul!) defeated the Franks at al-Balāṭ,[10] on Friday, the fifth of Jumāda I, in the year 513,[11] and annihilated them. He killed Roger [*rūjār*], the lord of Antioch, and all his cavalry. Thereupon my paternal uncle, 'Izz-al-Dīn abu-al-'Asākir Sulṭān (may Allah's mercy rest upon his soul!), set out to join Najm-al-Dīn, while my father (may Allah's mercy rest upon his soul!) remained behind in the Castle of Shayzar. My uncle had instructed my father to send me against Afāmiyah at the head of the men who were with me in Shayzar, and to call out the people, together with the Arabs,[12] for the pillage of the crops of Afāmiyah. A great number of the Arabs had recently joined us.

A few days after the departure of my uncle, the public announcer called us to arms, and I started at the head of a small band, hardly amounting to twenty horsemen, with full conviction that Afāmiyah had no cavalry in it. Accompanying me was a great body of pillagers and Bedouins. As soon as we arrived in the Valley of Bohemond,[13] and while the pillagers and the Arabs were scattered all over the planted fields, a large army of the Franks set out against us. They had been reinforced that very night by sixty horsemen

[8] Apamea, north of Shayzar, represented today by Qal'ah-al-Muḍīq

[9] "ibn-al-Ghāzi" in the manuscript He was the amīr of Māridīn

[10] A narrow gorge between two mountains north of al-Athārib Kamāl-al-Dīn, *Zubdah*, in *Recueil historiens orientaux*, vol III, p 617; R. Rohricht, *Beiträge zur Geschichte der Kreuzzuge* (Berlin, 1874), vol I, p 255

[11] August 14, 1119 This is the date of the second battle of Dānīth, with which this battle was evidently confused by the author The battle of al-Balāt, in which Roger was killed, took place June 28

[12] The reference is to nomadic Arabs — Bedouins.

[13] *wādi-abu-al-maymūn*

and sixty footmen. They repulsed us from the valley, and we retreated before them until we joined those of our number who were already in the fields, pillaging them. Seeing us, the Franks raised a violent uproar. Death seemed an easy thing to me in comparison with the loss of that crowd [24] in my charge. So I turned against a horseman in their vanguard, who had taken off his coat of mail in order to be light enough to pass before us, and thrust my lance into his chest. He instantly flew off his saddle, dead. I then faced their horsemen as they followed, and they all took to flight. Though a tyro in warfare, and having never before that day taken part in a battle, I, with a mare under me as swift as a bird, went on, now pursuing them and plying them with my lance, now taking cover from them.

In the rear guard of the Franks was a cavalier on a black horse, large as a camel, wearing a coat of mail and the full armor of war. I was afraid of this horseman, lest he should be drawing me further ahead in order to get an opportunity to turn back and attack me. All of a sudden I saw him spur his horse, and as the horse began to wave its tail, I knew that it was already exhausted. So I rushed on the horseman and smote him with my lance, which pierced him through and projected about a cubit in front of him. The lightness of my body, the force of the thrust and the swiftness of my horse made me lose my seat on the saddle. Moving backward a little, I pulled out my lance, fully assuming that I had killed him. I then assembled my comrades and found them all safe and sound.

In my company was a young mameluke holding the halter of an extra black mare which belonged to me. Under him was a good female riding mule with a saddle the tassels of which were silver. The mameluke dismounted from the mule, left it by itself and jumped on the back of the mare, which flew with him towards Shayzar.

On my return to my comrades, who had caught the mule, I asked about that boy. They said, "He's gone." I immediately knew that he would reach Shayzar and cause anxiety to my father (may Allah's mercy rest upon his soul!). I therefore called one of the soldiers and said to him, "Hasten to Shayzar and inform my father of what has happened."

In the meantime the boy had arrived and my father had him

brought before him and asked, "What things have ye met?" The boy said, "O my lord, the Franks have set out against us with a thousand men, and I doubt if any of our men would escape with the exception of my master. "But how would thy master," asked my father, "of all the men, escape?" "Well," replied the slave, "I have seen him covered with full armor riding on a green mare." Here he was interrupted in his conversation by the arrival of the horseman whom I had sent. The horseman related to my father the facts. I arrived right after him, and my father (may Allah's mercy rest upon his soul!) questioned me. So I said to him:

O my lord, that was the first fight in which I took part. But the moment I saw that the Franks were in contact with our men, then I felt that death would be an easy matter for me. So I turned back to the Franks, either to be killed or to protect that crowd.

My father (may Allah's mercy rest upon his soul!) quoted the following verse as illustrating my case:

The coward among men flees precipitately before danger facing his own mother,
But the brave one protects even him whom it is not his duty to shelter.

My uncle (may Allah's mercy rest upon his soul!) returned a few days later from his visit to Najm-al-Dīn Īlghāzi (may Allah's mercy rest upon his soul!). A messenger came to summon me to present myself before my uncle at a time in which it was not his custom to call me. So I hurried to him, and, behold, a Frank was in his company. My uncle said to me:

Here is a knight who has come from Afāmiyah in order to see the horseman who struck Philip [14] the knight, for verily the Franks have all been astounded [25] on account of that blow which pierced two layers of links in the knight's coat of mail and yet did not kill him.

"How," said I, "could he have survived?" The Frankish knight replied, "The thrust fell upon the skin of his side." "Fate is an impregnable stronghold," I exclaimed. But I never thought that the knight would survive that blow.

My comment is that he who is on the point of striking with his

[14] In F. Duchesne, *Historiae Francorum scriptores*, vol IV, p 92, and in *Recueil: historiens occidentaux*, vol V, p 361, there is a reference to a knight in the service of Bohemond named "Philippus de monte Aureo," but there is no way of identifying him with this knight

lance should hold his lance as tightly as possible with his hand and under his arm, close to his side, and should let his horse run and effect the required thrust; for if he should move his hand while holding the lance or stretch out his arm with the lance, then his thrust would have no effect whatsoever and would result in no harm.

A Moslem cavalier survives a Frankish thrust which cuts his heart vein. — I once witnessed in an encounter between us and the Franks one of our cavaliers, named Badi ibn-Talīl al-Qushayri, who was one of our brave men, receive in his chest, while clothed with only two pieces of garment, a lance thrust from a Frankish knight. The lance cut the vein in his chest and issued from his side. He turned back right away, but we never thought he would make his home alive. But as Allah (worthy of admiration is he!) had predestined, he survived and his wound was healed. But for one year after that, he could not sit up in case he was lying on his back unless somebody held him by the shoulders and helped him. At last what he suffered from entirely disappeared and he reverted to his old ways of living and riding. My only comment is: How mysterious are the works of him whose will is always executed among his creatures! He giveth life and he causeth death, but he is living and dieth not. In his hand is all good, and he is over all things potent.[15]

An artisan dies from a needle prick. — We had once with us an artisan, 'Attāb by name, who was one of the most corpulent and tall of men. He entered his home one day, and as he was sitting down he leaned on his hand against a robe which happened to be near him and in which there was a needle. The needle went through the palm of his hand and he died because of it. And, by Allah, as he moaned in the lower town [of Shayzar], his moan could be heard from the citadel on account of the bulk of his body and the volume of his voice. This man dies of a needle, whereas al-Qushayri is pierced with a lance which penetrates through his chest and issues out of his side and yet suffers no harm!

The exploits of al-Zamarrakal, the brigand. — In a certain year,[16] the lord of Antioch[17] (may Allah's curse be upon him!) came to attack us with his cavalry, infantry and tents. Mounting on our

[15] Cf. Koran III · 25. [16] About 1122. [17] Probably Baldwin II.

horses we went to meet them, assuming that they were ready for the combat. But they came and installed their camp in a place where they used to encamp, and settled down in their tents. We, on our part, made our way back until the end of the day. Then we mounted our horses, supposing that they would open battle with us. But they did not ride out of their tents.

My cousin, Layth-al-Dawlah Yaḥya, had a crop of grain ready for harvest in a field near the place where the Franks were. He brought together some beasts of burden in order to go to the crop and transport it. We went with him, numbering twenty well-equipped horsemen, and stationed ourselves between him and the Franks until he loaded his crop and went away. Then I turned from the main road, with one of our adopted men,[18] named Ḥusām-al-Dawlah Musāfir (may Allah's mercy rest upon his soul!), to a vineyard in which we had spied [26] certain objects on the bank of the river.[19] When we, as the sun was setting, got to these objects which we had spied, behold, they were an old man in a woman's clothing, accompanied by another man. Ḥusām-al-Dawlah (may Allah's mercy rest upon his soul!), who was an excellent man, full of fun, said to the old man, "O sheikh, what dost thou here?" The latter replied, "I wait until it is dark and then appropriate for myself, through Allah's aid, some of the horses of these unbelievers." Ḥusām-al-Dawlah asked, "And dost thou, O sheikh, cut off the ropes to detach their horses with thy teeth?" "No," replied the old man, "rather with this knife." And saying this he drew out of his waist a knife tied to a string and shining like a torch of fire. The man had no trousers [*sarāwīl*] on. We left him and departed.

Early the second morning I rode out in expectation of what the Franks were going to do, and, behold, the same old man was sitting on a stone in my way with the blood coagulated on his leg and foot. I said to him, "Happy recovery to thee! What hast thou done?" "I took from them," he replied, "a horse, a shield and a lance. But as I was making my way out from among their troops, a footman pursued me and thrust his lance through my thigh. But I ran away with the horse, shield and lance." He spoke thus, be-

[18] *muwallad*, meaning a foreigner, often a slave, not of Arab extraction, but brought up as an Arab

[19] The Orontes, *al-'Āṣi*.

littling the thrust in him as though it were in somebody else. This man, named al-Zamarrakal,[20] is one of the devils of brigands.

The following story was related to me about him by al-Amīr Mu'īn-al-Dīn [21] (may Allah's mercy rest upon his soul!), who said:

Once while I was staying at Hims,[22] I made a raid to Shayzar. At the end of that day I returned and camped in a village belonging to the territory of Hamāh, though I was an enemy of the lord of Hamāh. Then came to me a band of my men bringing an old man who had aroused their suspicions and whom they had therefore seized and brought before me. "O sheikh," asked I, "what art thou?" "I am a pauper," he replied, "an aged man with a chronic disease (saying this he put out his hand, which did have a chronic disease) The soldiers took away two goats of mine, and I went after them, hoping that they would be kind enough to bestow them on me." I then said to a group of my bodyguard,[23] "Guard him until tomorrow." The men made him sit between them, and they sat on the sleeves of a fur coat which was on him. Taking advantage of their inadvertence during the night, the old man sneaked out of his fur, left it under them and took to flight. They chased after him, but he beat them running and disappeared.

Mu'īn-al-Dīn continued thus:

Previous to this, I had dispatched some of my men on an errand. They now came back and one of them was a guard, named Sawmān [Shawmān?], who used to live in Shayzar I related to him the story of the old man and he exclaimed, "What a loss I have sustained by his escape! If I had only caught him, I would have gulped his blood. This is surely al-Zamarrakal!" "And what is there between him and thee?" asked I. He replied, "As the army of the Franks were once encamped around Shayzar, I came out and made a tour around them, hoping to be able to steal one of their horses. When darkness was complete, I walked towards a horses' picket line [*tuwālah*] which stood before me and, behold, this man appeared in front of me and said, 'Whereto?' 'To take a horse from this line,' I replied. He said, [27] 'Have I been here since supper time, watching this very place so that thou mayest take the horse!' 'Don't talk nonsense!' said I. He replied, 'Thou shalt not pass By Allah, I shall not let thee take anything.' I paid no attention to what he said and started in the direction of the horses, upon which he stood up and shouted at the top of his voice: 'Oh, poor me! Oh, what a disappointment to my toil and watchfulness!' And he kept on shouting

[20] In the absence of vowel marks it is not possible to tell whether this word should read "Zamarrakal," "Zumurrukul" or some other variant thereof.

[21] Mu'īn-al-Dīn Anar [22] Colloquially, "Ḥums"

[23] *jandar*, variant *jandār*, a Persian word meaning "bodyguard," "sword bearer" or "executioner."

until the Franks came out to me. As for him, he fled away like a bird. The Franks pursued me until I threw myself into the river, and I never imagined that I would escape from them. Had I caught him I would have gulped his blood. This man is a great brigand, and he had no object in pursuing thy troops except to steal from them."

This al-Zamarrakal was a man of whom no one who ever saw him could say he was capable of stealing even a loaf of bread from his own home.

Horse stealing. — One of the astonishing things that happened in the way of theft is the following:

There was a man in my service named 'Ali ibn-al-Dūdawayhi, originally an inhabitant of Muthkīr.[24] The Franks (may Allah's curse be upon them!) one day [25] camped around Kafartāb,[26] which then belonged to Ṣalāḥ-al-Dīn Muḥammad ibn-Ayyūb al-Ghisyāni [27] (may Allah's mercy rest upon his soul!). This 'Ali ibn-al-Dūdawayhi stole out, made a tour around them and took a horse which he mounted and rushed out of the camp galloping. He heard some noise behind him and, taking it to mean that someone was pursuing him on horseback, he pressed his horse as much as he could, but the noise persisted behind him. He galloped a distance of two parasangs while the noise accompanied him. Finally he turned back to see what could be behind him in the dark, and, behold! a female mule, which had kept company with the horse, had broken its halter and was following the horse. 'Ali stopped long enough to fasten his handkerchief around the neck of the mule, which he took along. The next morning he was with me in Ḥamāh, together with the horse and the mule. That horse was one of the finest breeds, one of the prettiest and swiftest among steeds.

The atābek appropriates for himself Usāmah's horse. — One day as I was in the presence of the atābek,[28] who was then laying siege to Rafaniyyah [29] and who had summoned me to him, he said to me,

[24] Possibly "Muthkīn," but I cannot find either in any of the Arab geographies. Derenbourg reads the word *tankīr* and considers it a common noun, translating it (*Autobiographie*, p 45) *dont la conduite était reprehensible.* Shumann, p 75, reads "Muthakīr"

[25] Between 1135 and 1138 A D

[26] A fortified place lying halfway between Shayzar and Ma'arrah-al-Nu'mān

[27] An abbreviated form of al-Yāghi-Siyāni, which is the Turkish original, meaning "belonging to (slave of) Yāghi-Siyān" *Recueil historiens orientaux*, vol I, p. 863.

[28] Zanki of Mawsil

[29] Between Ḥimṣ and Ḥamāh, about 1137 A.D.

"O Usāmah [*fulān*], what has become of thy horse which thou hast kept in hiding?" The atābek had been told the story of the horse. "No, by Allah, O my lord," said I, "I have no hidden horse. My horses are all in the army." "And the Frankish horse?" asked he. "It is ready," said I. "Then," said he, "dispatch someone and bring it here." I sent an attendant to fetch it and said to him, "Take it directly to the stable." But the atābek said, "Let it stay for the time being with me." The second morning the atābek rode the horse and made a race with other horses, which my horse won. He returned it to my stable. In the morning he ordered it brought out again and made another race, which it won too. Then I sent it into his stable.

Fatal blows in unusual parts of the body: In the throat. — In the battle which was the last to take place in this war, I witnessed the following event:

We had a soldier named Rāfi' al-Kilābi, a renowned cavalier. We were engaged in a fight with the banu-Qarāja,[30] who had massed Turkomans and others against us and were all mustered to meet us. We encountered them in a place away from the town. They proved too numerous for us, so we returned while some of us were defending the others. This Rāfi' was among those guarding the rear. He was wearing a quilted jerkin [31] and had on his head a helmet without a visor. He looked back in order to see whether he had a chance [28] to halt and attack his pursuers. As he turned aside, a jagged arrow hit him and gashed his throat, thus slaying him. He fell dead on the spot.

In the chest of a mare. — A similar episode I witnessed in the case of Shihāb-al-Dīn Maḥmūd ibn-Qarāja. The differences between him and us having been reconciled, he dispatched a messenger to my uncle,[32] saying to him, "Wilt thou order Usāmah to meet me with one horseman at Kar'ah [Lar'ah?] so that we may go together and find a place where we can lie in ambush for the attack of Afāmiyah?" My uncle having ordered me to go, I rode and met Shihāb-al-Dīn. We made a reconnoitre of the available positions.

[30] Ṣamṣām-al-Dīn Khīrkhān of Ḥimṣ and his brother, Shihāb-al-Dīn Maḥmūd of Ḥamāh

[31] Ar *kuzāghand*, from Persian *kazh-āghand*, a kind of jerkin of thick quilted cotton or silk, worn in battle and enclosing armor

[32] 'Izz-al-Dīn abu-al-'Asākir Sulṭān, the lord of Shayzar.

Then his army and ours united,[33] with myself leading the Shayzar army and he leading his. We set out together to Afāmiyah and encountered their [the Franks'] cavalry and infantry in the ruins in its vicinity. This was a place where horses could not move freely because of the stones, the columns and the lower parts of the walls which stood in ruins. We therefore failed to dislodge the enemy from their position. Thereupon one of the troops said to me, "Wouldst thou rout them?" "Of course," said I. "Let's direct ourselves," said he, "to the gate of the castle." "Start," said I to the troops The one who made the suggestion repented and realized that the enemy could trample us under their feet and reach the castle before us. So he tried to dissuade me. But I refused and marched on in the direction of the gate.

The moment the Franks saw us marching in the direction of the gate, their cavalry and infantry turned back against us, rode us down and passed us. The horsemen dismounted inside of the gate of the castle and sent their horses up to the castle. They arranged the iron heads of their lances in rows in the opening of the gate. All this took place while I, with a comrade, one of the adopted slaves [*muwallad*] of my father (may Allah's mercy rest up his soul!), whose name was Rāfi' ibn-Sūtakīn, was standing under the wall facing the gate while stones and arrows were falling on us in great quantities. In the meantime, Shihāb-al-Dīn was standing at a distance at the head of a detachment, for fear of the Kurds. One of our companions, named Ḥārithah al-Numayri, a relative of Jum'ah, received in the chest of his horse a blow of a lance coming sideways The lance pierced the mare, which struggled until the lance fell off. The whole skin of the chest peeled off and remained suspended on the forelegs of the mare.

In the bone of the lower arm. — Shihāb-al-Dīn, who held aloof from the combat, received an arrow from the castle, which struck in the bone of his lower arm. But it did not penetrate in the side of that bone as much as the length of a grain of barley. His messenger then came to me, saying in his behalf, "Leave not thy post until thou hast rallied all our men now scattered over the town, for I am wounded and I feel as if the wound were in my very heart. I am going back. Watch for our men."

[33] Year 1124.

Shihāb-al-Dīn went away and I led our men back and halted at Burj Khuraybah Musfān.[34] The Franks had installed in it a sentinel to spy us at a distance in case we intended to make a raid against Afāmiyah.

Late in the afternoon, I arrived in Shayzar and found Shihāb-al-Dīn in the home of my father trying to take the bandage off his wound and treat it. But my uncle prevented him, saying, "By Allah, thou shalt not take the bandage off thy wound except in thine own home." Shihāb-al-Dīn replied, "I am now in my father's home" (thus referring to my own father — may Allah's mercy rest upon his soul!). "Well," said my uncle, "when thou [29] hast arrived in thine own home and thy wound is healed, then shall thy father's home be at thy disposal."

Accordingly, Shihāb-al-Dīn mounted his horse at sunset and started for Ḥamāh. There he spent the second day and the day following, after which his arm turned black and he lost consciousness. Then he died. What happened to him was nothing but the ending of his predetermined days.

Noteworthy lance thrusts: One cuts ribs and elbow. — One of the terrible lance thrusts I witnessed was one administered by a Frankish knight (may Allah render them [the Franks] helpless!) to one of our cavaliers, named Sābah[35] ibn-Qunayb of the Kilābi tribe, which cut three of his ribs on the left side, and hit with its sharp edge his elbow, cutting it in two just as the butcher cuts a joint. He died on the spot.

One cuts coat of mail. — One of our troops, a Kurd named Mayyāḥ, smote a Frankish knight with a lance, which made a piece of the link in his coat of chain mail penetrate into his abdomen, and killed him. A few days later, the Franks made a raid against us. Mayyāḥ, who had just been married, went out to meet them with full armor but wearing over his coat of mail a red garment of his bridal clothes, making himself especially conspicuous. A Frankish knight smote him with a lance and killed him (may Allah's mercy rest upon his soul!).

O, how close to his funeral was his wedding!

[34] The watch-tower of Khuraybah (small ruins) Musfān (?) Original not clear. "Musfān" occurs in the text before "Khuraybah" but has a *mīm* above it, which may indicate that it should follow "Khuraybah"

[35] Original lacking in diacritical marks. *Autobiographie,* p. 48 "Sāya (?)."

His case brought to my memory the following story related about the Prophet (may Allah's blessing and peace rest upon him!). Somebody recited before him this verse by Qays ibn-al-Khaṭīm:

I kept on struggling against them on the day of combat while uncovered,
With the sword in my hand like a toy in the hand of a player.[36]

The Prophet (may Allah's blessing and peace rest upon him!) asked those of the Anṣārs[37] (may Allah's favor rest upon them!) who were present, "Did any one of you take part in the battle of al-Ḥadīqah?"[38] One of them replied, "I was present then, O Messenger of Allah, may Allah's blessing and peace rest upon thee! Qays ibn-al-Khaṭīm also was present, and, being newly married, he had on him a red mantle. And by him who sent thee on a mission of truth, Qays conducted himself during the fight exactly as he has said about himself."

One transpierces a Frankish knight. — Another marvelous thrust of the lance is the following:

There was a Kurd named Ḥamadāt who had been bound to us by old bonds of friendship and who had journeyed with my father (may Allah's mercy rest upon his soul!) to Iṣpahān to the court of Sultan Malik-Shāh.[39] But now he had become old and his eyesight had become weak. His children were grown. My uncle, 'Izz-al-Dīn (may Allah's mercy rest upon his soul!), said to him:

O Hamadāt, thou hast aged and become feeble. Thou hast claims on us because of thy service. If thou wilt only keep to thy mosque (he owned a mosque next to the door of his house), we will register thy children on the books with those receiving stipends Thou shalt also receive two dīnārs per month and a load of flour, as long as thou keepest to thy mosque.

"I shall do so, O amīr," replied Ḥamadāt. This arrangement was carried out for a short time only, at the end of which he came to my uncle and said, "O amīr! By Allah, I cannot force myself to stay indoors all the time. To be killed on my horse is more desirable

[36] Al-Isfahāni, *Kitāb al-Aghāni* (Būlāq, 1285 A H), vol. II, p 162

[37] Helpers The people of Yathrib (later al-Medīnah) who rallied to the support of Muḥammad when he fled there.

[38] A suburb of al-Medīnah where the Aws and Khazraj in pre-Islamic days had a battle, to which Qays referred in his verse quoted above. Yāqūt, *Mu'jam al-Buldān*, vol II, p 226

[39] The Seljūq who died in 1092. This visit took place in 1085.

to me than to die on my bed." "Do as thou pleasest," replied my uncle, who gave orders [30] that the old stipend for Ḥamadāt as a soldier be reassigned to him.

Only a few days had passed after this, when the count of Cerdagne,[40] the lord of Tripoli, made an incursion against us. Our men rushed to the encounter and Ḥamadāt was among those who rushed. He took his post on an elevation of the ground and faced south [*al-qiblah*]. As he stood there, a Frankish cavalier attacked him from the west. One of our comrades, seeing him, shouted, "O Ḥamadāt!" So he looked around and saw a horseman headed towards him. He immediately turned the head of his mare northward and, holding his lance with his hand, he thrust it straight into the chest of the Frank. He hit him so hard that the lance transpierced him. The Frank went back, hanging to the neck of the horse and breathing his last breath. When the battle was over, Ḥamadāt said to my uncle, "O amīr, had Ḥamadāt been in the mosque, who would then have struck this blow?"

One kills two horsemen at once. — This reminded me of something which al-Find al-Zimmāni [41] had said:

> O, what a thrust from a sheikh,
> Aged, decrepit and decayed!
> I was rejuvenated by it,
> While those of my age have no desire for arms.

This al-Find was already an aged man when he took part in a battle in the course of which he struck with one blow of his lance two horsemen approaching him and felled them both dead.

One kills two horsemen and two horses. — Something similar had happened to us previous to that. A farmer from al-'Alāh came running to my father and uncle (may Allah's mercy rest upon their souls!) and said, "I have seen a detachment of the Franks astray, coming from the direction of the desert. If ye set out against them ye shall capture them." My father and two paternal uncles immediately mounted their horses and marched at the head of the troops to meet the lost detachment. And, lo! that was the count of Cerdagne, the lord of Tripoli, at the head of three hundred horse-

[40] Ar *al-sardāni*, that is, William Jourdain, count of Cerdagne and nephew of Raymond of St. Gilles. This event took place in 1108

[41] His first name was Sahl ibn-Shaybān. He was a pre-Islamic poet.

men and two hundred Turcopoles,[42] the latter the archers of the Franks. As soon as they saw our companions, they mounted their horses, charged our troops at full speed, routed them and pursued them for a long distance. A mameluke belonging to my father, Yāqūt al-Ṭawīl [43] by name, swerved and turned back on his pursuers — as my father and uncle (may Allah's mercy rest upon their souls!) were looking at him — and smote with his lance a horseman of theirs, who together with another horseman by his side were pursuing our comrades. Both horsemen and both horses fell down. This slave was one addicted to appropriating money for himself illicitly and to committing other wrong deeds, for one of which my father was going to discipline him. But every time my father proposed to discipline him, my uncle would say, "O my brother, by thy life, grant me his guilt, and forget not that lance thrust!" My father would then pardon him because of the intercession of his brother.

This aforementioned Ḥamadāt was a most interesting conversationalist. My father (may Allah's mercy rest upon his soul!) related to me the following story:

One early morning as we were journeying on the way to Iṣpahān, I said to Ḥamadāt, "O Amīr Hamadāt, hast thou eaten anything today?" He replied, "Yes, amīr. I have eaten a sop" [44] I said to him, "We have been riding through the night, we did neither [31] alight nor strike a fire. How didst thou then get that sop?" "O amīr," he replied, "I have made it in my mouth I would mix up the bread in my mouth with the water which I would drink on top of it and that would result in something like a sop."

Usāmah's father: A warrior. — My father (may Allah's mercy rest upon his soul!) was greatly addicted to warfare. His body bore scars of terrible wounds. And withal he died on his own bed. One day he took part in a battle in full armor, wearing on his head a Moslem helmet with a nasal. Someone (in that period their

[42] *turkubūlī*, diacritical points lacking in the manuscript The word is defined by Usāmah as "the archers of the Franks" So these must have been native mercenaries in the service of the Franks Evidently they were the children of Turkish or Arab fathers and Greek mothers See Prutz, *Kulturgeschichte der Kreuzzuge* (Berlin, 1883), pp. 186, 539, 'Imād-al-Dīn, *al-Fath al-Qussī*, ed Landberg (Leyden, 1888), p 425; du Cange, *Glossarium ad scriptores mediae et infimae Latinitatis* (Paris, 1736), vol. VI, col 1349

[43] "Yāqūt the tall"

[44] *tharīdah*, a piece of bread soaked in broth

combats were generally with the Arabs) launched a javelin at him, which struck the nasal of the helmet. The nasal bent and made my father's nose bleed, but it caused him no harm. But if Allah (praise be to his name!) had decreed that the javelin should deviate from the helmet's nasal, then it would have killed him.

On another occasion he was hit with an arrow in his leg. In his slipper he had a dagger. The arrow struck the dagger and was broken on it, without even wounding him — thanks to the excellent protection of Allah (exalted is he!).

He (may Allah's mercy rest upon his soul!) took part in a fight on Sunday, the twenty-ninth of Shawwāl, in the year 497,[45] against Sayf-al-Dawlah Khalaf ibn-Mulā'ib al-Ashhabi,[46] the lord of Afāmiyah, in the territory of Kafarṭāb. He put on his byrnie, but the attendant in his haste neglected to fasten its hook on the side. A pike hit him right in the place which the attendant had failed to cover up, just above his left breast, and issued from above his right breast. The causes of his safety were due to what Providence had seen fit to execute in the way of marvels, just as the infliction of the wound was in accordance with what Allah (worthy of admiration is he!) had decreed in the way of marvels.

On that same day my father (may Allah's mercy rest upon his soul!) smote a cavalier with his lance, made his own horse shy a little to one side, bent his arm while holding the lance and withdrew the lance from the victim. Relating this story to me, he said:

> I felt something biting my forearm. I took it to be caused by the heat from the vambrace of the byrnie. But my lance fell from my hand I turned my arm to see, and all of a sudden realized that I had been pierced with a lance in my forearm, which weakened because of the cutting off of some of the nerves.

I was present with him (may Allah's mercy rest upon his soul!) when Zayd the surgeon was dressing his wound and an attendant was standing behind his head. My father said, "O Zayd, extract this pebble from the wound." The surgeon made no reply. He repeated and said, "Seest thou not this pebble? Wilt thou not remove it from the wound?" Annoyed by his insistence, the surgeon said, "Where is the pebble? This is the end of a nerve that

[45] July 25, 1104

[46] Mentioned many times by ibn-Taghri-Birdi, *al-Nujūm al-Zāhirah*, ed. Popper (University of California Press, 1909–12), vol. II, pt. II, pp. 284, 287.

has been cut off." In reality it was white as though it were one of the pebbles of the Euphrates.

My father received on that day another lance thrust. But Allah spared him until he died on his own bed (may Allah's mercy rest upon his soul!) on Monday, the twelfth of Ramaḍān, in the year 531.[47]

A Koran copier. — My father wrote a magnificent hand, which that lance thrust did not affect. But he used to copy nothing except the Koran. One day I asked him, "O my lord, how many full copies of the Koran hast thou made?" To this he replied, "Before long ye shall know." When he was on the point of death, he said, "In that box are different copies, each one of which contains the Koran in full. Place them [32] (referring to the copies) under my cheek in the grave." We counted them and they turned out to be forty-three copies, each containing the full text. One of the copies was a huge one which he wrote in gold and in which he included all the sciences of the Koran — its different readings, its obscure terms, its Arabic style and grammar, its abrogating and abrogated passages, its commentary, reasons for its revelation, and its jurisprudence. This copy, which he styled *al-Tafsīr al-Kabīr* [the great commentary], was written in black ink alternating with red and blue. Another copy he transcribed with letters of gold, but this had no commentary. The rest of the copies were written in black ink with the following in gold: the first words of the tenth and fifth parts of the book, the number of verses, the first word of the sūrahs, the titles of the sūrahs and the headings of the sections.[48]

My book does not require the mention of this fact. But I did mention it in order to appeal to those who read my book to solicit Allah's mercy upon my father.

I shall now return to the subject which I was treating before.

An exemplary attendant of Usāmah's uncle. — In the course of that day,[49] an attendant who belonged to my paternal uncle, 'Izz-al-Dawlah abu-al-Murhaf Naṣr (may Allah's mercy rest upon his soul!), and whose name was Muwaffaq-al-Dawlah Sham'ūn, received a terrific blow from a lance to which he exposed himself

[47] May 30, 1137

[48] The Koran is divided into 114 *sūrahs* and thirty sections, called *ajzā'*, singular *juz'*. Three sections constitute one tenth and six sections one fifth of the book.

[49] July 25, 1104.

in behalf of my other paternal uncle 'Izz-al-Dīn abu-al-'Asākir Sulṭān (may Allah's mercy rest upon his soul!). It happened that my uncle [Sulṭān] later sent this attendant on a mission to King Riḍwān ibn-Tāj-al-Dawlah Tutush in Aleppo. When Sham'ūn presented himself before Ridwān, the latter said to his attendants, "Like unto this one should all attendants and honest persons [50] be in their duties towards their masters!" And then he said to Sham'ūn, "Relate to them thy story in the days of my father and what thou didst for thy master." Sham'ūn said:

> O our lord, the other day I took part with my master in a battle. Some cavalier charged upon him to smite him with the lance. I immediately interfered between him and my master in order to redeem my master with my own life. So the cavalier hit me and cut off two of my ribs. These ribs, I swear by thy grace, I still keep in a casket.

Hearing this, King Riḍwān said to him, "By Allah, I shall give thee no answer to thy mission until thou hast sent and fetched that casket with the ribs." Accordingly, Sham'ūn tarried with the king and sent someone to fetch the casket. And there were in it two bones of his ribs. Riḍwān, struck with amazement, said to his followers, "Do ye likewise in my service."

As for the event about which Riḍwān had asked Sham'ūn and which happened in the days of his father, Tāj-al-Dawlah, it is this:

My grandfather, Sadīd-al-Mulk abu-al-Ḥasan 'Ali ibn-Muqallad ibn-Naṣr ibn-Munqidh (may Allah's mercy rest upon his soul!), sent his son, 'Izz-al-Dawlah Nasr (may Allah's mercy rest upon his soul!), to the service of Tāj-al-Dawlah, who was then encamping in the suburbs of Aleppo. Tutush seized him and put him in jail, intrusting his keep to a special guard. Nobody was allowed admission to him except this mameluke of his, Sham'ūn, who would be admitted while the guard would be standing around the tent. My uncle wrote to his father (may Allah's mercy rest upon their souls!) to this effect: "Thou shalt dispatch to me on such and such a night (which he designated) so and so of my companions (whom he named), together with horses, which I could ride to such and such a place." When that night came, Sham'ūn entered the tent and took off his clothes, which his master put on. The latter

[50] *awlād halāl*, literally "legitimate children," but also used in the sense of "ingenuous" or "faithful persons."

went out and passed by the night guard without arousing their suspicion. He marched on until he joined his companions, upon which he mounted his horse and went away. As for Sham'ūn, he slept in his master's bed.

It was customary for Sham'ūn to bring to his master early every morning water for his ablutions, he (may Allah's mercy rest upon his soul!) being one of those ascetics who spent [33] their nights reciting the Book of Allah (exalted is he!). When the guard, therefore, awoke in the morning and did not notice Sham'ūn come in, according to his custom, they entered the tent and found Sham'ūn — 'Izz-al-Dawlah having disappeared. They reported the case to Tāj-al-Dawlah, who ordered that Sham'ūn be brought into his presence. When the latter presented himself, Tāj-al-Dawlah asked, "How didst thou do it?" Sham'ūn replied, "I gave my clothes to my master, who put them on and went away while I slept in his bed." Tāj-al-Dawlah said, "And wert thou not afraid that I would strike off thy head?" Sham'ūn replied, "O my lord, if thou strikest off my head, and my master escapes and returns to his home, then I am happy indeed on account of it. He did not buy me and bring me up except to redeem him with my own life." Tāj-al-Dawlah (may Allah's mercy rest upon his soul!) then said to his chamberlain, "Deliver to this retainer the horses, beasts of burden, tents and all the baggage of his master and let him go and follow him." Tāj-al-Dawlah set no blame on him, nor cherished the least anger for what he had accomplished in the service of his master. It was this episode which Riḍwān meant when he said to Sham'ūn, "Relate to my companions what thou didst for thy master in the days of my father."

I shall now return to the story of the aforementioned battle with ibn-Mulā'ib.

Usāmah's uncle stabbed in eyelid. — My uncle, 'Izz-al-Dawlah (may Allah's mercy rest upon his soul!), received on that day a number of wounds, one of which was inflicted by a lance in the lower eyelid near the inner corner of the eye. The lance pierced through the eyelid to the outer corner. The whole eyelid fell down and remained suspended with its skin at the outer corner of the eye. And the eye kept all the time moving, being unable to settle in any definite position, for it is the eyelid which holds the eye in its proper place. The surgeon sewed the eye and treated it, and it returned to its former position; so much so that the stabbed eye could not be distinguished from the other one.

Acts of bravery by Usāmah's uncle and father. — These two [my father and my uncle] (may Allah's mercy rest upon their souls!) were among the bravest of their people. One day I was in their company when they went out in the direction of Tell-Milḥ [51] for the hunt with the falcons. That place abounded with waterfowl. Suddenly we became aware that the army of Tripoli [Ṭarābulus] had arrived on an incursion against our upper town [52] and was already camping outside of it. We immediately returned home. My father was just recuperating from sickness. As for my uncle, he hurried with the troops he had and marched until he crossed the river [53] at the ford towards the Franks, who were keeping an eye on him. And in regard to my father, he also started, riding on a trotting horse and holding in his hand a quince from which he was sucking, while I, as a lad,[54] was accompanying him. As we approached the Franks, he said to me, "Go by thyself and enter by the dam." But he crossed the river from the side where the Franks were.

On another occasion I observed my father, as the horsemen of Maḥmūd [55] ibn-Qarāja made an assault upon us [56] while we were at some distance from our town. The horsemen of Mahmūd were closer to it than we were. I was myself taking part in that battle, having then become well experienced in warfare, wearing my quilted jerkin and riding on my horse with my lance in my hand, while he (may Allah's mercy rest upon his soul!) was mounted on a female mule. So I said, "O my lord, dost thou not want to ride thy horse?" "Certainly," he replied, and advanced just as he was, unperturbed and unhurried; while I, fearing for his safety, was insisting that he should mount his horse. He continued on his mule until we got to the town. When the enemy went back and we felt safe, I said to my father, "Thou didst see the enemy standing between us and the upper town and still thou didst refuse to

[51] The Hill of Salt, not far from Shayzar

[52] Of Shayzar, *al-balad*, the part which was enclosed in the Castle (Qal'ah). This is the expedition of Count Bertrand of Tripoli in the summer of 1110.

[53] Orontes [54] Usāmah was then fifteen years old

[55] Shihāb-al-Dīn Maḥmūd of Ḥamāh. [56] Year 1120.

ride one of the extra horses led at thy side by a halter [34], while I was all the time addressing thee and thou didst pay no attention!" Then he said, "O my child, it is in my horoscope that I should feel no fear."

In fact my father (may Allah's mercy rest upon his soul!) was well versed in the science of the stars, in spite of his great piety and religion [57] and his habit of continual fasting and reciting the Koran. He always urged me to study the science of the stars, but I would refuse and hold back. So he would say, "At least thou shouldst know the names of those stars which rise and set." He used to point out to me the stars and acquaint me with their names.

A Frankish ruse on Shayzar foiled. — Here is something of men's intrepidity and gallantry in warfare which I saw:

One day [58] we arose early in the morning at the time of the dawn prayer only to find a band of Franks, about ten cavaliers, who had come to the gate of the lower town [59] before it was opened. They asked the gatekeeper, "What is the name of this town?" The gate was of wood with beams running across, and the gatekeeper was inside of the gate. "Shayzar," he replied. The Franks thereupon shot an arrow at him through the crack of the door, and they turned back with their horses trotting under them.

So we mounted our horses. My uncle (may Allah's mercy rest upon his soul!) was the first to ride, and I was in his company; while the Franks were marching along unworried. A few of our troops came following us. I said to my uncle, "Command only, and I shall take our companions, pursue the enemy and dislodge them from their saddles as long as they are not so far away." "No," replied my uncle, who was more of an expert in warfare than I was. "Is there a Frank in Syria who knows not Shayzar? This is a ruse."

He then called two of our cavaliers riding on two swift mares and said, "Go and reconnoitre Tell-Milḥ." This was the place where the Franks usually laid their ambuscade. As soon as our two men were in a position overlooking the Tell, the army of Antioch

[57] Moslem theologians, under the influence of a rigid monotheistic conception of the deity and the Aristotelian philosophy, have been almost unanimous in their condemnation of astrology, yet this science has always been deeply rooted among all lay classes of Islam.

[58] Probably in the year 1122

[59] *al-madînah*, that part of Shayzar which stood by the bridge.

set out against them *en masse.* We hastened to the encounter of those who were in the vanguard, desiring to take advantage of them before the battle was over. In our company were Jum'ah al-Numayri and his son, Maḥmūd. In fact, Jum'ah was our leading cavalier and our sheikh.[60] His son, Maḥmūd, somehow got into the midst of the ranks of the enemy. And Jum'ah cried, "O real cavaliers! My boy!" So we went back with him, numbering sixteen cavaliers, smote with our lances sixteen Frankish knights and carried back our comrade from among them. We got so much mixed up with them in the course of the encounter that the head of Jum'ah was held under the armpit of one of them, but he was soon delivered by those lance blows which we administered.

Usāmah and Jum'ah rout eight knights, but are themselves routed by one footman. — With all that, one should not put too much trust in his own courage, nor take too much pride in his own intrepidity. By Allah, I once [61] set out with my uncle (may Allah's mercy rest upon his soul!) on an incursion against Afāmiyah. It so happened that its men, who had gone out to see a caravan off, had done so and were on their way back when we came across them. We killed about twenty of their men. My eyes fell upon Jum'ah al-Numayri (may Allah's mercy rest upon his soul!) with half a lance shaft thrust into him. The lance struck the pad of the saddle, went through the stuffed lining beneath the saddle, hit his thigh and pierced it to its back part, where the lance broke. I was alarmed at the sight. But he said, "Fear not. I am safe." Then holding the point of the lance, he drew it out of him, while he and his horse were perfectly safe.

I said to him, "O abu-Maḥmūd, I wish I could come near [35] the castle and see it well." "Start," said he. So we both started with our horses trotting under us until we got to a point from which we clearly saw the castle, and behold! eight [Frankish] cavaliers were posted on our road. The castle stood on an elevation which overlooked the square,[62] from which we could not descend except by following that road. Jum'ah said to me, "Stop, that I may show thee what I can do with them." I replied, "This is not fair. We should rather make an open assault on them, both thou and I."

[60] Most experienced. [61] About 1124
[62] *maydān*, used for "open space" "race course," or "field."

"Start," said he. So we made an assault, routed them and turned back, thinking that we had done something which no one else could have done. We two routed eight knights of the Franks.

As we stopped near that elevation, looking at the castle, we were startled with the sudden appearance of a small footman, who had climbed that steep ascent carrying a bow and arrows. He shot his arrows at us while we had no way to hit back at him. So we ran away, hardly believing, by Allah, that we should escape with our horses safe. We made our way back until we entered the meadow around Afāmiyah, from which we drove before us a great body of buffaloes, cows and sheep. We then departed, with my heart laden with regret on account of that footman who put us to defeat while we had no access to him, though we had defeated eight knights of the Franks.

The battle at Kafarṭāb: Unexpected cures. — I took part in a battle in which the horsemen of Kafarṭāb, few in number, made an incursion against us. Taking advantage of their small number, we immediately rushed against them. But they had left a band of their number lying in ambush for us. The horsemen who made the incursion took to flight, so we pursued them until we got quite far from the town. The ambuscade then came out, and those whom we were pursuing turned back against us. We were convinced that if we retreated they would dislodge us all from our saddles. So we encountered them, fighting like men seeking death. But Allah gave us victory over them. We dislodged from them eighteen knights, of whom some received lance blows and died, others received lance blows and fell off their horses but survived, and still others escaped the blows which fell on their horses and became footmen. All those who survived and were on the ground now unsheathed their swords, stood on their feet and smote everyone who passed by them.

One of them by whom passed Jum'ah al-Numayri stepped towards him and struck him on his head, which was covered with a hood. The blow cut through the hood and wounded Jum'ah's forehead, from which blood flowed until it was all drained, leaving his forehead open like the mouth of a fish. I came upon Jum'ah while we were yet in the throes of our conflict with the Franks and said to him, "O abu-Maḥmūd, dost thou not bandage thy wound?"

He replied, "This is no time for putting bandages and dressing wounds." Now, Jum'ah had most of the time a black kerchief round his face, on account of an inflammation (i.e., ophthalmia) and enlarged veins, with which his eyes had for a long time been afflicted. When he received that wound from which gushed forth so much blood, the disease from which he was suffering in his eyes vanished. He no more had ophthalmia nor felt pain. "Thus it sometimes happens that bodies are cured by diseases."[63]

Narrow escape of Usāmah's cousin. — [36] As for the Franks, having lost of their number those whom we killed, they reunited and stood opposite to us. My cousin on my father's side, Dhakhīrah-al-Dawlah abu-al-Qana Khiṭām (may Allah's mercy rest upon his soul!), then came to me and said, "O cousin, thou hast two riding animals led at thy side, and here I am on this old ragged mare!" So I said to my attendant, "Offer him the red horse." The attendant offered it to him. The moment Khiṭām was firm in the saddle he made a charge, single-handed, upon the Franks. The latter made room for him until he got into their midst, and then they smote him with their lances, overthrowing him, and smote his horse. Reversing their lances, they then began to dig into him with them. But Khiṭām was wearing a coat of mail the links of which were so strong that their lances could have no effect upon it. Seeing this, we began to shout out to the others: "To the help of your comrade! To the help of your comrade!" And we made an onslaught on them and extricated him from their midst, safe and sound. As for the horse, it died on that same day. Mysterious are the works of him who gives safety, the all-powerful one!

That battle resulted in the happiness of Jum'ah and in the curing of his eyes. Praise be to him who says, "Yet haply ye are averse from a thing, though it be good for you."[64]

An unusual way of curing dropsy. — An analogous case happened to me. When I was in upper Mesopotamia[65] in the army of the atābek,[66] a friend of mine invited me to his home. I went there accompanied by a groom, named Ghunaym, who was afflicted with dropsy and whose neck had become thin and whose abdomen had become inflated. This servant kept me company on my sojourns

[63] A part of a well-known verse by al-Mutanabbi. [64] Koran II : 213.
[65] Al-Jazīrah, about 1132 A.D. [66] Zanki.

in foreign lands, and I always treated him with special consideration on account of it. Ghunaym took his mule into the stable of that friend, together with the grooms of the other persons invited. Among us was a young Turk who drank to the point of intoxication, went out to the stable, drew his dagger and rushed on the servants. They all took to flight and rushed out with the exception of Ghunaym, who, because of his weak condition and disease, had thrown the saddle under his head and lain down. He did not get up until everybody in the stable had gone out. Then the drunken man stabbed him with the dagger under his navel and cut in his abdomen a wound about four inches deep, which made him fall on the spot. The man who invited us, who was the master of the Castle of Bāsahra [?], had him carried to my home. The man who stabbed him was also carried there, with his hands tied behind his back. There I set him free. The surgeon made frequent visits to my servant, until he was better, could walk and do his work. But the wound would not heal. For two months it continued to excrete something like scabs and yellow water, at the end of which time the cut closed up, the abdomen of the man resumed its normal condition and he returned to perfect health. That wound was thus the cause of his regaining his health.

A falcon's eye cured in a strange way. — One day I saw the falconer standing before my father (may Allah's mercy rest upon his soul!), saying to him, "O my lord, this falcon is afflicted with ecdysis [67] and is dying. One of his eyes is already lost. Use it for the hunt, therefore. It [37] is a clever falcon, but it is doomed to perdition." We went out for the hunt. My father (may Allah's mercy rest upon his soul!) had with him several falcons. The sickly falcon was flown at a francolin. The francolin took cover [68] inside of a thicket of brambles. The falcon, which had on his eye something like a big point, followed the francolin, and a thorn from the thicket hit it on that particular spot and burst it open. The falconer brought back the falcon, whose eye while closed was flowing, and said, "O my lord, the eye of the falcon is lost." To this my father replied, "The whole bird is lost." But the second morning the bird opened its eye and lo, it was safe and sound.

[67] *haṣṣ*, any affliction which results in the loss of plumage.
[68] *nabaja* = dashed into covert or place of security.

The bird lived in our house in perfect condition until it molted twice. It was one of the cleverest of falcons.

I mentioned the case of this falcon in connection with what happened to Jum'ah and Ghunaym, though this is not the place for falcon stories.

I have seen the case of one afflicted with dropsy who was treated by bloodletting in his abdomen and who died; whereas Ghunaym, whose abdomen was cut open by that drunken man, recovered and returned to normal health. Mysterious are the ways of the Almighty!

In flight before the Franks of Antioch. — The army of Antioch made an incursion on us.[69] Our comrades met their vanguard and were retreating before them. I posted myself on their route, expecting their arrival and hoping thereby to be able to get an opportunity to attack the enemy. Our comrades began to pass by me in defeat. Among those who thus passed was Maḥmūd ibn-Jum'ah. I said, "Halt, O Maḥmūd!" He stopped for an instant; then he spurred his horse and left me. By that time the vanguard of the Frankish horsemen had reached me, so I retired before them, turning back my lance in their direction and my eyes towards them lest some one of their horse should prove too quick for me and pierce me with his lance. In front of me were some of our companions, and we were surrounded by gardens with walls as high as a sitting man. My mare hit with its breast one [70] of our companions, so I turned its head to my left and applied the spurs to its sides, whereupon it leaped over the wall. I so regulated my position until I stood on a level with the Franks. The wall only separated us. One of their horsemen hastened to me, displaying his colors in a green and yellow silk tunic, under which I thought was no coat of mail. I therefore let him alone until he passed me. Then I applied the spurs to my mare, which leaped over the wall, and I smote him with the lance. He bent sideways so much that his head reached his stirrup, his shield and lance fell off his hand, and his helmet off his head. By that time we had reached our infantry. He then resumed his position, erect in the saddle. Having had linked mail under his tunic, my lance did not wound him.

[69] About 1127. Antioch = Antākiyah.

[70] Arabic original *rajulun*, which should be corrected for *rajulan*. Cf. *Autobiographie*, p. 62.

His companions caught up with him, all returned together, and the footman recovered his shield, lance and helmet.

Even Jum'ah flees. — When the battle was over and the Franks withdrew, Jum'ah (may Allah's mercy rest upon his soul!) came to me apologizing in behalf of his son, Mahmūd, and said, "This dog fled away while in thy company!" I replied, "What of it?" He said, "He flees from thee and what of it?" "By thy life, [38] O abu-Maḥmūd," said I, "thou wilt also flee away while in my company." To this he replied, "O what shame! By Allah, my death would verily be easier for me than to flee away and leave thee."

Only a few days passed after that when the horsemen of Ḥamāh made an incursion on us. They took a herd of cattle which belonged to us and shut it up in an island under the Jalāli Mill [al-Ṭāḥūn al-Jalāli]. Their archers mounted on the mill in order to defend the herd. I went to them with Jum'ah and Shujā'-al-Dawlah Mādi, one of our adopted men [*muwallad*] who was a man of valor. I said to the two with me, "We will cross the water to the other side and take our animals." So we crossed. Māḍi's mare was hit with an arrow which caused its death. The mare carried him back to his companions with great difficulty. As for me, an arrow struck my mare at the nape of its neck and entered a span deep in it. But by Allah, my mare neither kicked nor was disturbed, but it went on as though it felt no cut. As regards Jum'ah, he went back, fearing for his horse. When we returned I said, "O abu-Maḥmūd, did I not tell thee that thou wouldst flee away from me, when thou wert blaming thy son Maḥmūd?" "By Allah," he replied, "I feared for nothing except for my mare. It is so dear to me." And he apologized.

Usāmah strikes the wrong man. — On that same day we had an encounter with the horsemen of Ḥamāh, after some of them had gone ahead of the others with the herd to the peninsula.[71] A fight ensued between them and us. Among them were the leading cavaliers of the army of Ḥamāh: Sarhank, Ghāzi al-Talli, Maḥmūd ibn-Baldāji, Ḥaḍr-al-Ṭūṭ and the Isbāslār Khuṭlukh.[72] Their

[71] *al-jazīrah* = "island" The reference is to the part of Shayzar which is surrounded by the Orontes on three sides.

[72] Ar *isbāslār*, variant *isfahsalār*, from Persian *sipah-sālāri* = commander of an army Khuṭlukh is "Khutlugh" in Kamāl-al-Dīn in *Recueil historiens orientaux*, vol. III, p. 595, the word is Tartar "Qutlugh"

army was more numerous than ours. But we made an onslaught on them and defeated them. I headed for a horseman of theirs, desiring to pierce him with the lance, and behold! that horseman turned out to be Ḥaḍr-al-Ṭūṭ, who shouted, "By thy benevolence [I beseech thee], O Usāmah!" I then turned away from him to another, whom I smote. The lance passed close under his armpit. Had he left it alone, he would not have been felled. But he pressed his arm on the lance, desiring to wrest it, while my mare was turning round with me. This caused him to fly off his saddle and fall on the neck of his horse and then down to the ground. He got up to find himself on the very edge of a precipice sloping down to al-Jalāli.[73] He then struck his horse and, driving it before him, went down. I thanked Allah (worthy of admiration is he!), for no damage whatever was inflicted on him by that blow of the lance, because the man turned out to be Ghāzi al-Talli. He (may Allah's mercy rest upon his soul!) was an excellent man.

Jum'ah saves a farmer and his cow. — The army of Antioch came and camped one day [74] in the same place where it always encamped when it came to attack us, while we on horseback stood facing them with the river [75] between us. Not one of them, however, ventured to approach us. They pitched their tents and established themselves in them. So we turned back and occupied our homes while we could still see them from inside the castle.[76] Then about twenty horsemen of our army went out to Bandar-Qanīn, a village near the upper town, in order to let their horses graze, and left their lances at home. Two Frankish riders detached themselves and came near those horsemen who were grazing their horses. On the way they happened to fall upon a man [39] driving a beast, and they made off with him and with his beast while we were watching from the castle. Those soldiers of ours mounted their horses and stood still, having no lances. My paternal uncle said, "Those are twenty men and yet cannot save a captive from two knights! If only Jum'ah were with them, then would ye know what he could do." No sooner had he said that than Jum'ah, fully armed, was seen galloping. My uncle thereupon said, "Watch now what he will do." When Jum'ah drew nigh to the two knights

[73] River, a tributary of the Orontes.
[74] About 1129.
[75] The Orontes, al-'Āṣi.
[76] Shayzar.

at full gallop, he turned the head of his mare and kept at some distance behind them. When my uncle, who was at the window of the castle looking out, saw Jum'ah stop his pursuit, he left the window and went in, furious, saying, "This is a case of disloyalty!" The fact is that Jum'ah stopped on account of a pit which lay ahead of the two knights and which he feared might be the hiding place of an ambuscade. But when he got to the pit and found nobody in it, he charged the two knights, saved the man and the animal, and chased the knights as far as their tents.

Bohemond,[77] the lord of Antioch, was watching what was taking place. No sooner had the two knights arrived than he sent and took their shields, which he converted into mangers for animals to feed from, pulled down their tents and expelled them, saying, "One single cavalier of the Moslems chases two cavaliers of the Franks! Ye are not men; ye are women." As for Jum'ah, my uncle rebuked him and was cross with him for desisting from their pursuit after having reached them. So he said, "O my lord, I was afraid they might have an ambuscade in the pit of Rābiyah-al-Qarāmiṭah,[78] from which they would make a sortie against me. But as soon as I spied the pit and found no one in it, I delivered the man and the beast and chased the two knights until they entered their camp." But my uncle, by Allah, neither accepted his excuse nor was satisfied with his conduct.

The high position enjoyed by the Frankish knights — The Franks (may Allah render them helpless!) possess none of the virtues of men except courage, consider no precedence or high rank except that of the knights, and have nobody that counts except the knights. These are the men on whose counsel they rely, and the ones who make legal decisions and judgments. I once [79] brought a case before them, relative to certain flocks of sheep which the lord of Bāniyās [80] had taken from the forest in the course of a period of truce between them and us. At that time, I was in Damascus. So I said to King Fulk, son of Fulk,[81] "This man has trespassed

[77] Bohemond II Ar *ibn-maymūn*

[78] The hill of the Qarāmiṭah, a Moslem sect allied to the Ismā'īliyyah and other extreme Shī'ah sects.

[79] In 1140

[80] Caesarea Philippi, Paneas, whose lord at this time was Renier, surnamed Brus.

[81] Fulk V, count of Anjou, who was installed on the death of his father-in-law, Baldwin II, fourth king of Jerusalem, in 1131.

upon our rights and taken away our flocks at the lambing time. The sheep gave birth and the lambkins died. Then he returned the sheep, after having lost so many of them." The king said to six, seven knights, "Arise and judge this case for him." The knights went out from his audience chamber, retired by themselves and consulted together until they all agreed upon one thing. Then they returned to the audience chamber of the king and said, "We have passed judgment to the effect that the lord of Bāniyās should be fined the amount of the damage he wrought among their sheep" The king accordingly ordered him to pay that fine. He pleaded with me, urged and implored me until I finally accepted from him four hundred dīnārs. Such a judgment, after having been pronounced by the knights, [40] not even the king nor any of the chieftains of the Franks can alter or revoke. Thus the knight is something great in their esteem.

The king said to me, "By the truth of my religion, I rejoiced yesterday very much indeed." I replied, "May Allah always make the king rejoice! What made thee rejoice?" He said, "I was told that thou wert a great knight, but I did not believe previous to that that thou wert a knight." "O my lord," I replied, "I am a knight according to the manner of my race and my people." If the knight is thin and tall the Franks admire him more.

Tancred's guarantee of safety proves worthless. — Tancred,[82] who was the first lord of Antioch after Bohemond, had previous to this pitched his camp against us.[83] After the fight, we had a reconciliation, and he sent a message requesting that a horse belonging to an attendant of my uncle, 'Izz-al-Dīn (may Allah's mercy rest upon his soul!), be given him. That was a noble steed. My uncle dispatched it to him mounted by one of our men, a Kurd named Ḥasanūn, one of our valiant cavaliers, young, good-looking and thin, in order to hold races with other horses in the presence of Tancred. Ḥasanūn ran a race and his horse out-ran all the horses which were in the course. He was brought before Tancred, and the knights began to inspect his arms and wonder at his thin physique and his youth, recognizing in him a valiant cavalier. Tancred bestowed a robe of honor on him.[84] But Ḥasanūn said to him, "O

[82] Ar. *dankari*, who succeeded Bohemond I, in 1104. [83] November 27, 1108

[84] *khala'a 'alayhi*, which in this case may simply mean "bestowed a prize on him"

my lord, I wish that thou wouldst give me thy guarantee of safety to the effect that if I should fall into thy hands at war time thou wouldst favor me and set me free." Tancred gave him his guarantee of safety — as Ḥasanūn imagined, for these people speak nothing but Frankish; we do not understand what they say.

A year or more passed.[85] The period of truce having expired, Tancred advanced anew at the head of the army of Antioch. A battle ensued near the wall of our lower town. Our horsemen had met their vanguard, and one of our men, a Kurd, named Kāmil al-Mashṭūb, had used his lance on them to great effect. Kāmil and Ḥasanūn were peers in valor. This took place while Ḥasanūn on his mare was standing near my father (may Allah's mercy rest upon his soul!) and awaiting his charger, which his attendant was bringing to him from the veterinary, and his quilted jerkin. The attendant was late and Ḥasanūn was getting impatient, seeing the lance blows of Kāmil al-Mashṭūb. So he said to my father, "O my lord, put at my disposal light equipment." My father replied, "Here are the mules laden with arms and standing still. Whatever suits thee, put on." I was at that time standing behind my father. I was a mere lad,[86] and that was the first day in which I saw actual fighting. Ḥasanūn examined the jerkins, in their cases on the backs of the mules, but none of them suited him. In the meantime, he was boiling in his desire to proceed and do what Kāmil al-Mashṭūb was doing. So he charged on horseback, void of arms. A Frankish knight intercepted his way and struck the mare in its croup. The mare, getting the bit in its teeth, rushed with its rider on its back until it threw him off amidst the lines of the Franks. They took him prisoner and inflicted on him all varieties of torture. They even wanted to put out his [41] left eye. But Tancred (may Allah's curse be upon him!) said to them, "Rather put out his right eye, so that when he carries his shield his left eye will be covered, and he will be no more able to see anything." So they put out his right eye in accordance with the orders of Tancred and demanded as a ransom from him one thousand dīnārs and a black horse, which belonged to my father, of Khafājah breed [87] and one of the most magnificent

[85] Spring of 1110.
[86] Fifteen years old.
[87] The Khafājah horses, so called after an Arab tribe, were one of the noblest breeds.

horses. My father (may Allah's mercy rest upon his soul!) ransomed him for that horse.

On that same day a large number of footmen had gone out of Shayzar. The Franks made an onslaught on them but did not succeed in dislodging them from their position. This made Tancred angry at them and say, "Ye are my knights, and every one of you receives a stipend equal to the stipends of a hundred Moslems. Those men ye met were sergeants [88] (by which he meant footmen) and ye cannot dislodge them from their position!" They replied, "Our fear was only for our horses. Otherwise we would have trampled them under our feet and used our lances fully on them." Tancred replied, "The horses are my property. Whosoever of you loses his horse shall have his horse replaced." Thereupon they made several charges on our men, in the course of which seventy of their horses were killed, without being able to drive our men out of their position.

Badrhawa the knight routs four Moslem cavaliers. — There was in Afāmiyah one of the most valiant Frankish knights named Badrhawa.[89] He used always to say, "Is it not possible that I shall some day meet Jum'ah in combat?" And Jum'ah used always to say, "Is it not possible that I shall some day meet Badrhawa in combat?"

The army of Antioch now camped against us, pitching their tents in the place where they used to pitch them. Between them and us was the water.[90] We had a detachment posted on an elevation opposite the enemy. One of their knights rode out of the camp and advanced until he stood just below our detachment, with the water separating him from us. And then he shouted to them, "Is Jum'ah among you?" "No," they replied. And, by Allah, Jum'ah was not present among them. That knight was Badrhawa.

The knight, looking around, saw four of our cavaliers on his side of the river: Yahya ibn-Ṣāfi al-A'sar,[91] Sahl ibn-abi-Ghānim al-Kurdi and Ḥārithah al-Numayri, together with a fourth cavalier. The knight charged upon them, put them to flight and overtook one of their number, whom he smote with his lance, missing

[88] *sarjand*, evidently an attempt to Arabicize French *sergeant*
[89] Derenbourg, *Vie d'Ousāma*, p 57, n 2, conjectures that this is the Arabicized form of "Pedrovant"
[90] The Orontes. [91] The left-handed.

him. His horse did not go fast enough to enable him to deal successive blows with the lance. So he returned to his camp.

On the return of our men to the town, their story was disclosed and the people disgraced them, blamed them and despised them, saying, "Four cavaliers put to flight by one single knight! Ye should have separated before him and he would have used his lance against one of you. Then the other three would have killed him, and ye would not have been put to such a shame." The bitterest one of all in his criticism was Jum'ah al-Numayri. But as though that defeat gave them hearts other than the ones they possessed and an amount of courage to which they never aspired before, these same cavaliers now became imbued with valor, and they fought and distinguished themselves in warfare, so much so that they became among the noted cavaliers after that defeat.

As for Badrhawa, he subsequently left Afāmiyah and proceeded on some business of his to Antioch On his way, a lion fell upon him from a forest in al-Rūj,[92] snatched him off his mule and carried him into the forest where he devoured him — may Allah's mercy not rest upon his soul!

Single-handed feats: One knight charges a Moslem army. — Among the cases of adventure in which one man faces a large group of men is the following:

[42] The Isbāslār Mawdūd[93] (may Allah's mercy rest upon his soul!) camped in the suburb of Shayzar on Thursday, the ninth of Rabī' I, in the year 505,[94] after Tancred, the lord of Antioch, had moved against him with a great army. My uncle and my father (may Allah's mercy rest upon their souls!) came out to Mawdūd and said:

The right thing would be for thee to break camp (he had his camp east of the upper town on the bank of the river) and install thyself inside of the town. The army will pitch their tents on the roofs in the lower town and we shall encounter the Franks after putting our tents and baggage in a place of security.

[92] A district of Aleppo lying between the city of Aleppo and al-Ma'arrah. Yāqūt, *op. cit*, vol. II, p 828

[93] Sharaf-al-Dīn Mawdūd ibn-Altūntikīn was the governor of al-Mawṣil (modern al-Mūṣul) in the name of the Seljūq sultan, Muḥammad-Shāh of Ispahān, and the leader of the army which the sultan, at the request of the 'Abbāsid caliph, put in the field against Tancred Ibn-Taghri-Birdi, *op. cit.*, vol. II, pt. II, p. 354.

[94] September 15, 1111.

He departed and established himself in accordance with what they said to him.

Early in the morning my uncle and father joined him, together with five thousand men from Shayzar, fully armed. The isbāslār rejoiced at seeing them, and was greatly encouraged by their presence. He himself (may Allah's mercy rest upon his soul!) had excellent men. He put his men in battle array on the south side of the water, while the Franks were encamped on the north side. All that day long they prevented the Franks from drinking and coming near the water. So when the night fell, the Franks departed, returning to their territory with our men around them. On their way they camped at Tell-al-Turmusi, and were again prevented from reaching the water as on the previous day. So they departed during the night and camped at Tell-al-Tulūl, pressed by our army, which prevented them from advancing and which surrounded the water in order to prevent them from reaching it. Again they departed in the nighttime, headed for Afāmiyah. Our army rushed and surrounded them while they were on the march. One of their knights now left the ranks and charged our men until he got in their midst. They killed his horse and inflicted several wounds on his body, but he fought his way on foot until he rejoined his comrades. As the Franks entered their territory, the Moslems left them and turned back. The Isbāslār Mawdūd (may Allah's mercy rest upon his soul!) departed for Damascus.

A few months later there came to us a letter from Tancred, the lord of Antioch, carried by a knight accompanied with attendants and followers. The letter read:

> This is a revered knight of the Franks who has completed the holy pilgrimage and is now on his way back to his country. He has asked me to introduce him to you so that he may see your cavaliers. Accordingly, I have sent him to you. Treat him well.

The knight was a young man, handsome in looks and well dressed, but his body bore traces of numerous cuts. His face showed the mark of a sword blow which had cut him from the middle of his head to the fore part of his face. I asked about him and was told: "This is the one who made a charge against the army of the Isbāslār Mawdūd, whose horse was killed and who fought until he rejoined his comrades." Exalted is Allah who can do what he pleases as he pleases! Holding aloof no more retards fate than adventure hastens it.

One man carries away booty from eight men. — A similar case is that related to me by al-'Uqāb, the poet, one of our combatants from al-Maghrib [Mauretania]. This is what he said: "My father left Tadmur [Palmyra], desiring to go to the market of Damascus, accompanied by four horsemen and four footmen driving eight camels for sale. [43] These are my father's words:

As we were on the march, behold! a horseman appeared, advancing towards us from the heart of the desert. He kept on advancing until he came close to us. He then said, "Let go the camels." We howled at him and cursed him He dashed his horse on us and struck with his lance one of our horsemen, unhorsing and wounding him. We pursued him. The horseman sped ahead at full gallop. After a while he turned back on us and said, "Let go the camels." Again we howled at him and cursed him. So he charged upon us and struck with his lance one of our footmen in whom he cut a deep wound. We followed him but could not overtake him Then he turned back, with two of our men already disabled, and made an onslaught on us. One of our men now received him and smote him with the lance. The blow fell on the pommel of the saddle and the lance broke. The knight hit our man with his lance and wounded him. Again he charged upon us and smote another of our men with his lance, felling him. Again he said, "Let the camels alone, otherwise I shall annihilate you." We said to him, "Come, take half of them." "No," said he. "Detach four of them. Leave them standing, and take four and depart." This we did, and we could hardly believe that we would escape with what was spared to us. He drove his four under our very eyes, for we were helpless with regard to him and had no hope with him. Thus he returned with his booty; and he was only one, while we were eight men.

One Frank captures a cavern. — A similar thing happened when Tancred, the lord of Antioch, made a raid on Shayzar and drove before him many of its animals after having killed and taken some of our men as prisoners. He then camped near a village called Zalīn in which was an inaccessible cavern as if suspended in the middle of the mountain. It had no way of descent to it from above and no way of ascent from below. He who seeks refuge in it can descend to it only by means of ropes. This happened on the twenty-fifth of Rabī' II, in the year 502.[95] A devil from among their

[95] November 27, 1108.

knights came to Tancred and said, "Make me a box of wood in which I will sit and ye shall lower me to the enemy from the top of the mountain by chains of iron which ye tie to the box, so that they cannot cut them with the swords and I be not hurled down." Accordingly they made a box for him and lowered it with chains to the hanging cavern, which he captured and from which he carried away to Tancred all who were in it. The way he did it was this: The cavern was an open court in which there was no place where one could secrete himself. He began to shoot arrows at them, and because of the narrowness of the place and the crowded condition of the people in it, not one of his arrows fell except on a person.

Usāmah's uncle ransoms a woman. — Among those who were taken captive [by the Franks] that day was a woman of noble Arab origin. Her description was once, prior to this, given to my uncle, 'Izz-al-Dīn abu-al-'Asākir Sulṭān (may Allah's mercy rest upon his soul!), when she was still in her father's home. My uncle on that occasion sent one of the old women of his entourage to inspect her. She came back dilating in her report [44] on the girl's great beauty and intelligence, either because of some bribe the old woman had received or because she was shown another girl My uncle was engaged to her and subsequently married her. When she uncovered before him, he saw something different from what was described to him. Besides, she was dumb. He therefore paid her the dowry and sent her back to her people. This woman was taken prisoner, on that day, from the home of her people. But my uncle said, "I shall not let a woman whom I had married and who had uncovered before me stay in the captivity of the Franks." So he bought her (may Allah's mercy rest upon his soul!) for five hundred dīnārs and delivered her to her own people.

A maiden's ingenuity saves the day. — A similar case was related to me by al-Mu'ayyad, the Baghdādi poet, in al-Mawṣil in the year 565.[96] This is what he said:

The caliph[97] bestowed upon my father as fief a village which my father used to frequent. That village was infested with vagabonds who carried on highway robbery and whom my father endeavored to please for fear of them and for profiting a little from what they seized. As

[96] September 25, 1169–September 13, 1170.
[97] The 'Abbāsid Caliph al-Mustanjid.

we were one day sitting in their village, there came a young Turk mounted on a horse, and with him a mule carrying a maiden riding on the saddlebag. He alighted, assisted the maiden to dismount and said, "O young men, help me put down the saddlebag." We came and put down the bag with him and lo! it was full of gold dīnārs and jewelry. He sat down with the maiden and ate something. Then he said, "Help me lift the saddlebag." We lifted it up with him. Then he said to us, "Where is the road to al-Anbār?" [98] My father said to him, "Here is the road (pointing it out with his hand), but there are on the road sixty vagabonds from whom I fear for thy safety." The man pooh-poohed my father, saying, "I fear the vagabonds!" My father left him and went to the vagabonds and told them the story of the man and what he carried. The vagabonds set off to intercept him on the way. When he saw them he pulled out his bow, put in it an arrow and bent it, desiring to shoot them. The string gave way. The vagabonds rushed at him and he fled away. So they took the mule and the maiden, together with the saddlebag. The maiden said, "O young men, by Allah, dishonor me not. Rather let me buy myself and the mule also for a necklace of gems, which is with the Turk and the value of which is five hundred dīnārs. Then take ye the saddlebag and all that is in it." "We accept," they replied. She said, "Send with me someone from among you so that I may speak with the Turk and take the necklace." Accordingly they sent with her someone to guard her until she came near the Turk and said to him, "I have bought myself and the mule for the necklace which is in the leg of thy left boot,[99] thy shoe. Deliver it to me." "All right," said he. Presently he went aside, took off his boot and lo! there was in it a bowstring, which he immediately fixed on his bow and turned back on them. They kept on fighting him while he was killing one after the other until he had killed forty-three men of their number. Looking around, he unexpectedly saw my father among [45] the vagabonds who survived. So he said, "Thou too among them! Dost thou desire that I should give thee thy share of arrows?" "No," replied my father. "Take them," said the Turk, "these seventeen who survive, lead them to the magistrate of the city to hang them." In the meantime those seventeen had stood staring with fear and put down their arms. The Turk drove his mule with all that was on it and continued his march. Thus Allah (exalted is he!) sent through him upon the vagabonds a calamity and great wrath.

Other single-handed feats. — Another illustration I witnessed in the year 509.[100] My father (may Allah's mercy rest upon his soul!)

[98] A town on the left bank of the Euphrates, in the northeast of 'Irāq.

[99] The word used in the manuscript is *mūza* which is Persian *mūzeh* = boot. That explains why some copyist probably added an explanatory modifier in Arabic *khuff*, which we translated "shoe."

[100] May 27, 1115–May 15, 1116.

had set out at the head of the army to join the Isbāslār Bursuq ibn-Bursuq (may Allah's mercy rest upon his soul!), who had arrived on an expedition ordered by the sultan.[101] Bursuq commanded a huge army including a large number of amīrs, among whom were the Amīr-al-Juyūsh [commander of the armies] Uzbeh[102] the lord of al-Mawṣil, Sunqur Dirāz the lord of al-Raḥabah, the Amīr Kundughadi, al-Ḥājib al-Kabīr [the grand chamberlain] Baktimur, Zanki ibn-Bursuq (who was a veritable hero), Tamīrak, Ismā'īl al-Bakji,[103] and others. They camped before Kafarṭāb, in which were the two brothers of Theophile at the head of the Franks, and attacked it. The troops from Khurāsān entered the trench and began to dig an underground tunnel. Convinced that they were on the point of perdition, the Franks set the castle on fire. The roofs were burned and fell upon the horses, beasts of burden, sheep, pigs and captives — all of whom were burned up. The Franks remained clinging to the walls at the top of the castle.

It occurred to me to enter the underground tunnel and inspect it. So I went down in the trench, while the arrows and stones were falling on us like rain, and entered the tunnel. There I was struck with the great wisdom with which the digging was executed. The tunnel was dug from the trench to the barbican [*bāshūrah*]. On the sides of the tunnel were set up two pillars, across which stretched a plank to prevent the earth above it from falling down. The whole tunnel had such a framework of wood that extended as far as the foundation of the barbican. Then the assailants dug under the wall of the barbican, supported it in its place, and went as far as the foundation of the tower. The tunnel was narrow. It was nothing but a means to provide access to the tower. As soon as they got to the tower, they enlarged the tunnel in the wall of the tower, supported it on timbers and began to carry out, a little at a time, the splinters of stone produced by boring. The floor of

[101] Muḥammad-Shāh ibn-Malik-Shāh the Seljūq sultan of Ispahān

[102] Or, Uzbek = "the lord of the army," referred to as "the Amīr-Juyūsh Bey" in abu-al-Fida in *Recueil historiens orientaux*, vol I, p 13, and ibn-al-Athīr, in *ibid*, pp 300, 345

[103] Original "al-Balkhi," lacking diacritical marks "Bakji" is a Turkish word meaning "grand" Ibn-al-Athīr, *al-Kāmil*, ed Tornberg (Leyden, 1864), vol X, p 422, mentions "Ismā'īl al-Bakji" Cf *Recueil historiens orientaux*, vol II, pt II, p 45, n 3

the tunnel, on account of the dust caused by the digging, was converted into mud. Having made the inspection, I went on without the troops of Khurāsān recognizing me. Had they recognized me, they would not have let me off without the payment of a heavy tribute.

They then began to cut dry wood and stuff the tunnel with it. Early the next morning they set it on fire. We had just at that time put on our arms and marched, under a great shower of stones and arrows, to the trench [46] in order to make an onslaught on the castle as soon as its tower tumbled over. As soon as the fire began to have its effect, the layers of mortar between the stones of the wall began to fall. Then a crack was made. The crack became wider and wider and the tower fell. We had assumed that when the tower would fall we should be able to enter as far as our enemy. But only the outer face of the wall fell, while the inner wall remained intact. We stood there until the sun became too hot for us, and then returned to our tents after a great deal of damage had been inflicted on us by the stones, which were hurled against us.

After resting until noontime, there set out all of a sudden a footman from our ranks single-handed and carrying his sword and shield He marched to the wall of the tower which had fallen, and the sides of which had become like the steps of a ladder, and climbed on it until he got as far as its highest point. As soon as the other men of the army saw him, about ten of them followed him hastily in full armor and climbed one after the other until they got to the tower, while the Franks were not conscious of their movements. We in turn put on our armor in our tents and advanced. Many climbed the tower before all our army had wholly arrived.

The Franks now turned upon our men and shot their arrows at them. They wounded the man who was first to climb. So he descended. But the other men continued to climb in succession until they stood facing the Franks on one of the tower walls between two bastions [*badan*]. Right in front of them stood a tower the door of which was guarded by a cavalier in full armor carrying his shield and lance, preventing entrance to the tower. On top of that tower were a band of Franks, attacking our men with arrows and stones. One of the Turks climbed, under our very eyes, and started walking towards the tower, in the face of death, until he approached the tower and hurled a bottle of naphtha on those who were on top of it. The naphtha flashed like a meteor falling upon those hard stones, while the men who were there threw themselves on the ground for fear of being burnt. The Turk then came back to us.

Another Turk now climbed and started walking on the same wall between the two bastions. He was carrying his sword and shield. There came out to meet him from the tower, at the door of which stood a knight, a Frank wearing double-linked mail and carrying a spear in his hand, but not equipped with a shield. The Turk, sword in hand, encountered him. The Frank smote him with the spear, but the Turk warded off the point of the spear with his shield and, notwithstanding the spear, advanced towards the Frank. The latter took to flight and turned his back, leaning forward, like one who wanted to kneel, in order to protect his head. The Turk dealt him a number of blows which had no effect whatsoever, and went on walking until he entered the tower.

Our men proved too numerous and too strong for the enemy. So the latter delivered the castle, and the captives came down to the tents of Bursuq ibn-Bursuq.

Among those who were assembled in the large tent of Bursuq ibn-Bursuq in order to set for themselves a price for their liberty, I recognized that same man who had set out with his spear against the Turk. He, who was a sergeant [*sarjandi*], stood up and said, "How much do ye want from me?" They said, "We demand six hundred dīnārs." He pooh-poohed them, saying, "I am a sergeant. My stipend is two dīnārs a month. [47] Wherefrom can I get you six hundred dīnārs?" And saying this, he went back and sat among his companions. And he was huge in size. Seeing him, the Amīr al-Sayyid al-Sharīf,[104] who was one of the leading amīrs, said to my father (may Allah's mercy rest upon his soul!), "O my brother, seest thou what manner of people these are? In Allah we seek refuge against them."

By the decree of Allah (worthy of admiration is he!) our army

[104] The noble (a descendant of the Prophet) chief, probably the leader of Bursuq's army. Cf. ibn-al-Athīr in *Recueil: historiens orientaux*, vol. I, p. 282.

departed from Kafarṭāb to Dānīth [105] and were surprised to meet early Tuesday morning, the twenty-third of Rabīʿ II,[106] the army of Antioch. The capitulation of Kafarṭāb took place on Friday, the thirteenth of Rabīʿ II.[107] The Amīr al-Sayyid (may Allah's mercy rest upon his soul!) was killed, together with a large body of Moslems.

My father (may Allah's mercy rest upon his soul!) with whom I had parted at Kafartāb returned [to Kafarṭāb] after the army had been defeated. We were still at Kafartāb guarding it with the intention of rebuilding it; for the isbāslār had delivered it into our hands. We were bringing out the captives, each two chained to one man from Shayzar. Some of them had half of their bodies burned and their legs remained. Others were dead by fire. I saw in what befell them a great object lesson.[108] We then left Kafarṭab and returned to Shayzar in the company of my father (may Allah's mercy rest upon his soul!), who had lost all the tents, loads, mules, camels and baggage he had, and whose army was dispersed.

A stratagem by the governor of Aleppo. — These reverses had befallen the army through a ruse effected by Lu'lu' al-Khādim,[109] who was then the lord of Aleppo. Lu'lu' had concerted with the lord of Antioch [110] to use a stratagem against the Moslems and divide them, upon which the latter would set out from Antioch with his army and defeat them. Accordingly Lu'lu' sent a message to the Isbāslār Bursuq (may Allah's mercy rest upon his soul!) to this effect:

> Dispatch unto me one of the amīrs with a company of soldiers, and I shall deliver unto him Aleppo; because I am afraid that the inhabitants may not agree with me regarding the delivery of the town. That is why I would like to have with the amīr a company of troops by whom I can get the upper hand over the Aleppines.

Bursuq dispatched to him the Amīr-al-Juyūsh Uzbeh at the head of three thousand horsemen, whom Roger [*rūjār*] (may Allah's

105 A city in the province of Aleppo situated between Aleppo and Kafarṭāb. Yāqūt, *op cit*, vol II, p 540

106 September 15, 1115

107 September 5, 1115

108 *'ibrah* is used here and in other places Hence the title of the book *al-iʿtibār*.

109 The servant His full name was Badr-al-Dīn Lu'lu', and he succeeded Riḍwān ibn-Tutush in 1117 in the governorship of Aleppo

110 Roger, prince of Antioch, December, 1112–June, 1119.

curse be upon him!) surprised one morning and defeated — through an execution of the divine will.

The Franks (may Allah's curse be upon them!) returned to Kafarṭāb, which they rebuilt and populated.

Allah (exalted is he!) decreed that the Frankish captives who were taken in Kafarṭāb be set free, since the amīrs divided them among themselves and kept them under their charge until they could buy themselves off; the only exception being the case of the isbāslār who, before departing for Aleppo, issued orders and all those captives who fell in his share had their heads struck off.

The army — those of them who survived the battle of Dānīth — disbanded and went into their home lands. But that man who single-handed climbed to the tower of Kafarṭāb was responsible for the capture of that fortress.

Numayr storms a cavern in which Franks were hiding. — Another illustration:

There was in my service a man named Numayr al-'Allārūzi. He was a footman, brave and strong. With a band of men from Shayzar, he set out to al-Rūj to attack the Franks. When still in our territory, they came across a caravan of the Franks hiding in a cavern, and each one began to say to the other, "Who should go in against them?" "I," said Numayr. And as he said it, he turned over to his companions his sword and shield, drew his dagger and went in [48] against them. As he entered, one of them came to receive him, but Numayr stabbed him immediately with the dagger, overthrew him and knelt upon him to slay him Behind the Frank stood another one with a sword in his hand and struck Numayr. The latter had on his back a knapsack containing bread, which protected him. Having killed the man under him, Numayr now turned to the man with the sword, intent upon attacking him. The Frank immediately struck him with the sword on the side of his face and cut through his eyebrow, eyelid, cheek, nose and upper lip, making the whole side of his face hang down on his chest. Numayr went out of the cavern to his companions, who bandaged his wound and brought him back during a cold rainy night. He arrived in Shayzar in that condition. There his face was stitched and his cut was treated until he was healed and returned to his former condition, with the exception of his eye which was lost for good. This Numayr was one of the three whom the Ismā'īlites hurled to the ground from the Castle of Shayzar, and whose story we have already related.[111]

One man routs many near Rafaniyyah. — The following was related to me by al-Ra'īs [112] Sahri, who was in the service of the Amīr Shams-al-Khawāṣṣ Āltūntāsh, the lord of Rafaniyyah, and who had a standing enmity and a dispute with 'Alam-al-Dīn 'Ali-Kurd, the lord of Ḥamāh. These are the words of Sahri:

Shams-al-Khawāṣṣ ordered me to go and appraise the crop of Rafaniyyah and inspect its cultivated fields. I set out, accompanied by a band of troops, and appraised the crops of the town One evening, I set up my camp in one of the villages of Rafaniyyah, which had a tower, and I climbed with my companions to the roof of the tower, where we had our supper. After supper we took our seats while our horses stood at the door of the tower. Before we knew it there appeared a man overlooking us from among the battlements of the tower. He yelled at us and threw himself into our midst, holding a dagger in his hand We all took to flight and made our descent on the first ladder while he pursued us. We made our descent on the second ladder with him in our pursuit until we got to the door. As we rushed out, we unexpectedly found that he had stationed for us certain men at the door who seized every one of us, bound us fast with cords and took us over to Hamāh, into the presence of 'Ali-Kurd We escaped decapitation only because our predestined day had not arrived. 'Ali imprisoned us and put a heavy ransom on us. And the one who brought all this on us was a single-handed man.

One man captures a whole castle. — A similar episode took place in the Castle of [Qal'ah] al-Khirbah. This castle belonged to Ṣalāḥ-al-Dīn Muḥammad ibn-Ayyūb al-Ghisyāni [113] (may Allah's mercy rest upon his soul!), and there was stationed in it its governor, al-Ḥājib [chamberlain] 'Īsa. It was an impregnable fortress crowning a high rock, steep on all sides. The only access to it was by climbing a wooden ladder, which would then be removed, leaving no other way to reach it. With the governor in the fortress were none but his son, his servant and the gateman. The last mentioned

[111] Evidently in the missing part of the manuscript. Abu-al-Fida and ibn-al-Athīr, in *Recueil historiens orientaux*, vol I, pp 10, 272, mention this attack by the Ismā'īlites under a date corresponding to April, 1109, Sibṭ ibn-al-Jawzi in *ibid*, vol. III, p 548, in April, 1114

[112] "The chief," used for the head cook, sailor, muleteer, artisan, etc. In this case, the man is head appraiser

[113] An abbreviated form of al-Yāghī-Siyāni.

had a friend named ibn al-Marji [Murahhi?], who used to come up to him from time to time on certain business. This man conferred with the Ismā'īlites and made with them a pact assuring him a satisfactory amount of money and a fief on condition that he would deliver the Castle of al-Khirbah to them. He then came to the castle, asked permission to be admitted and mounted. Starting with the gateman, he put him to death. The servant who met him next he also killed. Then he entered the room of the governor and killed him Returning to the son of the governor, he also killed him, and delivered the castle to [49] the Ismā'īlites, who fulfilled their part of the contract with him.

When men strengthen themselves to do a thing, they usually do it.

Superiority among men in zeal: A native Christian muleteer.—Other illustrations relate to the differences between men in zeal and magnanimity. My father (may Allah's mercy rest upon his soul!) used to say to me:

The good among all species may have among the bad in its species what is equivalent to it in value [114] For instance, a good horse may be worth a hundred dīnārs, five bad horses may also be worth a hundred dīnārs. The same holds true in the case of camels. The same holds true in the case of the different varieties of clothing. The only exception is the son of Adam,[115] because one thousand bad men are not worth one good man.

And my father (may Allah's mercy rest upon his soul!) was right.

I once [116] dispatched a mameluke of mine on urgent business to Damascus. It so happened that in the meantime the Atābek Zanki (may Allah's mercy rest upon his soul!) had captured Ḥamāh and established his camp outside of Ḥimṣ Thus the return route was closed in the face of my man, who had to make his way to Ba'labakk [117] and thence to Tripoli, where he hired the mule of a Christian called Yūnān [118] The latter transported him to the place agreed upon, bade him farewell and returned As for my man, he joined a caravan with the intention of reaching Shayzar via the forts [119] of the mountains.[120] On the way they met a man who said

[114] Cf *Autobiographie*, pp 79–80. [115] That is, man. [116] In 1129 or 1130
[117] Colloquially, "Ba'albak" [118] Jonah
[119] *huṣūn*, which, for lack of diacritical marks, may be *huḍūn* = "sides," "passes"
[120] The pass between Tripoli and Shayzar had Mt Lebanon to the south and the Nuṣayriyyah mountain to the north, which was infested with assassins.

to the owners of the beasts, "Proceed not, for on your way in such and such a place lies a band of robbers, numbering sixty or seventy men, who will capture you." My servant, relating the story, said:

Here we stopped, not knowing what to do, neither cherishing the idea of turning back nor feeling bold enough to advance, on account of fear. As we were in this dilemma, behold! al-Ra'īs [121] Yūnān appeared, hurrying toward us. We said, "What is the matter with thee, O Ra'īs?" He replied, "I heard that there were robbers on your way, so I came to see you off. Proceed." Accordingly we advanced with him to that place, and lo! a great multitude of robbers fell upon us from the mountain, desiring to capture us. Yūnān met them and said, "O young men, keep your place! I am Yūnān, and these are under my guardianship. By Allah, there isn't one among you who would come near them." Thus, by Allah, he repelled them all from us, without having eaten even a loaf of our bread. Yūnān kept walking with us until we were in perfect safety and then bade us farewell and departed.

The fidelity of a Bedouin. — This same servant of mine, who in the year 538 [122] had accompanied me to Egypt, told me a story about the son of the lord of al-Ṭūr [Mt. Sinai] who told it to him in the following words (al-Ṭūr being a distant province belonging to Egypt and close to the land of the Franks and over which al-Ḥāfiẓ li-Dīn-Allāh — may Allah's mercy rest upon his soul! — would appoint as governor any one of his amīrs whom he desired to banish):

My father was appointed governor of al-Ṭūr, and I went out with him to the province. I was fond of hunting. So I went out one day to hunt and a group of Franks fell upon me, captured me and took me to Bayt-Jibrīl. There they shut me up all alone in a dungeon. The master of Bayt-Jibrīl fixed my ransom at two thousand dīnārs. I remained in the dungeon a year without anybody inquiring about me.

But one day as I was in my dungeon, behold! the trapdoor was uplifted [50] and a Bedouin was lowered towards me. I said, "Where did they take thee from?" "From the road," he replied. After staying with me a few days, his ransom was fixed at fifty dīnārs. One day he said to me, "Dost thou want to know that none can deliver thee from this dungeon but me? Deliver me, therefore, so that I may deliver thee." I said to myself, "Here is a man who, finding himself in distress, seeks for himself a way of deliverance." So I answered him not. A few days later he repeated the same request to me. So I said to myself, "By

[121] In the manuscript, *al-rayyis*, variant of *al-ra'īs*.
[122] This year ended July 3, 1144.

Allah, I will surely make an effort to deliver him, for maybe Allah will deliver me in recompense." So I shouted to the jailer and said, "Tell the lord I wish to confer with him." The jailer went away and returned. Then he made me mount out of the dungeon and presented me before the lord. I said to the lord, "I have been in thy prison for one year without anybody inquiring about me, and nobody knows whether I am alive or dead. Then thou hast imprisoned with me this Bedouin and fixed his ransom at fifty dīnārs. Now, add his ransom to mine and let me send him to my father so that he may buy me off" "Do so," replied the lord. Accordingly I returned and notified the Bedouin, who went out, bade me farewell and departed

I awaited results from him for two months, but I saw no trace of him nor heard any news about him. So I despaired of him But one night, to my great surprise, he appeared before me from a tunnel in the side of the dungeon and said, "Arise. By Allah, I have been five months digging this subterranean passage from a village in ruins until I got to thee" I arose with him and we went out through that subterranean passage. He broke my chain, and accompanied me to my own home. And now I know not what to admire more — his fidelity in carrying out his promise or his precision in digging a tunnel that hit the side of the dungeon.

When Allah (worthy of admiration is he!) decrees that relief should come, then how easy become the causes which bring it about!

Usāmah ransoms captives. — I used to visit frequently the king of the Franks [123] during the truce between him and Jamāl-al-Dīn Muḥammad ibn-Tāj-al-Mulūk [124] (may Allah's mercy rest upon his soul!), on account of the fact that King Baldwin, father of the queen,[125] who was the wife of King Fulk, son of Fulk, was under obligation to my father (may Allah's mercy rest upon his soul!). During these visits the Franks used to bring before me their captives so that I might buy them off, and I would buy off those of them whose deliverance Allah (exalted is he!) would facilitate.

Once a devil of a Frank named William Jiba [126] set out in his vessel for a piratical raid, and captured a vessel in which were Maghribi pilgrims numbering about four hundred souls, men and women. Now some of these Maghribis would be brought to me

[123] Fulk V of Anjou, king of Jerusalem.

[124] Tāj-al-Mulūk Būri ibn-Ṭughtakīn, the lord of Damascus, June 24, 1139–March 29, 1140. He was the brother and successor of Shihāb-al-Dīn Maḥmūd

[125] Queen Mélisende. This Baldwin was Baldwin II, king of Jerusalem, whose daughter married Fulk V in 1129.

[126] Ar. *kilyām jiba*, the exact Frankish equivalent of which is unknown.

by their owners, and I would buy from among them those whom I could buy. One of the captives was a young man who would salute and sit without uttering a word. I inquired about him and was told that he was an ascetic owned by a tanner. So I said to the tanner, "For how much wilt thou sell me this one?" The tanner replied, "By the truth of my religion, I will not sell him except in conjunction with this sheikh, and that for the same price that I paid for them, namely forty-three dīnārs." I bought them both, and I bought for my own use a few others. I also bought for the Amīr Mu'īn-al-Dīn [127] (may Allah's mercy rest upon his soul!) a few others costing one hundred twenty dīnārs. I paid [51] the money that I had with me and offered a bond for the balance.

Later I came to Damascus and said to the Amīr Mu'īn-al-Dīn (may Allah's mercy rest upon his soul!), "I have purchased some captives especially for thee, but I did not have their full price. And now that I have arrived in my home, if thou wantest them thou shalt pay their price, otherwise I shall pay it myself." "O no," said he, "I would, by Allah, rather pay their price myself. And of all men, I desire most the reward that comes thereby." In truth, Mu'īn-al-Dīn (may Allah's mercy rest upon his soul!) was the quickest of men in doing good and in gaining the reward thereof He paid their price. A few days afterwards I returned to 'Akka [Acre]

There remained with William Jiba thirty-eight of the captives, among whom was the wife of one of those whom Allah had delivered through my hand So I bought her off without paying her price on the spot Soon after, I rode to Jiba's home (may Allah's curse be upon him!) and said, "Wilt thou sell me ten of the captives?" "By my religion," he replied, "I won't sell them but all together." "I haven't got on my person the price of them all," I replied. "So I will now buy some, and then another time I will buy the rest " "I will not sell them to thee but all together," he repeated. So I departed. But Allah (worthy of admiration is he!) decreed and they fled away that very night, all of them. The inhabitants of the villages of 'Akka being all Moslems, whenever a captive came to them they would hide him and see that he got into Moslem territory. That accursed one sought his runaways, but succeeded

[127] Mu'īn-al-Dīn Anar, the minister of Damascus and Usāmah's patron.

in capturing none, for Allah (worthy of admiration is he!) made their deliverance good.

The second morning he began to demand from me the price of the woman whom I had purchased but whose price I had not paid and who was one of those who had fled away. I said to him, "Deliver her to me and then take her price." He replied, "Her price is mine by right since yesterday before she fled away." And he forced me to pay her price. So I paid it and considered it an easy thing since I was so happy at the deliverance of those miserable ones.

Cases of miraculous escape: An unsuccessful attempt at Āmid. — The following is a case of miraculous escape due to the intervention of destiny and the previous decision of divine will.

Al-Amīr Fakhr-al-Dīn Qara-Arslān ibn-Suqmān ibn-Urtuq [128] (may Allah's mercy rest upon his soul!) made a number of attempts on the city of Āmid,[129] while I was in his service, without accomplishing his object. In the course of the last attempt [130] he made on it, a Kurdish amīr, who was in charge of the register at Āmid, heading a group of followers, entered into correspondence with Fakhr-al-Dīn and agreed with him that on a certain night, which they appointed, the army of Fakhr-al-Dīn would arrive near his place and he would help them climb [the walls of the city] by means of ropes, and thus Fakhr-al-Dīn would come into possession of the city.

Fakhr-al-Dīn intrusted the execution of this momentous plan to a Frankish servant of his, named Yārūq, whom the whole army hated and despised because of his evil character.

Yārūq rode forward at the head of some troops. The rest of the amīrs rode behind him. Then he began to slow down. So the rest of the amīrs got to Āmid ahead of him. That Kurdish amīr with his companions looked down upon them from the tower and suspended the ropes to them saying, "Climb." But not one of them did climb. So they descended from the tower and broke the locks of the [52] city gate and said, "Enter." But they would not enter. All this was due to the fact that Fakhr-al-Dīn intrusted

[128] This amīr was the lord of Ḥisn-Kayfa in Dīyār-Bakr

[129] The capital of the province of Diyār-Bakr Diyār-Bakr, formerly the name of a province, is at the present day the name given to the ancient town of Āmid

[130] *Al-Rawḍatayn*, vol. II, p 40, refers to an attack which may be the one meant.

the execution of his momentous plan to an ignorant lad instead of intrusting it to the great amīrs.

Al-Amīr Kamāl-al-Dīn 'Ali ibn-Nīsān,[131] as well as the inhabitants of the city and the army, knew of the treachery. They fell upon the conspirators and killed some of them; others threw themselves over the walls. Some of them they seized. As one of those who threw themselves over was falling down through the air, he stretched out his arm, as if seeking something to take hold of, and his hand fell upon one of those ropes which had been suspended in the early part of the night and up which nobody climbed So he hung to it and escaped alone of all the company. But the skin of his two palms was stripped off from contact with the rope. All this took place in my presence.

The second morning the governor of Āmid pursued all those who had taken part in the conspiracy against him and killed them. The only man who escaped was that man. Worthy of admiration is he, therefore, who in case he decrees the safety of a man delivers him even from the jaws of the lion. This is a statement of a fact and not merely an illustration.

Delivered from the jaws of the lion. — In the Citadel of the Bridge[132] was one of our companions of the banu-Kinānah known by the name of ibn-al-Aḥmar. He mounted his mare at the citadel, intending to go to Kafarṭāb for some business of his. He passed through Kafarnabūdha[133] at the same time that a caravan was passing along the road. The caravan saw a lion. Ibn-al-Aḥmar had a javelin which was shining [in the sun]. The members of the caravan shouted to him, "O thou with the shining wood, attack the lion!" Moved by shame on account of their cries, he charged the lion. The mare shied with him in the saddle; so he fell. The lion came and crouched on his back. But, since Allah desired his safety, the lion was satiated with food. The lion bit a mouthful of his face and forehead, wounded his face and began to lick the blood while crouching over him without killing him. These are the words of ibn-al-Ahmar:

[131] The vizier of the governor of Āmid

[132] *hisn al-jisr* at Shayzar This citadel occupied a strategic position at the Bridge, which was the only means of communication from Shayzar to the right side of the Orontes The *jisr* is the *Gistrum* of Gauthier le Chancelier in *Recueil. historiens occidentaux*, vol V, p 89

[133] "Kafarnabu" in Yāqūt, *op. cit.*, vol. IV, p. 291.

something analogous to that, but it was not in course of war. The Franks massed their troops in great numbers against Bāniyās [139] accompanied by the patriarch.[140] The patriarch pitched a huge tent which he used as a church in which they held their prayers. The church services were conducted by an old deacon [*shammās*], who had covered its floors with bulrushes [141] and grass, which resulted in a pest of fleas. It occurred to that deacon to burn the bulrushes and grass in order to burn thereby the fleas. So he started the fire in the bulrushes and grass, which were all dried up by this time, and the fire sent flames which caught the tent and left it in ashes. This man acted with his reason absent.

Presence of mind when attacked by a lion. — Here is something to the contrary. One day we left Shayzar on horseback for a hunt. [54] My paternal uncle (may Allah's mercy rest upon his soul!) accompanied us, together with a detachment of troops. As we entered a reed bank in pursuit of a francolin, a lion came out facing us. One of our men, a Kurd known by the name of Zahr-al-Dawlah Bakhtiyār al-Qubruṣi,[142] so called[143] on account of his elegant physique, who was (may Allah's mercy rest upon his soul!) one of the best Moslem cavaliers, charged the lion. The lion met his charge. The horse shied with the man in the saddle and threw him. The lion came towards Zahr-al-Dawlah while he lay prostrate on the ground. He lifted his leg high and the lion bit at it. We rushed at the lion, killed it and pulled the man out safe and sound. Then we said to him, "O Zahr-al-Dawlah, why didst thou lift thy leg to the mouth of the lion?" He replied:

My body, as ye see it, is thin and lean; and I have on me only a garment and a tunic. There is nothing in me better clothed than my foot, with its stockings, boots and leggings. I therefore thought that I would keep the lion busy with it rather than with my ribs, hand or head until such time as Allah (exalted is he!) should provide relief.

Now, this man acted with presence of mind in a situation in which minds are lost, but the others did not act with presence of

[139] Paneas.

[140] Patriarch William of Jerusalem. R. Rohricht, *Geschichte des Konigreichs Jerusalem* (Innsbruck, 1898), p 221.

[141] *halfā'*, a kind of cane which grows in the water and on the banks of rivers. The word is used colloquially for papyrus.

[142] From *qubruṣ* (a variant of *qubrus*) = "Cyprus" *Autobiographie*, p. 87, reads "al-Qarsi."

[143] Zahr-al-Dawlah means "flower of the dynasty."

mind. Above all things, therefore, man stands primarily in need of reason.[144] Reason is praised by both the intelligent and the ignorant.

Wise administrations: The case of Usāmah's uncle. — Another illustration:

Roger [*rūjār*], the lord of Antioch, wrote[145] to my uncle, saying, "I am dispatching one of my knights on urgent business to Jerusalem, and I ask thee to send an escort of horsemen to take him from Afāmiyah and conduct him to Rafaniyyah." My uncle organized the escort and sent them to fetch him. When the knight met my uncle he said to him, "My lord has dispatched me on business and a secret mission. But seeing that thou art an intelligent man, I shall disclose it to thee." My uncle said to him, "How dost thou know that I am an intelligent man, and thou hast never seen me before this moment?" The knight replied, "Because I noticed that the whole region through which I passed was in ruins, with the exception of thy region, which is flourishing. I therefore reasoned that thou couldst not have made it flourish except through thy intelligence and good administration." Then he revealed to him the object of his mission.

The case of the lord of Diyār-Bakr. — The following story was told me by al-Amīr Fadl ibn-abi-al-Hayjā', the lord of Irbil,[146] who said, "It was related to me by abu-al-Hayjā', who said to me:

"When the Sultan Malik-Shāh[147] arrived in Syria he sent me to al-Amīr ibn-Marwān, the lord of Diyār-Bakr, in order to claim from him thirty thousand dīnārs. Arriving there, I held an interview with ibn-Marwān and read to him the message I carried To this he replied, 'Thou shalt first have thy rest, and then we shall discuss the matter.' The second morning he ordered that I should be admitted into his bath and sent to me the bath outfit, all made of silver, together with a complete suit of clothes, and told my valet that all the bath outfit was our property. On leaving the bath, however, I put on my own clothes and sent back all the articles that were offered. Ibn-Marwān let me go for a few days and then ordered again that I be conducted into his bath, without showing displeasure for not accepting the articles They now carried with me to the bath an outfit superior to the one brought before,

[144] *'aql*, used for both reason and intelligence [145] About 1116.

[146] Ancient Arbela, in Mesopotamia, south of Mawsil Ibn-Khallikān in his biography of Usāmah, *Ta'rīkh*, vol I, p 110 = *Dictionary*, vol I, p 177, mentions Usāmah's visit to Irbil See also Yāqūt, *op cit*, vol I, pp 186–89.

[147] The Seljūq governor of Iṣpahān. He was the son and successor of Alp-Arslān.

and a suit of clothes richer than the other one. His valet said to mine the same thing he said before. On leaving the bath, I again put on my own clothes and sent back the articles and the suit. He let me go again for three or four days and then made me enter [55] the bath. They also took in with me an outfit of silver superior to the one brought on the previous occasions and a suit of clothes richer than the other two. On leaving the bath I put on my own clothes and sent back all the articles. When I presented myself before the amīr, he said to me, 'O my son, I have dispatched unto thee clothes which thou didst not wear, and bath outfits which thou didst not accept and which thou hast sent back. What can be the reason for this?' I replied, 'My lord, I have come on a mission from the sultan regarding some business which has not yet been transacted. Shall I then accept what thou hast been kind to offer to me and return without transacting the business of the sultan, as if I had come here only in my own interest?' 'O my son,' said he, 'seest thou not how flourishing my country is, with its varied resources and gardens, its numerous farmers and prosperous estates? Dost thou suppose that I would expose all that to ruin for the sake of thirty thousand dīnārs? By Allah, I have verily put the gold for thee in sacks since the day of thy arrival I was only waiting so that the sultan might pass away from my territory, after which thou wouldst follow him with the money; for I feared that in case I paid on the spot the amount, he might demand from me as he approached my territory many times over the required sum Worry not, therefore, about it. Thy business is already transacted' He then sent to me all three suits which he had sent before and which I had refused, together with all the bath outfits which he had sent on the previous three occasions, and I accepted all of them. After the sultan had passed by Diyār-Bakr, ibn-Marwān delivered to me the money, which I carried, and I followed the sultan."

The case of the lord of Badlīs — Good administration results in a great advantage for the prosperity of the land. Here is an illustration. The Atābek Zanki (may Allah's mercy rest upon his soul!) was engaged to the daughter of the lord of Khilāṭ,[148] whose father [149] was dead and whose mother was the regent over the district. Ḥusām-al-Dawlah ibn-Dilmāj,[150] who was the lord of Badlīs,[151] now also sent a messenger demanding the hand of the daughter

[148] The capital of Armenia This took place in 1134

[149] Sukmān or Suqmān al-Quṭbi, founder of the Shāh-Armīn dynasty, who died in 506 = 1112–13 *Recueil historiens orientaux*, vol I, pp 11, 17, abu-al-Fida *Ta'rīkh* (Constantinople, 1286 A H), vol. II, p 237

[150] Probably identical with Ṭughān-Arslān ibn-Ālṭakīn Ibn-al-Athīr, *al-Kāmil*, vol X, pp. 389, 436 = *Recueil: historiens orientaux*, vol I, pp 325 354.

[151] Turkish Bidlīs or Bitlīs, the modern capital of the district of Kurdistān in Turkish Armenia.

for his son. The atābek marched at the head of a good-sized army to Khilāṭ, taking a route other than the frequented one which leads through Badlīs. This route led us through mountains. We used to spend our nights en route without tents, each one stopping in his own place on the road, until we arrived in Khilāṭ. The atābek installed his camp outside the city and we entered its castle and wrote the marriage contract, including dowry.

When the business was concluded,[152] the atābek ordered that Ṣalāḥ-al-Dīn[153] should take the greater part of the army and march to Badlīs to attack it. So we mounted in the early part of the evening and marched, arriving in Badlīs early the second morning. Ḥusām-al-Dawlah, its lord, came out and met us at a distance from the town, and he installed Ṣalāḥ-al-Dīn in the public square. Having offered Ṣalāḥ-al-Dīn fine hospitality, waited on him and drunk in his tent on the public square, Ḥusām-al-Dawlah said, "O my lord, what dost thou prescribe? Thou hast certainly toiled and tired thyself out in coming here." Ṣalāḥ-al-Dīn replied, "The atābek was angered against thee because of thy demand in marriage of the same girl to whom he was engaged. And thou hast offered to pay to those people ten thousand dīnārs, which we now demand from thee." "Most willingly," replied Ḥusām-al-Dawlah, who presently produced some of the amount required and asked permission for a delay of a few days, the number of which he fixed, for the payment of the balance. We turned back, leaving his region, thanks to his good policies, in its flourishing condition and without having suffered the least damage.

The case of the lord of Ja'bar. — [56] That is somewhat similar to what happened to Najm-al-Dawlah Mālik ibn-Sālim[154] (may Allah's mercy rest upon his soul!). This is the way it happened. Joscelin[155] [*jūslīn*] made a raid on al-Raqqah and al-Qal'ah, seized all that was in their neighborhood, took many captives, drove before him a great booty of animals and encamped just across from al-Qal'ah with the Euphrates between. Najm-al-Dawlah Mālik rode in a bark accompanied by three or four attendants and crossed

[152] Cf Kamāl-al-Dīn, *Zubdah* in *Recueil· historiens orientaux,* vol III, pp 666–67.
[153] Ibn-Ayyūb al-Ghisyāni.
[154] The master of Qal'ah-Ja'bar on the Euphrates not far from al-Raqqah. The word Qal'ah means "fortress."
[155] Joscelin I of Tell-Bāshir.

the Euphrates to Joscelin. Between the two was a bond of old acquaintance; in fact, Mālik had done Joscelin favors which put the latter under obligation to him. Joscelin assumed that in the bark was a messenger from Mālik, so when one of the Franks came to him and said, "Here is Mālik in the bark," he replied, "This is not true." Another one came to him and said, "Mālik has disembarked and has come on foot as far as the place where I was." Then Joscelin arose, met Mālik and received him with special honors. He also restored to him all the booty and captives which he had taken. Had it not been for the diplomacy of Najm-al-Dawlah his region would have been devastated.

Courage of no avail in the face of destiny: The case of ibn-Sarāya. — When the days are over, courage and strength are of no avail. I witnessed a battle resulting from an advance made against us by the army of the Franks,[156] some of whom had joined the Atābek Ṭughdakīn [157] in an attack upon the Citadel of the Bridge [*ḥiṣn al-jisr*]. The atābek had concerted in Afāmiyah with Īlghāzi [158] ibn-Urtuq and the Franks for a joint fight against the army of the sultan.[159] The army of the sultan had already arrived in Syria under the Isbāslār Bursuq ibn-Bursuq, who camped in Ḥamāh on Sunday, Muḥarram 19, year 509 [160] As for us, the enemy opened battle against us near the city wall, but we won over them and repulsed them, setting them at naught. I then saw one of our comrades in arms, named Muḥammad ibn-Sarāya, who was a young man hard and strong, charged by a Frankish knight (may Allah's curse be upon him!) who smote Muḥammad with a lance in his thigh. The lance pierced through the thigh. Muḥammad got hold of it while it was still in his thigh. The Frank started to pull the lance back in order to take it out, while Muḥammad pulled it [on the other side] in order to keep it, thus making the lance go back and forth through his thigh until the thigh was made hollow. The lance was finally retained by him after the thigh was irreparably injured. The man died two days later — may Allah's mercy rest upon his soul!

[156] This was a joint expedition by Baldwin I of Jerusalem, Roger of Antioch and Pontius of Tripoli

[157] More commonly "Ṭughtakīn" from Turkish *tughān* (or *dughān*)-*tikīn* = "warrior falcon," the *Doldequin* of occidental historians. He was first the vizier of Duqāq and later assumed the title Sayf-al-Islām

[158] The copyist, taking the first syllable for a definite article, wrote the word "al-Ghāzi" here and below. [159] Muḥammad-Shāh of Iṣpahān. [160] June 14, 1115.

Usāmah's cousin saved by him. — On that same day, as I was engaged in battle on one wing of our army, I saw one of the enemy cavaliers charge one of our cavaliers and kill his horse with a lance thrust. Our comrade became a footman, standing on the ground, but I could not make out who he was on account of the distance between us. I immediately dashed my horse towards him, fearing for his safety from the Frank who had stabbed at him. The lance was left in the horse, which lay dead with its intestines falling out. In the meantime the Frank withdrew a short distance from the man, drew his sword and stood facing him. When I reached the man I found him to be my paternal cousin Nāṣir-al-Dawlah Kāmil ibn-Muqallad (may Allah's mercy rest upon his soul!). I stopped beside him, removed my foot [57] from the stirrup for him and said to him, "Mount." As soon as he was in the saddle, I turned the head of my horse westward while the city was to our east. He said to me, "Where goest thou?" I said, "To the man who killed thy horse, for it is now a splendid opportunity to get him." Stretching his hand out, Kāmil seized the reins of my horse saying, "Thou shouldst never engage in a stabbing contest while two men in armor are on thy horse. Deliver me to a safe place and then return and engage him in combat." Accordingly I rode off, delivered him and returned to that dog, who had by that time penetrated among his companions.

Under Allah's protection: An ascetic overlooked by the Franks. — I have witnessed the following manifestation of Allah's benevolence (exalted is he!) and good protection. The Franks (may Allah's curse be upon them!) camped [161] against us with their cavalry and infantry, with the Orontes, whose water was so extremely high that they could neither pass to our side nor we to their side, intervening between them and us. Their tents they pitched on the mountain, and a party of them came down to the gardens which were on their side [of the river] and left their horses at large among the green fodder and went to sleep. A few young men from the infantry of Shayzar addressed themselves to this matter, took off their clothes, carried their swords and swam to those sleepers, of whom they killed some. The enemy became too numerous for our comrades, so they threw themselves into the water and crossed

[161] This is the same attack, which took place in the summer of 1115.

while the army of the Franks was riding down the mountain like a flood. On the side of the Franks was a mosque called Masjid abi-al-Majd ibn-Sumayyah, in which lived a man named Ḥasan al-Zāhid [the ascetic]. Ḥasan was then standing on a roof by the mosque reciting a supererogatory prayer. He had on him a black garment of wool. We could see him, but had no access to him The Franks came and alighted at the door of the mosque, and climbed to him as we were repeating, "There is no force and no strength except by Allah![162] They shall soon kill him." But he, by Allah, neither discontinued his prayer, nor stirred from his place. The Franks turned back, descended, mounted their horses and departed while he was still standing in his place reciting his prayer. We have no doubt that Allah (worthy of admiration is he!) blinded them so they could not see him and concealed him from their sight. How worthy of admiration, therefore, is the Almighty, the Merciful!

The case of a Moslem captive ransomed by an unknown man.— Another illustration of Allah's benevolence:

When the Byzantine emperor[163] camped against Shayzar in the year 532,[164] a group of footmen went out of Shayzar for the combat. The Byzantines isolated them, killed some of them and took others captive. Among those whom they took captive was an ascetic of the banu-Kardūs, one of the freedmen of al-Ṣālih, i.e., he was an adopted slave of Maḥmūd ibn-Ṣāliḥ,[165] the lord of Aleppo. When the Byzantines returned, he went with them as a captive and arrived in Constantinople. One day as he was in that city he met a man who said to him, "Art thou ibn-Kardūs?" "Yes," he replied. The other man said, "Come with me and show me thy master." So he went with him until he pointed out to him his master. The man bargained with the Byzantine regarding the price of ibn-Kardūs until they agreed upon a price which satisfied the Byzantine. [58] The man paid the price and gave ibn-Kardūs some money for expenses, saying, "This will see thee home. Depart in the keeping of Allah (exalted is he!)." Ibn-Kardūs left Constantinople and succeeded in returning to Shayzar. All that took place through the relief of Allah (exalted is he!) and through his

[162] Cf Koran XVIII: 37.
[163] *malik al-rūm* This was John II Comnenus (1118–43). [164] 1138.
[165] Tāj-al-Mulūk Maḥmūd ibn-Nāsir ibn-Ṣāliḥ (1060–74) of the Mirdāsi dynasty.

unseen beneficence; for ibn-Kardūs never knew who the man was who bought him and released him.

An angel comes to the succor of Usāmah. — Something similar to this happened to me when the Franks attacked[166] us on our way out of Egypt and killed 'Abbās ibn-abi-al-Futūḥ and his eldest son, Naṣr, and we fled to a neighboring mountain. Our army climbed the mountain on foot, leading their horses behind them. As for me, I was on a pack horse.[167] As I was unable to walk, I climbed the mountain on horseback, while its slopes were all covered with pieces of stone and pebbles which slipped backwards under the feet of the horse every time its hoofs struck them. I beat the pack horse in order to make it climb, but it could not do so; it slipped backward, with the pebbles and chips of stone sliding under it, and fell. So I dismounted, assisted the horse to its feet and stopped, unable to move. At that moment a man came down to me from the mountain and held me by the hand, my other hand holding the pack horse, until he got me to the summit. No, by Allah, I did not know who the man was and never saw him again.

At that perilous time people would put you under obligation to them for a slight favor and would demand some recompense for it. I received a drink of water from a Turk and gave him two dīnārs. Still he did not cease, even after our arrival in Damascus, to ask me to render services for him and to use me for accomplishing his purposes — all because of that drink he gave me. As for the other person who gave me succor, he was none other than an angel whom Allah, moved by compassion toward me, sent to my aid.

The Prophet comes to the rescue of a prisoner. — Another illustration of the beneficence of Allah (exalted is he!) was related to me by 'Abdallāh al-Mushrif [al-Musharraf?] in the following words:

I was put in prison in Hayzān,[168] chained and treated with severity. As I was in prison, with the door-guard at the door, I saw the Prophet (may Allah's blessing and peace rest upon him!) in my dream. He said to me, "Remove the chain and go out." I then awoke, removed the chain, which came off from my foot, and went towards the door, desiring to open it. But I found it already open. So I passed by the guard to a

[166] In 1154.

[167] *kadīsh* or *ikdīsh* (Persian *akdish*, *ikdish* = "of mixed breed"), a horse of low breed and often castrated, used in Syria for carrying loads or pulling wagons and sometimes as a mount

[168] A city in Armenia near Shirwān. Yāqūt, *op. cit.*, vol. II, p 380.

small opening in the outer wall, which was so small that I did not suppose my hand would go through it, and went out through it. As I went out I fell into a dunghill where traces of my fall and my footprints were marked. Then I descended into a valley outside the wall and entered a cavern in the slope of the mountain which was on the side where I happened to be. I was saying to myself all the time, "Now shall they come out, see my traces and capture me." But Allah (worthy of admiration is he!) sent snow which covered those traces. They came out, [59] hunting for me all day long in plain sight of me. When the evening came and I felt secure against their pursuit, I came out from that cavern and went to a place of safety.

This man, al-Mushrif, was in charge of the cuisine of Ṣalāḥ-al-Dīn Muḥammad ibn-Ayyūb al-Ghisyāni (may Allah's mercy rest upon his soul!).

Fighting for heavenly reward: A jurisconsult and an ascetic. — Among men there are those who battle, just as the Companions of the Prophet (may Allah's favor be upon them!) used to battle, for the hope of Paradise and not in order to satisfy a desire or win a reputation. Here is an illustration.

When the Frankish king of the Germans [169] (may Allah's curse be upon him!) arrived in Syria,[170] all the Franks who were in Syria assembled under him, and they moved against Damascus. The army and the inhabitants of Damascus came out to meet them in battle.[171] Among them were the jurisconsult al-Findalāwi and the ascetic Sheikh 'Abd-al-Raḥmān al-Ḥalḥūli [172] (may Allah's mercy rest upon their souls!), who were among the most virtuous of the Moslems. When they approached the enemy, the jurisconsult said to 'Abd-al-Raḥmān, "Are these not the Byzantines?" "Yes, of course," replied 'Abd-al-Raḥmān. "Well," said the former, "until when, then, are we going to keep still?" "Advance," replied 'Abd-al-Raḥmān, "in the name of Allah (exalted is he!)." They then both advanced and battled until they were killed (may Allah's mercy rest upon their souls!) on the same spot.[173]

Fighting because of loyalty: Fāris the Kurd. — Others fight because of loyalty. An illustration of this is the case of a Kurd named Fāris [cavalier], who, true to his name, was a cavalier, and

[169] Conrad III. [170] April, 1148. [171] July 24, 1148.
[172] Yāqūt, *op cit*, vol. II, p 316
[173] Cf. story as quoted in *al-Rawḍatayn*, vol I, p 52, whose author seems to have used a more accurate copy of Usāmah's work than our copy.

what a cavalier he was! My father and paternal uncle (may Allah's mercy rest upon their souls!) fought a battle[174] with Sayf-al-Dawlah Khalaf ibn-Mulā'ib,[175] who planned a conspiracy against them and treated them treacherously, for he had mustered his troops and assembled them, while they were not prepared for the enemy. The reason for this was that he had communicated with them, saying, "Let us go to Asfūna[176] where the Franks are and capture it" But our comrades went before he did, dismounted, marched against that castle and undermined it. As they were engaged in the combat, ibn-Mulā'ib arrived. He seized the horses of those of our company who had dismounted, so the fight turned against him after it had been directed against the Franks. The battle raged furiously. Fāris al-Kurdi fought most impetuously and was wounded a number of times He continued to fight, however, and to be wounded until his body was all covered with cuts. Then the battle ceased. My father and uncle (may Allah's mercy rest upon their souls!) passed by Fāris while he was carried in the midst of our men, stopped beside him and congratulated him on his safety, to which he replied, "By Allah, I fought not with the hope of safety for myself but because I am under great obligation and moral debt to you and I never saw you in a more perilous condition than this day. So I thought I would fight in your behalf and repay you for your benevolence, offering my life for your sake." In accordance with the decree of Allah (worthy of admiration is he!) the man was healed of his wounds.

Fāris departed after that to Jabalah,[177] in which was Fakhr-al-Mulk ibn-'Ammār.[178] The Franks were in al-Lādhiqiyyah [Laodicea]. Certain cavaliers set out from Jabalah for an attack on al-Lādhiqiyyah at the same time in which certain cavaliers set out from al-Lādhiqiyyah for an attack on Jabalah. The two parties camped en route with a hill between them. A Frankish knight [60] climbed from the Frankish side of the hill to reconnoitre the enemy at the same time in which Fāris al-Kurdi climbed

[174] In 1109.
[175] Lord of Afāmiyah Ibn-Taghri-Birdi, *op cit*, vol II, pt II, p 286.
[176] In the neighborhood of Ma'arrah-al-Nu'mān, west of Kafartāb. E. Rey, *Les colonies franques de Syrie* (Paris, 1883), p 330
[177] On the seashore south of al-Lādhiqiyyah
[178] Fakhr-al-Mulk abu-'Ali 'Ammār ibn-Muḥammad ibn-'Ammār succeeded to the amirate of Tripoli in 1107.

from the other side to reconnoitre for his party. The two cavaliers met at the top of the hill and each one charged the other. Each dealt a lance blow to the other, and both fell dead. While the two cavaliers lay dead, their horses went on attacking each other at the top of the hill.

This Fāris left with us a boy named 'Allān. He belonged to the army, possessed magnificent horses and an excellent outfit, but was not like his father. One day[179] Tancred, the lord of Antioch, fell upon us and started the combat before he pitched his tents. This 'Allān ibn-Fāris was riding on a beautiful, nimble horse, one of the best steeds. He was stationed upon a little elevation of the ground, and as he stood there absent-minded a Frankish knight charged him and thrust the lance into his horse's neck. The lance penetrated through the neck and the horse jumped, throwing 'Allān off. The Frank turned back holding the horse to his side with the lance in its neck, as though he was holding it with a leash, proud of his rich booty.

Stories of horses: An enduring horse. — Having made mention of horses, I might add that there are among them, as among men, those which are enduring and others which are faint-hearted. Here is an illustration of the former kind. Among our troops was a Kurd named Kāmil al-Mashṭūb[180] who was a repository of valor, religion and benevolence (may Allah's mercy rest upon his soul!). He possessed a horse of solid black color as big as a camel. An encounter took place between him and a Frankish knight. The Frank dealt a blow to the horse beside the throatlatch. The violence of the blow made the neck of the horse bend to one side so that the lance came out through the lower part of the neck and hit the thigh of Kāmil al-Mashṭūb, transpiercing it. Neither the horse nor the horseman budged on account of that blow. I have often seen the scar of that wound in the thigh after it was healed and closed up. No wound could have been bigger than it. The horse also survived, and Kāmil had occasion to mount it again for a battle in which he had an encounter with a Frankish knight who thrust his lance into the frontal bone of the horse and made the whole bone cave in. Again the horse did not budge, and survived the second blow. Even after it healed up, one could close his hand

[179] In 1110. [180] "Kāmil the slashed one."

and stick it in the frontal of the horse where the wound was inflicted and have room for it.

An amusing thing that happened in connection with this horse was the following:

My brother, 'Izz-al-Dawlah abu-al-Ḥasan 'Ali (may Allah's mercy rest upon his soul!), bought the horse from Kāmil al-Mashṭūb. After it had become slow of gait, my brother gave it as a part of the rent of a village which was owned by a Frankish knight from Kafarṭāb. The horse remained in the possession of the knight for a year, after which it died. So the knight sent word to us, claiming its price. We told him, "Thou hast bought it and used it and it died in thy possession. What right hast thou to demand its price?" He replied, "Ye must have given it something to drink and of which it would die after a year." His ignorance and low intelligence amazed us.

A horse with its heart cut carries its rider. — A horse was wounded under me as we engaged in combat at Ḥimṣ. The thrust of the lance cut its heart asunder and a number of arrows hit its body. But it, nevertheless, carried me out of the battle with its two nostrils flowing [61] blood like two bucket spouts, and I felt nothing unusual in its conduct. After having reached my companions, it died.

Another feels normal with three wounds. — Another horse was wounded under me three times in Shayzar during the battle against Maḥmūd ibn-Qarāja, and I continued fighting on its back without realizing, by Allah, that it was wounded, because I did not feel anything unusual in its conduct.

Usāmah's horse fails him on account of a little scratch. — As for the faint-heartedness of horses and their inability to stand wounds, here is an example. The army of Damascus encamped [181] against Ḥamāh, which then belonged to Ṣalāḥ-al-Dīn Muḥammad ibn-Ayyūb al-Ghisyāni, while Damascus belonged to Shihāb-al-Dīn Maḥmūd ibn-Būri ibn-Ṭughdakīn. I was then in Ḥamāh. The army came [182] to attack us in great numbers. The governor [*wāli*] of Ḥamāh was Shihāb-al-Dīn Aḥmad ibn-Ṣalāḥ-al-Dīn, who was then on Tell [hill]-Mujāhid. His chamberlain, Ghāzi al-Talli,

[181] In 1137 or 1138

[182] In 1135, 1137 or 1138. Cf Kamāl-al-Dīn in *Recueil historiens orientaux*, vol. III, p. 670.

came to him and said, "The infantry of the enemy are in battle formation, the helmets are shining among the tents and in a minute the men will charge ours and annihilate them." Shihāb-al-Dīn replied, "Go and bring them back." "By Allah," replied Ghāzi, "no one can bring them back other than thou or so and so," referring to me. Then Shihāb-al-Dīn said to me, "Thou shalt go out and bring them back." Accordingly I took a coat of linked mail which an attendant of mine was wearing, put it on and went out to turn the men back by means of a club, having under me a chestnut horse which was of the finest of breeds, and of the longest-necked horses. As I started to turn back our men, the enemy advanced towards us and no cavaliers of our company remained outside the wall of Ḥamāh but myself, for some of them, realizing that they would be captured, went inside the walls, and others dismounted and marched in my escort. When the enemy would charge us, I would pull the reins of the horse and make it go slow, keeping my face turned towards them, and when they would turn back, I would march behind them stealthily, for the place was narrow and the crowd was thick. My horse was hit in its leg with an arrow which only scratched it, and it fell to the ground with me on its back. Then it arose and fell again while I was beating it so hard that the men who were in my escort said to me, "Go into the barbican and get another mount." But I said, "By Allah, I shall not dismount." Thus I experienced in the case of this horse a weakness which I never experienced in any other horse.

Ṭirād's horse does not give up with its entrails out. — An illustration of the long endurance of horses is the following: Ṭirād ibn-Wahīb al-Numayri took part in a battle between the banu-Numayr, who had killed 'Ali ibn-Shams-al-Dawlah Sālim ibn-Mālik, the governor of al-Raqqah, and took possession of the town and of the latter's brother, Shihāb-al-Dīn Mālik ibn-Shams-al-Dawlah. Under Ṭirād ibn-Wahīb was a horse of his belonging to one of the best breeds and of great value. In the course of the battle the horse was hit by a lance in its side and its entrails came out. Ṭirād bound the surcingle around the wound, lest the horse should step on them and tear them, and continued to fight until the battle was over. After that he entered al-Raqqah with his horse, which immediately died.

Always prepared for battle: Usāmah's case. — To go back to my own experience. The mention of horses has brought back to my mind something which happened to me with Ṣalāḥ-al-Dīn Muḥammad ibn-Ayyūb al-Ghisyāni (may Allah's mercy rest upon his soul!). It took place as follows:

The Malik-al-Umarā'[183] Zanki (may Allah's mercy rest upon his soul!) camped against Damascus in the year 530[184] pitching his tents in Dārayya.[185] The lord of Ba'labakk, Jamāl-al-Dīn Muḥammad ibn- [62] Būri ibn-Ṭughdakīn[186] (may Allah's mercy rest upon his soul!), had corresponded with the atābek with a view to joining him, and set out from Ba'labakk, going to Damascus in order to put himself in his service. The atābek, informed that the army of Damascus had gone out to capture Jamāl-al-Dīn, issued orders to Ṣalāḥ-al-Dīn to the effect that we should mount and meet the army in order to repel the Damascenes and save Jamāl-al-Dīn. Ṣalāḥ-al-Dīn's messenger came to me in the night, saying, "Mount thy horse." My tent was next to his, and he was already on horseback standing by his tent. I instantly mounted, upon which he asked, "Didst thou know about my having mounted my horse?" "No, by Allah," I replied. He said, "I have this very moment sent thee word, and thou hast instantly mounted." I said, "O my lord, my horse ordinarily eats its barley and the groom fixes the bit in its mouth and sits at the door of the tent holding the reins in his hand. In the meantime I put on my armor, gird on my sword and sleep So when thy messenger came to me there was nothing to retard me."

Ṣalāḥ-al-Dīn stood in his place until a part of the army joined him. He then said, "Put on your armor." The majority of those present did so while I remained standing at his side. After a while he said again, "How many times must I say 'Put on your armor'?" I said, "O my lord, thou dost not mean me?" "Surely," said he. I replied, "By Allah, I cannot put on anything more. We are in the early part of the night, and my quilted jerkin [*kuzāghand*] is furnished with two coats of mail, one on top of the other. As soon

183 A title of honor meaning "king of amīrs."

184 Probably a mistake for 532 = 1137–38

185 The largest and richest village of the Ghūtah of Damascus. It is still standing, four miles from Damascus

186 At the death of his father, Tāj-al-Mulūk Būri, the lord of Damascus, this Jamāl-al-Dīn took possession of Ba'labakk.

as I see the enemy I shall put it on." Ṣalāḥ-al-Dīn did not reply, and we set off.

In the morning we found ourselves near Ḍumayr.[187] Ṣalāḥ-al-Dīn said to me, "Shall we not dismount and eat something? I am hungry, having been up all night." I replied, "I shall do what thou orderest." So we dismounted, and no sooner had he set foot on the ground than he said, "Where is thy jerkin?" Upon my order, my attendant produced it. Taking it out from its leather bag, I pulled out my knife and ripped it at the breast and disclosed the side of the two coats of mail. The jerkin enclosed a Frankish coat of mail extending to the bottom of it, with another coat of mail on top of it reaching as far as the middle. Both were equipped with the proper linings, felt pads, rough silk [188] and rabbits' hair. On seeing it, Ṣalāḥ-al-Dīn turned to an attendant of his and addressed him in Turkish, which I did not understand. The attendant presently brought before him a roan horse, which the atābek had given him in earlier days and which looked like a solid rock chipped from the summit of a hill. Ṣalāḥ-al-Dīn then said, "This horse fits in nicely with this jerkin. Deliver it to the attendant of so and so." Accordingly the attendant of Ṣalāḥ-al-Dīn delivered it to my attendant.

Testing Usāmah's presence of mind. — Another experience of mine:

My paternal uncle 'Izz-al-Dīn (may Allah's mercy rest upon his soul!) used to investigate my presence of mind in time of combat and test me with questions. One day when we were at war with the lord of Ḥamāh,[189] who had recruited and mustered his troops and stationed them in one of the villages of Shayzar, where they were burning and pillaging, my uncle picked out about sixty or seventy cavaliers of the army and said to me, "Take them and march against the enemy." So we started galloping as fast as we could, met the vanguard of their horsemen, defeated them, wielded our lances freely on them and dislodged them from the position which they had occupied.

I then dispatched one of the cavaliers in my company to my

[187] A village to the north of Damascus.

[188] *al-lāsin*, which I take to be what is called today *al-laysin*, the silk waste produced in the process of spinning the silk threads from the cocoons.

[189] Shihāb-al-Dīn Maḥmūd ibn-Qarāja (1115–24).

uncle and father (may Allah's mercy rest upon their souls!), who were waiting behind with the rest of the army and the numerous infantry, saying to them, "Advance with the infantry. I have defeated the enemy." So they proceeded towards me, and when they came near we charged together against the enemy and routed them. They threw their horses into the Shārūf,[190] which was then overflowing with water, and swam across it. As they departed, we turned back victorious. My uncle said to me, [63] "What was that message which thou didst dispatch to me?" I replied, "I dispatched to thee a message saying, 'Advance with the infantry, for we have defeated the enemy.'" He further asked, "With whom didst thou dispatch that message?" I replied, "With Rajab al-'Abd."[191] "That is right," he remarked. "I see that thou hadst presence of mind and that thou wert not confused by the combat."

On another occasion we were engaged in a combat with the army of Ḥamāh. Maḥmūd ibn-Qarāja had secured in his fight against us the aid of the army of his brother Khīrkhān ibn-Qarāja, the lord of Ḥimṣ. At that time they had just developed the use of the compound lance, which was formed by attaching one lance to another until the weapon became twenty cubits [*dhirā'*] or eighteen cubits in length. There stood facing me a detachment of the enemy while I was at the head of a company of fifteen cavaliers From the detachment 'Alwān al-'Irāqi, one of their best cavaliers and braves, charged us. When he came near us and found that we did not give ground, he turned back and dragged his lance behind him. I saw the lance trailing on the ground like a rope, with the warrior unable to lift it. So I rushed my horse against him and smote him with my lance. By that time he had gotten as far as his comrades. I then turned back with their streamers floating over my head. My comrades, including my brother Bahā'-al-Dawlah Munqidh[192] (may Allah's mercy rest upon his soul!) met my pursuers and repulsed them. When I hit 'Alwān, the weapon broke in half, leaving one portion in his quilted jerkin, while we were near my uncle, who was then looking at me. So when the battle was over, my

[190] A tributary of the Orontes.
[191] "Rajab the black slave"
[192] One of the three brothers of Usāmah.

uncle said to me, "Where didst thou thrust 'Alwān al-'Irāqi?" "I meant to thrust him in his back," I replied, "but the effect of the wind on my streamer made my weapon swerve and fall on his side." "Thou art right," said he. "Thou certainly hadst presence of mind on that occasion."

6. ADVENTURES WITH LIONS AND OTHER WILD ANIMALS

A glimpse into Usāmah's breeding. — I never saw my father (may Allah's mercy rest upon his soul!) forbid my taking part in a combat or facing a danger, in spite of all the sympathy and preference he cherished towards me and of which I was cognizant. This is what I noticed in regard to him on a certain day[1] We had with us in Shayzar certain hostages, consisting of Frankish and Armenian knights, whom Baldwin,[2] the king of the Franks, had offered as security for a financial obligation which he owed to Ḥusām-al-Dīn Timurtāsh ibn-Īlghāzi[3] (may Allah's mercy rest upon his soul!). When the amount due was paid and the hostages were waiting to go back home, Khīrkhān, the lord of Ḥims, dispatched some horsemen who lay in ambush for them in the suburbs of Shayzar As the hostages were on their way home, the men in ambush came out and captured them When the cry for help reached us, my uncle and my father (may Allah's mercy rest upon their souls!) mounted their horses and stood in a certain spot, sending to the release of the hostages everyone who came I then arrived My father said to me, "Pursue the marauders with thy men, hurl yourselves on them and deliver your hostages." Accordingly I pursued them, overtook them after a race covering most of the day and delivered those of the hostages who had fallen into their hands, in addition to capturing some of the Ḥimṣ' horsemen But the thing that surprised me was my father's word. "Hurl yourselves on them."

Once I was with him (may Allah's mercy rest upon his soul!) while he was standing in the interior court of his house, when a big serpent stuck its head out on the frieze of the arches of the portico over the court. My father stood in his place watching it as I carried a ladder which was on one side of the court and put it in a position [64] below the serpent. Climbing to the serpent, under

[1] In 1124. [2] Baldwin II of Jerusalem. [3] The lord of Māridīn.

the very eyes of my father, who was watching me but not forbidding me, I pulled out a little knife from my belt, applied it to the neck of the serpent, while it was sleeping, with less than a cubit between my face and itself, and began to saw the neck. The serpent pulled its body out and wound itself around my lower arm, where it remained until I cut its head off and threw its body down to the floor of the house lifeless.

On one occasion only I saw my father (may Allah's mercy rest upon his soul!) act differently. One day we set out to kill a lion which had made its appearance at al-Jisr.[4] When we reached the place, the lion jumped on us from a thicket in which it lay hidden. It hurled itself on our horses, then it stopped while my brother, Bahā'-al-Dawlah Munqidh (may Allah's mercy rest upon his soul!), and I stood between the lion and the procession headed by my father and my uncle (may Allah's mercy rest upon their souls!) and including a small body of troops. The lion then crouched on the very edge of the river, beating its chest against the ground and roaring. Presently I made an onset on it, but my father (may Allah's mercy rest upon his soul!) yelled at me, saying, "Face it not, thou crazy one! It will get thee!" But I smote it with the lance and, by Allah, it stirred not from its place, and died on the spot. I never saw my father forbid me a fight except on that day.

How men differ: A weak Turkoman.—Allah (mighty and majestic is he!) has created his creatures of different categories, varying in nature and temperament: among them are the white and the black, the beautiful and the ugly, the tall and the short, the strong and the weak, the brave and the coward — all according to his own wisdom and universal power.

I saw the son of one of the Turkoman amīrs who were in the service of the Malik-al-Umarā' Atābek Zanki (may Allah's mercy rest upon his soul!) when an arrow hit him and did not penetrate as deep as a grain of barley in his skin He immediately dropped down, his muscles relaxed, his power of speech ceased, and he became unconscious, although he was a man as big as a lion; no bulkier man could be. They brought him the physician and the surgeon. The physician said, "No fear for him now, but if he is wounded again he dies." So the man was calmed, and began to

[4] The bridge of Shayzar spanning the Orontes.

ride his horse and conduct himself as he used to before. A short time later, however, he received another arrow wound which was slighter and less harmful even than the former one; and he died.

A hornet's sting proves fatal to a miller. — I saw something else analogous to that. We had with us in Shayzar two brothers known by the name of banu-Majāju. The name of the one was abu-al-Majd and of the other Maḥāsin.[5] They rented the Mill of the Bridge [6] for eight hundred dīnārs. Near the mill was a slaughter place where the butchers [7] of the town used to slay their sheep and where hornets gathered in great numbers because of the blood. One day as Maḥāsin ibn-Majāju was on his way to the mill, a hornet stung him As a consequence he became paralyzed, lost his power of speech and stood on the threshold of death. After remaining thus for a while, he regained consciousness. But for some time he did not frequent the mill. Therefore, his brother abu-al-Majd remonstrated with him, saying, "O my brother, we have rented this mill for eight hundred dīnārs and yet thou dost not care to oversee it or inspect it! Tomorrow [8] we may fail to pay its rent and shall die in prison as a result of it" Mahāsin said [65] to him, "It is thy object that some other hornet should sting me and put me to death!" The second morning, however, he came to the mill A hornet stung him, and he died. The simplest of things therefore may kill when the allotted days are over, and a good omen is superior to logic.

A slave singled out by a lion. — Another illustration is when a beast of prey [9] appeared in our land of Shayzar. We rode towards it and found a slave of al-Amīr Sābiq ibn-Waththāb ibn-Mahmūd ibn-Ṣālih, named Shammās, pasturing his mare on the very spot where the lion had appeared. My uncle asked him, "Where is the lion?" Shammās replied, "In that thicket of brambles." My uncle said, "March before me to it." The slave remarked, "It is thy object that the lion should come out and seize me!" And he marched before him. The lion thereupon came out as if he were

[5] Or "Muḥāsin"; both forms occur as proper nouns See al-Dhahabi, *al-Mushtabih*, ed Jong (Leyden, 1863), p 266

[6] *rahāt al-jisr* The bridge spanned the Orontes at Shayzar

[7] *jazzāri* which should be corrected for *jazzāru* and which Derenbourg, *Autobiographie*, p 104, translates *le seigneur terrier*

[8] Ar *ghadan*, used to designate any day after the present

[9] *sab'*, used by the people of Syria until the present day as a synonym of *asad*, i.e., "lion"

sent on purpose to Shammās, seized him and killed him, singling him out of the whole party. The lion was in turn killed.

Usāmah's experience with a fearless lion. — I have seen lions do many things which I never expected them to do. Nor did I ever before believe that lions, like men, have among their number the courageous and the cowardly. This is the way it happened.

One day the herder of our horses came to us running and said, "There are three lions in the thicket of Tell-al-Tulūl "[10] So we mounted and rode out to them and lo, there was a lioness with two lions behind it. As we reconnoitred that thicket, the lioness came out to attack us and then stopped. My brother, Bahā'-al-Dawlah abu-al-Mughīth Munqidh (may Allah's mercy rest upon his soul!), charged the lioness and gave it a blow with his lance which killed it. The lance was shattered within its body. On our return to the thicket, one of the two lions came out to attack us. It chased the horses, and my brother, Bahā'-al-Dawlah, and I stood in its way as it was coming back from the pursuit of the horses, for whenever a lion goes out from a place, it is sure to return to that same place, without the least doubt. As we stood in its way, we had the backs of our horses turned towards it and held our lances backward, pointed in its direction, believing that it would attack us, upon which we would dart our lances into it and kill it. All of a sudden, we were surprised to see the lion pass by us, like wind, and go to one of our comrades, named Sa'dallāh al-Shaybāni, and give his mare a blow which felled it to the ground. I thrust my lance into the lion, hitting it in the middle part of its body, and it died on the spot.

We then turned back to the other lion with about twenty footmen of Armenian troops who were good archers. The other beast, which was the biggest of all three in size, now came out, walking. The Armenians covered its route with a shower of arrows, as I was standing on one side of them, waiting for the lion to charge them and seize one of their number, upon which I would apply my lance on it But it kept straight on. Every time an arrow struck it, it would roar and lash its tail and I would say, "Now it will charge " But it would start to walk again. It kept on doing this until it fell dead. Thus I saw on the part of this lion something which I never imagined before.

[10] A hill in the vicinity of Shayzar.

A lion flees before a sheep. — Later I witnessed on the part of another lion something even more marvelous than that. There was in the city of Damascus a lion cub which a lion trainer had brought up until it became big and began to seek horses and cause damage to some men. Al-Amīr Mu'īn-al-Dīn (may Allah's mercy rest upon his soul!) was told in my presence, "This beast has caused damage to some people, and horses are frightened away from it while it is on the road" The lion used to spend its days and nights in a [66] mastaba adjoining the home of Mu'īn-al-Dīn. Mu'īn-al-Dīn said, "Tell the trainer to bring it here." Then he said to his table master, "Bring out from the animals to be slaughtered for the kitchen a sheep and leave it in the inner court so that we may see how the lion annihilates it." Accordingly the table master brought out a sheep to the inner court. Then the trainer came in accompanied by the lion. As soon as the sheep saw the lion, whose trainer had set it free from the chain which was around its neck, he rushed to it and butted at it. The lion took to flight and began to circle around the pool [11] with the sheep following behind, chasing and goring it. We were all overcome with laughter. The al-Amīr Mu'īn-al-Dīn (may Allah's mercy rest upon his soul!) said, "This is a miserable [12] lion. Take it out, slay and flay it, then bring its skin here" Accordingly they slew the lion and flayed it. As for the sheep, it was exempted from slaughter.

A dog saves its master from a lion. — Another surprising thing about lions. A lion appeared in our land of Shayzar. So we went out against it accompanied by some footmen of Shayzar, including a slave of al-Mu'abbad, to whom the people of the mountain [13] owed allegiance and whom they almost worshiped That slave had a dog with him. All of a sudden a lion came out to attack the horses, which galloped away, startled, before it. The lion fell upon the footmen, seized that slave and crouched over him. The dog immediately jumped on the back of the lion, which left off attacking the man and ran back to the thicket. The man presented himself before my father (may Allah's mercy rest upon his soul!)

[11] The houses of Damascus are still today built with the rooms arranged in a rectangular form opening into an inner court surrounded by a portico with arches. In the center of the court is a fountain with a little pool of water around it

[12] *manhūs*, literally "of ill omen"

[13] This is evidently a reference to the Assassins, *al-mu'abbad* means "the one revered to the point of worship"

laughing and said, "O my lord, by thy life, the lion did neither wound me nor hurt me." Subsequently the lion was killed and the man went back to his home. But that same night he died, having received no wound except that his heart gave way on account of the shock. I have often since admired the adventurous character of that dog in the face of the lion, although all animals flee from the lion to avoid it

All animals fear the lion. — I have seen the head of a lion carried to one of our houses, whereupon the cats were seen fleeing from that house and throwing themselves from the roofs without having ever before seen a lion.[14] We used to skin a lion and throw the carcass between the castle [Shayzar] and the barbican [*bāshūrah*], and no dogs or any kind of bird would come near it. Even the crows, seeing flesh, would descend upon it, but the moment they approached it, would scream and take to flight. The awe which the lion inspires in animals is very much like the awe which the eagle [15] inspires among birds. For the eagle, if seen by a chicken which never saw an eagle before, makes the chicken shriek and flee. Such is the awe which Allah (exalted is he!) has lodged in the hearts of animals for these two animals.

Kills a lion but is killed by a scorpion. — Since I am discussing lions, I might by the way add that we had among our companions two brothers named banu-al-Ru'ām who were footmen and plied back and forth between Shayzar and al-Lādhiqiyyah (al-Lādhiqiyyah at that time belonged to my uncle 'Izz-al-Dawlah abu-al-Murhaf Naṣr, and was in charge of his brother 'Izz-al-Dīn abu-al-'Asākir Sulṭān — may Allah's mercy rest upon their two souls!) carrying correspondence between the two [uncles]. They related the following story:

We set out from al-Lādhiqiyyah [67] and looked down from 'Aqabah-al-Mandah, which is a rugged hill ['*aqabah*] overlooking all the lowland below, and saw a lion lying on the bank of a river right beneath the hill. So we stopped in our place, not daring to descend for fear of the beast. Presently we saw a man advancing. We called loudly to him and waved our clothes to him in order to warn him against the lion, but he did not heed us. He tightened his bowstring, fixed an arrow in it and marched

[14] Cf F C Selous, *African Nature, Notes and Reminiscences* (London, 1908), p 95.
[15] '*uqāb*, a term applied in Syria to all smaller eagles and buzzards H B. Tristram, *The Fauna and Flora of Palestine* (London, 1888), p 98

along. The lion saw him and sprang toward him, but the man instantly shot his arrow, which did not miss the heart of the lion, and killed it. Then he advanced towards the lion and finished it off Thereupon the man took his arrow and came to the river. He removed his shoes, took off his clothes and went down to bathe in the water. Then he went up and put on his clothes — while we were still looking at him — and he began to shake his hair in order to dry it from the water. After that he put on one shoe and leaned upon his side and remained leaning for a long time. We said to ourselves, "By Allah, he did very well, but for whom is he showing off?" We descended to him while he was still in the same position and found him dead. We could not tell what afflicted him. Then we took off the shoe from his foot and, behold! a small scorpion which was in it had bitten him in his big toe, and he died on the spot. So we were amazed at the case of this hero who killed a lion, but was killed by a scorpion as big as a finger. How mysterious, therefore, are the works of Allah, the Almighty, whose will is always executed among his creatures!

The habits of the lion as studied by Usāmah. — To return to my own experience. I have battled against beasts of prey on occasions so numerous that I cannot count them all, and I have killed of them quite a number, single-handed, in addition to those which I have killed conjointly with others. Indeed I have had more experience with lions and knowledge about fighting them than any other person. I know, for instance, that the lion, like all other animals, fears man and flees from him. It is in a state of inattentiveness and stupidity except when it is wounded. But once it is wounded, then it becomes the real lion it is. That is the time in which it is to be feared. Whenever a lion goes out of a forest or thicket in order to assault horsemen, it is sure to return to the same thicket from which it had gone — even though fires be set on its way[16] Having discovered that myself, through experience, I never failed to wait for it on its return, whenever it went out to attack our horsemen, provided it was not wounded. And as it would come back I would let it alone until it passed me, and then I would pierce it with the lance and kill it.

Usāmah and his companions riddle a leopard. — As for the leopards, battling with them is even more difficult than battling with lions because of their swiftness and their long leaps. Besides,

[16] Arabs believed that lions kept away from fire Therefore whenever they camped in the desert and were in fear of lions, they always built fire around their camp. To this fire they applied the specific name *nār al-asad* = "the lion-fire."

leopards go into caverns and holes as hyenas do, whereas lions go only into forests and thickets.

A leopard once appeared to us in a village belonging to the region of Shayzar known by the name of Ma'arzaf. My uncle, 'Izz-al-Dīn (may Allah's mercy rest upon his soul!), mounted his horse to go and attack the leopard and sent me a cavalier, while I was on my horse attending to a personal affair, who said, "Follow me to Ma'arzaf." Accordingly I followed him, and together we came to the place in which [68] the leopard was said to be But we could not find it There was at that place a pit. I dismounted and sat at the mouth of the pit, armed with a lance. The pit was not deep, about one fathom, and in its side was a fissure that looked like a burrow. I moved the lance inside of that fissure which was in the pit, and the leopard stuck out its head from the fissure in order to seize the lance. Seeing that it was in that place, some of my comrades came down to me. One of our party now began to poke his lance inside of the burrow so that when the leopard should come out the other men could stab at it with their lances. Every time the leopard tried to climb out of the pit, we pierced it deep with our lances until we killed it. This leopard was of huge size, but it had just fed so much on the animals of the village that it had become too heavy to protect itself. Of all animals the leopard is the only one which can jump over forty cubits.

A leopard jumps from a church window and kills a Frank. — In the church of Ḥunāk [17] was a window forty cubits high. Every day at noontime a leopard would come and jump to the window, where it would sleep until the end of the day, at which time it would jump down and go away. At that time Ḥunāk was held as a fief by a Frankish knight named Sir Adam, one of the devils of the Franks. Sir Adam was told the story of the leopard and he said, "As soon as ye see it, let me know" The leopard came as it was wont to do and jumped into the window. One of the peasants came and told Sir Adam about it. The latter put on his coat of mail, mounted his horse, took his shield and lance and came to the church, which was all in ruins with the exception of one wall which was standing

[17] One of the castles defending Ma'arrah-al-Nu'mān. Yāqūt, *op. cit.*, vol. II, p. 345.

and in which the window was. As soon as the leopard saw him, it jumped from the window upon him while he was on his horse, broke his back and killed him. It then went away. The peasants of Ḥunāk used to call that leopard, "the leopard that takes part in the holy war" [*al-namir al-mujāhid*]

One of the characteristics of the leopard is that in case it wounds a man and a mouse urinates on the wound, the man dies. It is very difficult to keep the mouse away from one wounded by a leopard In fact, they sometimes go so far as to fix a bed for him in the midst of water and tie cats all around him for fear of the mice

Distinction between a leopard and a cheetah. — It is well-nigh impossible to get a leopard to become familiar with human beings or to act tamely in their presence. I was once [18] passing through Ḥaifa by the coast which belongs to the Franks, when one of the Franks said to me, "Wilt thou buy from me an excellent cheetah?" "Yes," I replied The man brought me a leopard which he had brought up until it became the size of a dog "No," said I, "this does not suit me This is a leopard [*namir*] and not a cheetah [19] [*fahd*]." Nevertheless I was amazed at its tractability and conduct with the Frank.

The difference between the leopard and the cheetah is this: The face of the leopard is long like the face of the dog and its eyes are blue, whereas the cheetah has a round face and black eyes.

A leopard turned loose in a lord's sitting room. — An Aleppine caught a leopard and brought it in a sack [20] to the lord of al-Qadmūs,[21] which belonged to one of the banu-Muḥriz. The latter was at the time drinking with some friends. As soon as the Aleppine opened the sack, the leopard rushed to the attack of all those in the sitting room. As for the amīr, he happened to be near a window in the tower, so he entered through it and closed the casement behind him. The leopard roamed about the house killing some and wounding others until it was itself killed.

An adventure with a tiger. — I have often heard [69] that among

[18] Between 1140 and 1143 [19] Cf Tristram, *op cit*, pp 18, 19

[20] Ar *'idl* which Derenbourg, *Texte arabe*, p 83 reads *'adl* and translates, *Autobiographie*, p 110, *demandant justice* and *la séance* Shumann, p 161, follows suit

[21] One of the strongest fortresses in the Nuṣayriyyah region lying to the south-west of Shayzar.

beasts is a variety called tiger [*babr*],[22] but I never saw one myself. And I could not believe that the animal existed until the Sheikh al-Imām Ḥujjah-al-Dīn abu-Hāshim Muḥammad ibn-Muḥammad ibn-Ẓafar (may Allah's mercy rest upon his soul!) related to me the following story. These are his words:

I went on a journey to al-Maghrib [Mauretania] accompanied by an aged slave who belonged to my father and who had traveled much and experienced many things. On the way our water supply was exhausted and we got thirsty. We had no third person, being only two, he and I, on two camels of good breed We made our way towards a well on our route and found by it a tiger [23] sleeping. After retreating a little my companion dismounted from his camel, handed me its reins, took his sword and shield, together with the waterskin which we had, and said to me, "Look after the head of the camel" He then advanced towards the well. As soon as the tiger saw him, it arose and jumped, facing him. When it passed by him it growled as if calling its cubs, which rushed out and ran after it. It neither barred our way nor did us the least harm. So we drank, provided ourselves with water and continued our march.

This is what he (may Allah's mercy rest upon his soul!) related to me, and he was one of the best of Moslems in his religion and learning.

[22] This Arabic word is Persian *babr* = "tiger" The Indian language at first borrowed Persian *shīr* = "lion" and applied it to the tiger, there being no lions in India When, later, the necessity was felt to distinguish between a lion and a tiger, Indian littérateurs helped themselves to Persian *babr*, making it *babar* and applying it to the lion (A Siddiqi, *Journal Royal Asiatic Society*, July, 1927, p 560) The *babr* is mentioned by al-Qazwīni, *'Ajā'ib al-Makhlūqāt*, ed F Wustenfeld (Gottingen, 1849), vol I, p 391, who defines it as "an Indian animal, stronger than the lion, between which and the lion and leopard exists hostility" This would seem to indicate that the Arabs borrowed the word from India and applied it to the tiger and any other beasts of prey with which they were not familiar.

[23] As there are no tigers in Mauretania, this animal [*babr*] may have been a leopard

7. OTHER WAR EXPERIENCES

Byzantine mangonels at the siege of Shayzar. — One of the marvels of destiny was the following:

When the Byzantines camped around Shayzar in the year 532,[1] they set up against it frightful mangonels which they had brought with them from their land for hurling weights. These mangonels could throw a stone to a distance farther than the distance covered by the arrow, their stone being twenty to twenty-five rotls in weight.

One time they hurled a large millstone against the house of a friend of mine, named Yūsuf ibn-abi-al-Gharīb (may Allah's mercy rest upon his soul!). This one stone destroyed the whole building from top to bottom.

Above a tower in the residence of the amīr stood a lance bearing a banner. The road by which the inhabitants of the castle passed lay right beneath the banner. The stone from the mangonel hit the lance and broke it in the middle. The part which broke away and which held the spearhead toppled over and fell down to the road just at the moment when one of our men happened to be passing by. The half lance, with the spearhead, falling from that height hit the man between his collar bones and ran through him clear to the ground. It killed him instantly.

Khuṭlukh, a mameluke of my father's (may Allah's mercy rest upon his soul!), related to me the following story:

During the siege [of Shayzar] by the Byzantines, we were once sitting in the hallway at the entrance of the castle with our full equipment and swords. All of a sudden an old man appeared running towards us and said, "O Moslems! Your harem! The Byzantines have entered the town." We immediately grasped our swords and went out to find that they had already climbed through a breach in the outer wall, which their mangonels had opened. So we applied our swords on them until

[1] 1138.

we repulsed them, and we pursued them until we got them as far back as their comrades. Then we returned and dispersed. I remained alone with the old man who had raised the alarm. He stood up and turned his face to the wall in order to pass water. So I turned away from him, but soon heard the crash of a fall. I looked around and, behold! [70] a mangonel stone had hit the head of the old man, crushed it, and stuck it to the wall, making the brain flow on the wall I carried him away and, after conducting the funeral service, we buried him in his place — may Allah's mercy rest upon his soul!

Another mangonel stone struck one of our men on his lower leg and broke it. They carried him to the presence of my uncle, who was then sitting in the hallway of the castle and who said, "Fetch the bonesetter." Now there was in Shayzar an artisan named Yahya who was an expert in bonesetting He came and sat down in a recess outside the castle gate, and began to set the bones of the leg. A stone hit the head of the man with the broken leg and crushed it. The bonesetter reentered the hallway, upon which my uncle said to him, "How quickly thou hast set his bone!" "O my lord," he replied, "another stone hit him and saved him the trouble of undergoing the operation of setting."

The unlucky march of the Franks against Damascus. — Another illustration of the execution of divine will in the fates and ages of men.

The Franks (may Allah render them helpless!) unanimously agreed to direct their forces against Damascus and capture it. Accordingly they concentrated a considerable army,[2] which was joined by the lord of al-Ruha [3] and Tell-Bāshir [4] and the lord of Antioch.[5] On his way to Damascus, the lord of Antioch stopped in front of Shayzar. The princes were so sure of the conquest and possession of Damascus that they had already bargained amongst themselves for the houses of Damascus, its baths and its bazaars, and in turn sold them to the bourgeois [*al-burjāsiyyah*], who paid the prices in cash.

Kafartāb at that time belonged to the lord of Antioch. He now detached from his troops a hundred picked horsemen, whom he

[2] This was the army of Baldwin I of Jerusalem in the year 1113
[3] Edessa, modern Urfa, Ar al-Ruha
[4] Tell-Bāshir, the "Turbessel" of the Franks, lay between Aleppo and al-Ruha. The lord was Joscelin I See E. Rey, *op. cit.*, p. 322.
[5] Roger

ordered to stay in Kafarṭāb as a check against us and against Ḥamāh. When he marched against Damascus, the Moslems of Syria assembled to attack Kafarṭāb. They dispatched one of our men, named Qunayb ibn-Mālik, to spy for them on Kafarṭāb during the night. Arriving in the city, he made a tour around it and returned, saying, "Rejoice at the booty and safety [awaiting you]!" The Moslems marched against the troops in it, had an encounter with them at an ambush,[6] and Allah (worthy of admiration is he!) gave victory to the Moslems, who killed all the Franks.

Qunayb, who had spied on Kafartāb for our men, had noticed in its moat a large number of animals. Now that the Moslems defeated the Franks and killed them, Qunayb wanted to capture those animals, and he hoped to appropriate the booty all for himself. So he went running to the trench. One of the Franks from the citadel threw a stone on him and killed him. He left with us a mother, a very old woman, who used to chant dirges at our funerals and who would on every occasion sing a lamentation for her son. Whenever she wailed in memory of her son, Qunayb, her breasts would always overflow with milk to the point of soaking all her clothes. But the moment she stopped her wailing [71] over him and her anguish subsided, then her breasts would become once more like two pieces of dry skin with not a drop of milk in them. Worthy of admiration is he who saturates the hearts with tender affection for the children!

When the lord of Antioch, who was then fighting against Damascus, was told "The Moslems have killed thy men," he replied, "This is not true. I have left in Kafartāb a hundred knights who can meet all the Moslems put together."

By the decree of Allah (worthy of admiration is he!) the Moslems in Damascus, too, won the victory over the Franks and slaughtered of them a great number, capturing all their animals. So they departed from Damascus in the most miserable and humiliating manner — praise be to Allah the lord of the worlds!

A Kurd carries his brother's head as a trophy. — One of the amazing things that happened in connection with the Franks in the course of that combat was the following: In the army of Ḥamāh

[6] *mutakamman*, orthography not clear. The word may be the name of a place, *Milkin*, *Bikkin*, or something like it

were two Kurdish brothers, one named Badr and the other 'Annāz.[7] The latter, 'Annāz, was feeble of sight. When the Franks were overpowered and massacred, their heads were cut off and tied to the belts of the horses. 'Annāz cut off one head and tied it to the belt of his horse Seeing him, the army of Ḥamāh said to him, "O 'Annāz, what is this head with thee?" He replied, "Worthy of admiration is Allah because of what happened between me and him which resulted in my killing him!" They said to him, "Man, this is the head of thy brother, Badr!" 'Annāz looked at the head and investigated it, and behold! it was the head of his brother. He was so ashamed of himself before the men that he left Ḥamāh and we do not know where he went. In fact, we never heard a word about him since. It was, however, the Franks who killed his brother, Badr, in that battle.

Blows of sharp swords: One breaks an Ismā'īlite skull. — The crushing of the head of that old man (may Allah's mercy rest upon his soul!) by the mangonel stone has brought to my mind stories of blows administered by sharp swords. Here is one of them. One of our comrades, named Hammām [8] al-Ḥājj [the pilgrim] had an encounter with one of the Ismā'īlites, when they attacked the Castle of Shayzar,[9] in a portico of the residence of my uncle (may Allah's mercy rest upon his soul!) The Ismā'īlite held in his hand a dagger, while al-Ḥājj held a sword. The Bāṭinite [10] rushed on him with the knife, but Hammām struck him with the sword above his eyes. The blow broke his skull, and his brains fell out and were scattered over the ground. Hammām, laying the sword from his hand, vomited all that he had in his stomach, on account of the sickening he felt at the sight of those brains.

Usāmah's blow cuts a blade and a forearm. — On that day I had an encounter with an Ismā'īlite, who had a dagger in his hand, while I had my sword. He rushed on me with the dagger, and I hit him in the middle of his forearm as he was grasping the handle of the dagger in his hand and holding the blade close to his forearm. My blow cut off about four inches of the blade and cut his forearm in two in the middle. The mark of the edge of the dagger was left

[7] Cf al-Dhahabı, *al-Mushtabih*, p 376.
[8] Or "Humām" [9] In 1109 or 1114
[10] One belıevıng ın an inner, esoteric meanıng of the Koran, the Ismā'īlıte in thıs case

on the edge of my sword. An artisan in our town, seeing it, said, "I can remove this dent from it." But I said, "Leave it as it is. This is the best thing in my sword." The trace is there to the present day. Whenever one sees it he knows it is the trace of a knife.

Usāmah's father cuts his groom's outfit and arm with a sheathed sword. — [72] This same sword has a story, which I am about to relate. My father (may Allah's mercy rest upon his soul!) had a groom named Jāmiʻ. The Franks made an incursion against us and my father put on his jerkin and went out of his house to mount his horse, but did not find it. So he stood for a while waiting for it. After great delay, Jāmiʻ, the groom, brought the horse. My father hit him with the same sword while it was still in its sheath girded around him. The sword cut through the outfit, the silver sandal, a mantle and a woolen shawl which the groom had on, and then cut through the bone of his elbow. The whole forearm fell off. After this my father (may Allah's mercy rest upon his soul!) used to support him, and his children after him, because of that blow. The sword was since then known by the name of al-Jāmiʻi, after the name of that groom.

Two blows kill two men. — Among noteworthy sword blows is the following·

Four brothers related to al-Amīr Iftikhār-al-Dawlah abu-al-Futūḥ ibn-ʻAmrūn, the lord of the Castle of abu-Qubays,[11] went up to him in the castle while he was sleeping, inflicted many deep wounds on him, as he had no one with him in the castle except his son, and then went out, believing that they had killed him, and sought his son. This Iftikhār-al-Dawlah was endowed by Allah with unusual strength. Rising from his bed all naked, he took his sword, which was hanging in the room near him, and went out against his assailants. One of them, their leader and bravest, encountered him. Iftikhār-al-Dawlah struck this man with the sword and then jumped aside for fear that he might be reached with a knife which his assailant held in his hand. When he looked back he saw him lying prone on the ground, dead from that blow. He then proceeded to the second man, hit him with the sword and killed him. The other two took to flight and threw themselves

[11] The colloquial form *būqbays* occurs in the manuscript. This castle lies west of Shayzar and is mentioned by Yāqūt, *op. cit.*, vol I, p 103.

down to the ground from the castle. One of them was instantly killed and the other escaped.

The news having reached us in Shayzar, we dispatched a messenger to congratulate Iftikhār-al-Dawlah on his safety. Three days later we went to the Castle of abu-Qubays to make him a visit, for his sister lived with my uncle, 'Izz-al-Dīn, and he had children by her. He related to us his story and how it happened to him. He then said, "The back of my shoulder is itching in a place where I cannot reach it," and he called an attendant of his to see what had bitten him in that particular place. The attendant looked and behold! there was a cut in which was lodged the head of a dagger which had broken in his back and about which he had known nothing. Nor was he conscious of it until pus formed and it began to itch.

The strength of this man was such that he could hold a mule at the ankle and give the mule a beating without its being able to free its foot from his hand. He could hold a horseshoe nail between his fingers and drive it into a board of oak wood. His appetite for food was commensurate with his physical strength — nay, it was even greater

Heroic deeds by women. — I have thus far given some accounts of men's deeds, and shall now proceed to give some accounts of women's deeds, after presenting some details by way of introduction.

Baldwin succeeds Roger in Antioch. — Antioch belonged to a devil of the Franks named Roger [*rūjār*]. Roger went on a holy pilgrimage to Jerusalem,[12] whose lord was Baldwin, the prince,[13] an aged man, while Roger was a young man. The latter said to Baldwin, "Make a contract between thee and me [73] that in case I die before thee, Antioch shall be thine; and in case thou diest before me, Jerusalem shall be mine." They mutually agreed to this and bound themselves by it.

And now by the decree of Allah (exalted is he!) Najm-al-Dīn Īlghāzi ibn-Urtuq (may Allah's mercy rest upon his soul!) had an encounter with Roger at Dānīth on Thursday, the fifth of Jumāda I, in the year 513,[14] killed him[15] and slaughtered his entire army,

[12] *al-bayt al-muqaddas* = "the sanctified house"
[13] *baghdawin al-bruns*. This was Baldwin II [14] August 14, 1119.
[15] Roger was not killed at Dānīth but at al-Balāṭ, as Usāmah himself has mentioned above.

of which less than twenty men returned to Antioch. Baldwin then proceeded to Antioch and seized it.

Forty days later, Baldwin stood in battle array against Īlghāzi. The latter was so constituted that whenever he drank wine he would feel drunk for twenty days. Now it happened that after he had routed the Franks and put them to the sword,[16] he drank wine and entered his period of intoxication, from which he did not recover until King Baldwin, the prince, had arrived in Antioch with his army.

Ṭughdakīn beheads Robert. — The second battle between Īlghāzi and Baldwin had even results. Certain Franks routed certain Moslems, and other Moslems routed other Franks. From both sides a large number were killed. The Moslems took captive Robert, the lord of Ṣihyawn,[17] Balātunus [18] and the adjoining region. The latter was a friend of the Atābek Ṭughdakīn, the lord of Damascus at that time, and had been in the company of Najm-al-Dīn Īlghāzi when the latter joined the Franks in Afāmiyah against the army of the Orient on its arrival in Syria headed by Bursuq ibn-Bursuq [19]

This Robert, the leper,[20] had said to the Atābek Ṭughdakīn, "I know not what to offer thee in the way of hospitality But I have put at thy disposal my land. Let thy horsemen pass through it and take whatever they find, provided ye do not take captive or kill anyone. Animals, money and crops are theirs to use as they wish "

Now, when Robert was taken prisoner in this battle, in which the Atābek Ṭughdakīn took part in support of Īlghāzi, he fixed his own ransom at ten thousand dīnārs. Then Īlghāzi said, "Take him to the atābek. Perhaps the latter will scare him and we shall get a higher ransom from him." They took him there and found the atābek in his tent, drinking. As soon as he saw Robert coming towards him, the atābek arose, tucked up the lower extremities of his robe under his sword belt, held his sword and went out to Robert and struck off his head. Īlghāzi sent a messenger, reproach-

[16] This is evidently a reference to the battle of al-Balāt

[17] A citadel between al-Lādhiqiyyah and Ḥims Ibn-al-Athīr, in *Recueil: historiens orientaux*, vol I, p 721, Yāqūt, *op cit*, vol III, p 438

[18] Latin *Platanus*, a fortified place between al-Lādhiqiyyah and Antioch Ibn-al-Athīr, *ibid*, vol. I, p. 723, Yāqūt, *op cit*, vol I, p 710

[19] In 1115

[20] *rūbart al-abraṣ*. Kamāl-al-Dīn in *Recueil historiens orientaux*, vol III, pp. 621, 629.

ing the atābek, saying, "We are in need of even one dīnār to pay our Turkoman soldiers. Here was a man who had fixed his own ransom at ten thousand dīnārs and whom I dispatched to thee so that thou mightest scare him and he might increase for us the sum, and thou hast killed him!" The atābek replied, "I have no other way of scaring but this."

Baldwin exempts Usāmah's uncle from payment of an indemnity.— After this, Baldwin, the prince, took possession of Antioch. My father and uncle (may Allah's mercy rest upon their souls!) had him under great obligation to them because Nūr-al-Dīn Balak[21] (may Allah's mercy rest upon his soul!) had taken him captive, and after the death of Balak[22] he passed into the possession of Ḥusām-al-Dīn Timurtāsh ibn-Īlghāzi, who brought Baldwin to us in Shayzar so that my father and my uncle (may Allah's mercy rest upon their souls!) might act as an intermediary in determining the price of his ransom. Both of them treated him with benevolence.[23] Now when he became king and we owed indemnity[24] to Antioch, Baldwin exempted us from its payment. After that, we became very influential in the affairs of Antioch.

Baldwin cedes Antioch to Bohemond's son. — As Baldwin was occupying his position as king and while he was receiving an envoy [74] of ours, there arrived[25] at al-Suwaydiyyah[26] a ship carrying a lad in rags. This lad presented himself before Baldwin and introduced himself to him as the son of Bohemond [*ibn-maymūn*]. Baldwin thereupon delivered Antioch to him, left it and pitched his tents outside of the city. Our envoy, who was then visiting him, stated to us on his oath that he, that is, King Baldwin, bought the fodder for his horses that night from the market, while the granaries of Antioch were overflowing with provisions. Baldwin then returned to Jerusalem.

Bohemond II in battle against Usāmah's people. — That devil, the son of Bohemond, proved a terrible calamity to our people.

[21] Ibn-Bahrām, a brother of Īlghāzi, and the lord of a certain fortification in Malatyah (colloquially, "Malātiyyah") to the north of Edessa

[22] May 6, 1124

[23] For the exact ransom agreed upon see Kamāl-al-Dīn, *Zubdah* in Rohricht, *Beiträge*, vol I, p 279, and *Recueil historiens orientaux*, vol III, p 643

[24] This was four thousand gold pieces, which was imposed on the amīrs of Shayzar after Tancred's victory over them in 1110 Rohricht, *Geschichte des Konigreichs Jerusalem*, p 88.

[25] In 1126.

[26] The seaport of Antioch.

One day he came to attack us with his army and pitched his tents. By that time we had mounted our horses and stood facing them, but none of them came out to encounter us. They remained in their tents. As we were on horseback on an elevation, we could see them well, with the Orontes between them and us.

An encounter with the son of Bohemond. — My paternal cousin, Layth-al-Dawlah Yaḥya ibn-Mālik ibn-Ḥumayd (may Allah's mercy rest upon his soul!), left our ranks and went down to the Orontes. We thought he was giving his mare a drink. But he waded through the water, crossed over and proceeded towards a detachment of the Franks standing near their tents. As soon as he approached them, one knight came to encounter him. The two now charged each other, and each one swerved from the lance blow of the other. I, together with those of my companions who, like myself, were young, dashed at that moment towards the two combatants The rest of the detachment now came to encounter us The son of Bohemond and his troops also mounted and advanced like a flood. In the meantime, the mare of our man [my cousin] had been wounded. The van of our cavalry met the van of their cavalry. Among our troops was a Kurd named Mīkā'īl, who now came fleeing before the van of their infantry, followed by a Frankish knight and hard pressed by him. The Kurd was screaming before the Frank and howling aloud. As I met him, the Frank turned aside from the Kurdish cavalier and deviated from my path in pursuit of certain horsemen of ours stationed by the water beyond us. I kept behind him and spurred my horse forward to overtake him, so that I might give him a blow with the lance; but my horse could not overtake him, nor did the Frank look back towards me, his only objective being those assembled horsemen. This went on until he got to our horsemen, with me on his heels. My comrades then dealt a lance blow to his horse which all but finished it. Soon his comrades were coming to his assistance in such great number that we should be powerless before them. The Frankish knight now turned back, with his horse gasping its last, met his comrades and ordered them all to retire. He too returned with them. This knight was none other than the son of Bohemond, the lord of Antioch, who, being still a lad,[27] had his heart filled with

[27] Bohemond II was now eighteen years old.

fright. Had he let his comrades alone, they would have defeated us and chased us back to our town.

The story of Buraykah. — All that took place while an aged female slave, named Buraykah, owned by one of our men, a Kurd named 'Ali ibn-Maḥbūb [Majnūb?], was standing in the midst of our horsemen on the bank of the river, with a jar in her hand, filling it with water and giving our men to drink. Most of our men, who were on the elevation of the ground, seeing the Franks advancing in such great numbers, rushed away towards the city, [75] while that devil of a woman stood there undisturbed by that grave event.

I shall now mention something with regard to this Buraykah, although this is not the place for it; but the discussion leads from one point to another. Her master, 'Ali, was a pious man and never drank wine. One day he said to my father, "By Allah, O amīr, I consider it not legitimate for me to live on a stipend from the public treasury. I refuse to subsist on anything but the income from Buraykah." That ignorant man was of the opinion that that illicit income was a more legitimate thing than the state treasury by which he was employed.

This maid had a son named Naṣr, who was an elderly man and who was supervisor of a village belonging to my father (may Allah's mercy rest upon his soul!), in conjunction with another man called Baqiyyah ibn-al-Uṣayfir. Baqiyyah related to me the following story. He said:

I went at night to the town, desiring to go into my home on some personal business. As I approached the town, I saw among the tombs in the moonlight a living being which was neither human nor animal. I halted at a distance from it and was frightened by it. Then I said to myself, "Am I not Baqiyyah? What is this fear from a single object?" Taking up my sword, my leather shield and my javelin, which were with me, I advanced step by step, while I could hear some singing and a voice coming out of that object. When I was close by it, I jumped over it, holding my dagger in my hand, and got hold of it and behold! it was Buraykah with her hair spread all over, riding on a reed and neighing and roaming among the tombs. "Woe unto thee," said I, "what dost thou at this hour here?" "I am exercising sorcery," she replied. I said, "May Allah abominate thee, abominate thy sorcery and thy art from among all arts!"

A woman warrior in Shayzar. — The undaunted spirit of this bitch brought to my mind the memory of events which happened to our women in the battle which took place [28] between the Ismā'īlites and ourselves, though the two categories of women are quite different.

On that day the leader of the Ismā'īlites, 'Alwān ibn-Ḥarrār,[29] had an encounter in our castle with my cousin, Sinān-al-Dawlah Shabīb ibn-Ḥāmid ibn-Ḥumayd (may Allah's mercy rest upon his soul!). Sinān was my contemporary, having been born on the same day as myself, on Sunday, the 27th of Jumāda II, in the year 488.[30] But he had never taken part in a combat previous to that day, whereas I had already become by that time a master at it 'Alwān, desiring to put Shabīb under obligation to himself, said to him, "Return to thy house. Carry away from it whatever thou canst carry, and depart lest thou be killed, for we have already taken possession of the castle." Shabīb returned to his home and said, "Whoever has a thing, let him give it to me." This he said to his paternal aunt and his uncle's wives, every one of whom gave him something While he was at this, there suddenly entered the house a person wearing a coat of chain mail and a helmet and carrying a sword and a shield As soon as Shabīb saw the person, he felt certain of death. The person laid down the helmet and behold! it was none other than the mother of his cousin, Layth-al-Dawlah Yahya (may Allah's mercy rest upon his soul!). She said to him, "What dost thou want to do?" He replied, "Take whatever I can, descend from the castle by means of a rope and live in the world " To this she replied:

> What a wretched thing thou doest! Thou leavest thy uncle's daughters and the women of thy family to the ravishers [31] and goest away! What kind of life [76] will thine be when thou art dishonored by thy family and when thou fleest away, leaving them? Get out, fight in behalf of thy family until thou art killed in their midst! May Allah do this and that with thee! [32]

And thus she (may Allah's mercy rest upon her soul!) prevented him from flight. After this he became one of our noteworthy cavaliers.

28 In April, 1109

29 Lack of diacritical marks makes reading uncertain, possibly "Jarrār," "Jazzār," "Khazzār," "Khazzāz," "Ḥazāz," "Ḥarrāz," "Ḥazzār," or "Ḥarāz" See al-Dhahabi, *op. cit*, pp 99–100

30 July 4 1095

31 *hallājūn*, literally "cotton carders."

32 That is, she cursed him violently.

Usāmah's mother as a warrior. — On that day my mother (may Allah have mercy upon her soul!) distributed my swords and quilted jerkins. She came to a sister of mine who was well advanced in years and said, "Put on thy shoes and thy wrapper." [33] This she did. My mother then led her to the balcony in my house overlooking the valley from the east. She made her take a seat there, and my mother herself sat at the entrance to the balcony. Allah (praise be to him!) gave us victory over the enemy [the Ismā'īlites] I then came to my house seeking some of my weapons, but found nothing except the scabbards of the swords and the leather bags of the jerkins. I said, "O mother, where are my arms?" She replied, "My dear son, I have given the arms to those who would fight in our behalf, not believing that thou wert still alive." I said, "And my sister, what is she doing here?" She replied, "O my dear son, I have given her a seat at the balcony and sat behind her so that in case I found that the Bāṭinites had reached us, I could push her and throw her into the valley, preferring to see her dead rather than to see her captive in the hands of the peasants and ravishers." I thanked my mother for her deed, and so did my sister, who prayed that mother be rewarded [by Allah] in her behalf. Such solicitude for honor is indeed stronger than the solicitude of men.

An aged maid also fights. — On the same day an aged woman named Funūn,[34] who was one of the slaves of my grandfather, al-Amīr abu-al-Ḥasan 'Ali (may Allah's mercy rest upon his soul!), veiled herself and, sword in hand, rushed to battle. She continued to fight until we joined her and became too numerous for the enemy.

Usāmah's grandmother gives him wise advice. — No one can deny magnanimity, enthusiasm and sound judgment in the case of noble women. One day I went out with my father (may Allah's mercy rest upon his soul!) to the hunt. My father was especially fond of hunting and had a collection of falcons, shahins,[35] sakers, cheetahs and braches such as hardly anybody else possessed. He used to ride at the head of forty cavaliers from among his children and mamelukes, each one of whom was an expert hunter knowing all

[33] *izār*, a thin cover for the body, worn by Moslem women over their clothes and veiling their faces

[34] Orthography not clear. The word may be "Futūn." Al-Dhahabi, *op cit*, p 397.

[35] Ar. *shāhīn*, from Hindi *shāhīn*, is a falcon of the peregrine type, as is also the saker. The braches, mentioned below, were hounds

about the chase. He had in Shayzar two hunting grounds. One day he would ride to the marshy fields and streams to the west of the town, where he would hunt the francolins, waterfowl, hares and gazelles and kill the wild boars, and another day he would ride to the mountain south of the town to hunt partridges and hares. One day as we were in the mountain, the time came for the afternoon prayer. So he dismounted and we dismounted, praying each for himself, and behold! an attendant came running and said, "Here is the lion!" I brought my prayer to a conclusion before my father (may Allah's mercy rest upon his soul!) did, so that he might not prevent me from fighting the lion, mounted my horse, and, lance in hand, charged the lion. The lion faced me and roared. My horse shied with me in the saddle, and the lance, on account of its weight, fell from my hand. The lion chased me for a long distance. Then it returned to the slope of the mountain and stood there. It was one of the biggest of lions, as big as an arch, and it was famished. Every time we approached it, it would descend from the mountain and chase the horses away. Then it would resume its former position. And not once did it descend without [77]
leaving a great impression on our companions.

Finally, like a flash, I saw it leap over the haunches of the horse of one of my uncle's slaves, named Bastakīn Gharzah, and tear with its claws the clothes and leggings of the slave. It then returned to the mountain. Thus I had no way of attacking it until I climbed above it on the slope of the mountain and rushed my horse against it, giving it in the meantime a thrust with my lance which pierced its body. I left the lance in its body. The lion rolled over to the foot of the mountain with the lance in it and died. The lance was broken. This took place while my father (may Allah's mercy rest upon his soul!) was standing watching us, and with him were the children of his brother, 'Izz-al-Dīn, who, being young lads, were closely observing what was going on.

We then made our way to the town and entered it early in the evening carrying the lion. As we entered, my grandmother on my father's side (may Allah have mercy on both of their souls!) met me in the dark, holding in front of her a lighted candle. She was a very aged woman, almost a hundred years old. I entertained no doubt that she had come to congratulate me on my safety and acquaint me with her great satisfaction at what I had done. So I met her and kissed her hand. But she said to me with anger and with irritation, "O my boy, what makes thee face these adventures in which thou riskest thine own life and the life of thy horse, breakest thy weapons and increasest the antipathy and ill feeling which thine uncle cherishes in his heart against thee?" I replied, "O my grandmother,[36] the only thing that makes me expose myself to danger in this and similar cases is to endear myself to the heart of my uncle." She said, "No, by Allah! This does not bring thee nearer to thine uncle, but, on the contrary, it alienates thee from him and makes him feel more antipathy and ill will towards thee." I then realized that my grandmother (may Allah's mercy rest upon her soul!) was giving me wise counsel and was telling me the truth. By my life, such are the mothers of men!

The piety of Usāmah's grandmother.—This old woman (may Allah's mercy rest upon her soul!) was one of the most virtuous among Moslems, following the most strict paths of religion, almsgiving, fasting and prayer. I was once present on the night of the middle day of Sha'bān when she was praying in the home of my father, who (may Allah's mercy rest upon his soul!) was one of the best chanters of the Book of Allah (exalted is he!) and whose mother was then following him in her prayer. My father felt sympathy for her and said to her, "O my mother, if thou wouldst only keep sitting, thou couldst say thy prayer in that position." She replied, "O my dear son, are there days left of my life to enable me to survive to another night like this? No, by Allah, I shall not sit down." At that time my father was seventy years old,[37] while she was almost a hundred—may Allah's mercy rest upon her soul!

'Ali, the far-sighted, is killed by his wife for his betrayal of the Moslem cause.—I have witnessed wonderful manifestations of women's zeal, as illustrated in the following case:

One of the men of Khalaf ibn-Mulā'ib,[38] named 'Ali 'Abd[39] ibn-abi-al-Raydā', was endowed by Allah (exalted is he!) with a faculty of sight that rivaled that of Zarqā'[40] al-Yamāmah. He

[36] *sitt*, colloquial for "grandmother," also used for "lady."
[37] He was born in 460 = 1068
[38] Sayf-al-Dawlah, lord of Afāmiyah
[39] "'Abd" may be his *laqab*, meaning "the slave of"
[40] Who was proverbial in her far-sightedness, and who, according to Arab authors, could see at a distance of three days' journey.

used to rise with ibn-Mulā'ib and see caravans at a distance of one full day's march.

The following story was related to me by a companion of his, named Sālim al-'Ijāzi, who passed into the service of my father after the assassination of Khalaf ibn-Mulā'ib:[41]

We arose one day and sent out 'Ali 'Abd ibn-abi-al-Raydā' early in the morning [78] to act as a lookout. After a while he returned to us, saying, "Rejoice at the forthcoming booty. Here is a big caravan coming towards us." We all looked but saw nothing So we said to him, "We see neither a caravan nor anything else." He replied, "By Allah, I verily see a caravan in the van of which are two spotted horses shaking out their manes." We remained in the ambuscade until late in the afternoon, at which time the caravan with the two spotted horses preceding it arrived. So we made a sortie and captured the caravan.

Sālim al-'Ijāzi related to me also the following story:

After we arose one day, 'Ali 'Abd ibn-abi-al-Raydā' went up as our lookout. There he fell asleep and before he knew it a Turk from a Turkish detachment on a foray had seized him. The Turks asked him, "What art thou?" He replied, "I am a pauper and have rented my camel to a merchant in a caravan. Give me thy hand as a token that thou wilt give me back my camel and I will guide you to the caravan" Their leader gave him his hand. So he walked in front of them until he delivered them to our hand in the ambuscade. We made a sortie against them and captured them As for 'Ali, he got hold of the man who was in front of him and took his horse and his outfit. The booty we won from them was very rich indeed.

When ibn-Mulā'ib was killed, 'Ali 'Abd ibn-abi-al-Raydā' passed into the service of Theophile the Frank [*tūfīl al-ifranji*], the lord of Kafarṭāb. He then began to lead the Franks against the Moslems and secure booty for them, and went to the limit in doing harm to the Moslems, taking their property and shedding their blood — so much so that he rendered the roads unsafe for travelers. He had a wife with him in Kafartāb, in the hands of the Franks, who always objected to his behavior and tried to prohibit him from doing so, but to no avail. Finally, she sent and brought a relative of hers from one of the villages, who I think was her brother, and hid him in the house until nightfall, upon which both together

[41] In 1106 Ibn-al-Athīr in *Recueil historiens orientaux*, vol. I, pp. 232–35, and abu-al-Fida, *ibid.*, pp 8–9.

attacked her husband, 'Ali 'Abd ibn-abi-al-Raydā', killed him and ran away with all her possessions. The second morning she was with us in Shayzar. There she said, "I was angered on behalf of the Moslems because of what this infidel perpetrated against them." Thus she brought relief to our people from this devil. We took into consideration what she did, and she remained with us treated with special regard and respect.

A Frankish woman inflicts a wound on a Moslem with her jar. — Among the amīrs of Egypt was one named Badi al-Ṣulayḥi, whose face bore two scars, the one extending from his right and the other from his left eyebrow up to his hair. I once asked him about these two scars and he replied:

When I was a young man I used to undertake raids on foot from 'Asqalān One day I started towards the road to Jerusalem, having the Frankish pilgrims in mind. We came across a group of them. I encountered one of their number, who carried a lance and had his wife behind him holding a small wooden jar containing water The man gave me this first lance thrust, upon which I smote him and killed him. Then as I walked towards his wife, she struck me with the wooden jar and inflicted on me this other wound. [79] Both cuts left their marks on my face.

A Shayzar woman captures three Franks. — The following will serve as an illustration of women's love of adventure:

A group of Frankish pilgrims, after making the pilgrimage, returned to Rafaniyyah, which at that time belonged to them. They then left it for Afāmiyah. During the night they lost their way and landed in Shayzar, which at that time had no wall They entered the city, numbering about seven or eight hundred men, women and children. The army of Shayzar had already gone out of the town in the company of my two uncles, 'Izz-al-Dīn abu-al-'Asākir Sulṭān and Fakhr-al-Dīn abu-Kāmil Shāfi' (may Allah's mercy rest upon their souls!), to meet two brides, whom my uncles had married, who were sisters and belonged to the banu-al-Ṣūfi, the Aleppines. My father (may Allah's mercy rest upon his soul!) remained in the castle. One of our men, going out of the city at night on business, suddenly saw a Frank. He went back and got his sword, then went out and killed him. The battle cry sounded all over the town. The inhabitants went out, killed the Franks and took as booty all the women, children, silver and beasts of burden they had.

At that time there was in Shayzar a woman named Nadrah, daughter of Būzarmāṭ, who was the wife of one of our men. This woman went out with our men, captured a Frank and introduced him into her house. She went out again, captured another Frank and brought him in. Again she went out and captured still another. Thus she had three Franks in her house. After taking as booty what they had and what suited her of their possessions, she went out and called some of her neighbors, who killed them.

During the same night my two uncles, with the army, arrived. Some of the Franks had taken to flight and were pursued by certain men from Shayzar, who killed them in the environs of the town. The horses of my uncles' army, on entering the town in the night-time, began to stumble over corpses without knowing what they were stumbling over, until one of the cavaliers dismounted and saw the corpses in the darkness. This terrified our men, for they thought the town had been raided by surprise. In fact, it was booty which Allah (exalted and majestic is he!) had delivered into the hands of our people.

Prefers to be a Frankish shoemaker's wife to life in a Moslem castle. — A number of maids taken captive from the Franks were brought into the home of my father (may Allah's mercy rest upon his soul!) The Franks (may Allah's curse be upon them!) are an accursed race, the members of which do not assimilate except with their own kin. My father saw among them a pretty maid who was in the prime of youth, and said to his housekeeper, "Introduce this woman into the bath, repair her clothing and prepare her for a journey." This she did. He then delivered the maid to a servant of his and sent her to al-Amīr Shihāb-al-Dīn Mālik ibn-Sālim, the lord of the Castle of Ja'bar, who was a friend of his. He also wrote him a letter, saying, "We have won some booty from the Franks, from which I am sending thee a share." The maid suited Shihāb-al-Dīn, and he was pleased with her. He took her to himself and she bore him a boy, whom he called Badrān[42] [80] Badrān's father named him his heir apparent, and he became of age. On his father's death, Badrān became the governor of the

[42] Mentioned later by Kamāl-al-Dīn in *Recueil: historiens orientaux*, vol. III, p. 728.

town and its people, his mother being the real power. She entered into conspiracy with a band of men and let herself down from the castle by a rope. The band took her to Sarūj,[43] which belonged at that time to the Franks. There she married a Frankish shoemaker, while her son was the lord of the Castle of Ja'bar.

A Frank and his children revert to Christianity. — Among the Frankish captives who were carried into my father's home was an aged woman accompanied by her daughter — a young woman of great beauty — and a robust[44] son. The son accepted Islam, and his conversion was genuine, judging by what he showed in the practice of prayer and fasting. He learned the art of working marble from a stonecutter who had paved the home of my father. After staying for a long time with us my father gave him as wife a woman who belonged to a pious family, and paid all necessary expenses for his wedding and home. His wife bore him two sons The boys grew up. When they were five or six years old, their father, young Rā'ūl, who was very happy at having them, took them with their mother and everything that his house contained and on the second morning joined the Franks in Afāmiyah, where he and his children became Christians, after having practiced Islam with its prayers and faith. May Allah, therefore, purify the world from such people!

[43] In Mesopotamia, southwest of Edessa Cf ibn-al-Athīr in *Recueil historiens orientaux*, vol I, p 207

[44] *mushtadd*, which may here mean "who was of age"

8. AN APPRECIATION OF THE FRANKISH CHARACTER

Their lack of sense. — Mysterious are the works of the Creator, the author of all things! When one comes to recount cases regarding the Franks, he cannot but glorify Allah (exalted is he!) and sanctify him, for he sees them as animals possessing the virtues of courage and fighting, but nothing else; just as animals have only the virtues of strength and carrying loads. I shall now give some instances of their doings and their curious mentality.

In the army of King Fulk, son of Fulk, was a Frankish reverend knight who had just arrived from their land in order to make the holy pilgrimage and then return home. He was of my intimate fellowship and kept such constant company with me that he began to call me "my brother." Between us were mutual bonds of amity and friendship. When he resolved to return by sea to his homeland, he said to me:

> My brother, I am leaving for my country and I want thee to send with me thy son (my son,[1] who was then fourteen years old, was at that time in my company) to our country, where he can see the knights and learn wisdom and chivalry. When he returns, he will be like a wise man.

Thus there fell upon my ears words which would never come out of the head of a sensible man, for even if my son were to be taken captive, his captivity could not bring him a worse misfortune than carrying him into the lands of the Franks. However, I said to the man:

> By thy life, this has exactly been my idea. But the only thing that prevented me from carrying it out was the fact that his grandmother, my mother, is so fond of him and did not this time let him come out with me until she exacted an oath from me to the effect that I would return him to her.

Thereupon he asked, "Is thy mother still alive?" "Yes." I replied. "Well," said he, "disobey her not."

[1] Abu-al-Fawāris Murhaf.

Their curious medication. — A case illustrating their curious medicine is the following:

The lord of al-Munayṭirah [2] wrote to my uncle asking him to dispatch a physician to treat certain sick persons among his people. My uncle sent him a Christian physician named Thābit. Thābit was absent but ten days when he returned. So we said to him, "How quickly hast thou healed thy patients!" He said:

They brought before me a knight in whose leg [81] an abscess had grown; and a woman afflicted with imbecility [3] To the knight I applied a small poultice until the abscess opened and became well, and the woman I put on diet and made her humor wet. Then a Frankish physician came to them and said, "This man knows nothing about treating them." He then said to the knight, "Which wouldst thou prefer, living with one leg or dying with two?" The latter replied, "Living with one leg." The physician said, "Bring me a strong knight and a sharp ax." A knight came with the ax. And I was standing by. Then the physician laid the leg of the patient on a block of wood and bade the knight strike his leg with the ax and chop it off at one blow. Accordingly he struck it — while I was looking on — one blow, but the leg was not severed. He dealt another blow, upon which the marrow of the leg flowed out and the patient died on the spot. He then examined the woman and said, "This is a woman in whose head there is a devil which has possessed her. Shave off her hair." Accordingly they shaved it off and the woman began once more to eat their ordinary diet — garlic and mustard. Her imbecility took a turn for the worse. The physician then said, "The devil has penetrated through her head." He therefore took a razor, made a deep cruciform incision on it, peeled off the skin at the middle of the incision until the bone of the skull was exposed and rubbed it with salt. The woman also expired instantly. Thereupon I asked them whether my services were needed any longer, and when they replied in the negative I returned home, having learned of their medicine what I knew not before.

I have, however, witnessed a case of their medicine which was quite different from that.

The king of the Franks [4] had for treasurer a knight named Bernard [*barnād*], who (may Allah's curse be upon him!) was one of the most accursed and wicked among the Franks. A horse kicked him in the leg, which was subsequently infected and which opened

[2] In Lebanon near Afqah, the source of Nahr-Ibrāhīm, i e., ancient Adonis.

[3] Ar. *nashāf*, "dryness," is not used as a name of a disease. I take the word therefore to be Persian *nishāf* = "imbecility."

[4] Fulk of Anjou, king of Jerusalem.

in fourteen different places. Every time one of these cuts would close in one place, another would open in another place. All this happened while I was praying for his perdition. Then came to him a Frankish physician and removed from the leg all the ointments which were on it and began to wash it with very strong vinegar. By this treatment all the cuts were healed and the man became well again. He was up again like a devil.

Another case illustrating their curious medicine is the following: In Shayzar we had an artisan named abu-al-Fath, who had a boy whose neck was afflicted with scrofula. Every time a part of it would close, another part would open. This man happened to go to Antioch on business of his, accompanied by his son. A Frank noticed the boy and asked his father about him. Abu-al-Fatḥ replied, "This is my son." The Frank said to him, "Wilt thou swear by thy religion that if I prescribe to thee a medicine which will cure thy boy, thou wilt charge nobody fees for prescribing it thyself? In that case, I shall prescribe to thee a medicine which will cure the boy." The man took the oath and the Frank said:

> Take uncrushed leaves of glasswort, burn them, then soak the ashes in olive oil and sharp vinegar. Treat the scrofula with them until the spot on which it is growing is eaten up. Then take burnt lead, soak it in ghee butter [*samn*] and treat him with it. That will cure him.

The father treated the boy accordingly, and the boy was cured. The sores closed and the boy returned to his normal condition of health.

I have myself treated with this medicine many who were afflicted with such disease, and the treatment was successful in removing the cause of [82] the complaint.

Newly arrived Franks are especially rough: One insists that Usāmah should pray eastward. — Everyone who is a fresh emigrant from the Frankish lands is ruder in character than those who have become acclimatized and have held long association with the Moslems Here is an illustration of their rude character.

Whenever I visited Jerusalem I always entered the Aqsa Mosque, beside which stood a small mosque which the Franks had converted into a church. When I used to enter the Aqsa Mosque, which was occupied by the Templars [*al-dāwiyyah*], who were my friends, the Templars would evacuate the little adjoining mosque so that I might pray in it. One day[5] I entered this mosque, repeated the first formula, "Allah is great," and stood up in the act of praying, upon which one of the Franks rushed on me, got hold of me and turned my face eastward saying, "This is the way thou shouldst pray!" A group of Templars hastened to him, seized him and repelled him from me. I resumed my prayer. The same man, while the others were otherwise busy, rushed once more on me and turned my face eastward, saying, "This is the way thou shouldst pray!" The Templars again came in to him and expelled him. They apologized to me, saying, "This is a stranger who has only recently arrived from the land of the Franks and he has never before seen anyone praying except eastward." Thereupon I said to myself, "I have had enough prayer." So I went out and have ever been surprised at the conduct of this devil of a man, at the change in the color of his face, his trembling and his sentiment at the sight of one praying towards the *qiblah*.[6]

Another wants to show to a Moslem God as a child. — I saw one of the Franks come to al-Amīr Mu'īn-al-Dīn (may Allah's mercy rest upon his soul!) when he was in the Dome of the Rock[7] and say to him, "Dost thou want to see God as a child?" Mu'īn-al-Dīn said, "Yes." The Frank walked ahead of us until he showed us the picture of Mary with Christ (may peace be upon him!) as an infant in her lap. He then said, "This is God as a child." But Allah is exalted far above what the infidels say about him!

Franks lack jealousy in sex affairs. — The Franks are void of all zeal and jealousy. One of them may be walking along with his wife. He meets another man who takes the wife by the hand and steps aside to converse with her while the husband is standing on one side waiting for his wife to conclude the conversation. If she lingers too long for him, he leaves her alone with the conversant and goes away

Here is an illustration which I myself witnessed:

When I used to visit Nāblus,[8] I always took lodging with a man named Mu'izz, whose home was a lodging house for the Moslems. The house had windows which opened to the road, and there stood

[5] About 1140. [6] The direction of the Ka'bah in the holy city, Mecca.
[7] *al-ṣakhrah*, the mosque standing near al-Aqṣa in Jerusalem.
[8] Neapolis, ancient Shechem

opposite to it on the other side of the road a house belonging to a Frank who sold wine for the merchants. He would take some wine in a bottle and go around announcing it by shouting, "So and so, the merchant, has just opened a cask full of this wine. He who wants to buy some of it will find it in such and such a place." The Frank's pay for the announcement made would be the wine in that bottle.[9] One day this Frank went home and found a man with his wife in the same bed. He asked him, "What could have made thee enter into my wife's room?" The man replied, "I was tired, so I went in to rest." "But how," asked he, "didst thou get into my bed?" The other replied, "I found a bed that was spread, so I slept in it." "But," said he, "my wife was sleeping together with thee!" The other replied, "Well, the bed is hers. How could I therefore have prevented her from using her own bed?" [83] "By the truth of my religion," said the husband, "if thou shouldst do it again, thou and I would have a quarrel" Such was for the Frank the entire expression of his disapproval and the limit of his jealousy.

Another illustration:

We had with us a bath-keeper named Sālim, originally an inhabitant of al-Ma'arrah,[10] who had charge of the bath of my father (may Allah's mercy rest upon his soul!). This man related the following story.

I once opened a bath in al-Ma'arrah in order to earn my living To this bath there came a Frankish knight. The Franks disapprove of girding a cover around one's waist while in the bath So this Frank stretched out his arm and pulled off my cover from my waist and threw it away. He looked and saw that I had recently shaved off my pubes. So he shouted, "Sālim!" As I drew near him he stretched his hand over my pubes and said, "Sālim, good! By the truth of my religion, do the same for me." Saying this, he lay on his back and I found that in that place the hair was like his beard So I shaved it off. Then he passed his hand over the place and, finding it smooth, he said, "Sālim, by the truth of my religion, do the same to madame [*al-dāma*]" (*al-dāma* in their language means the lady), referring to his wife He then said

[9] *wa-ijratuhu 'an nidā'ihi al-nabīdh alladhi fi tilka al-qannīnah*, which Derenbourg, *Autobiographie*, p 132, translates "*Je lui fournirai de ce vin autant de bouteilles qu'il en désirera*" all of which he includes within quotation marks Landberg, *Critica Arabica*, No II (Leyden, 1888) pp 38–39 says that he spent two hours trying to make sense out of the Arabic phrase but without the least result

[10] Ma'arrah-al-Nu'mān, between Ḥamāh and Aleppo

to a servant of his, "Tell madame to come here." Accordingly the servant went and brought her and made her enter the bath. She also lay on her back. The knight repeated, "Do what thou hast done to me." So I shaved all that hair while her husband was sitting looking at me. At last he thanked me and handed me the pay for my service.

Consider now this great contradiction! They have neither jealousy nor zeal but they have great courage, although courage is nothing but the product of zeal and of ambition to be above ill repute.

Here is a story analogous to the one related above:

I entered the public bath in Ṣūr [Tyre] and took my place in a secluded part. One of my servants thereupon said to me, "There is with us in the bath a woman." When I went out, I sat on one of the stone benches and behold! the woman who was in the bath had come out all dressed and was standing with her father just opposite me. But I could not be sure that she was a woman. So I said to one of my companions, "By Allah, see if this is a woman," by which I meant that he should ask about her. But he went, as I was looking at him, lifted the end of her robe and looked carefully at her. Thereupon her father turned toward me and said, "This is my daughter. Her mother is dead and she has nobody to wash her hair. So I took her in with me to the bath and washed her head." I replied, "Thou hast well done! This is something for which thou shalt be rewarded [by Allah]!"

Another curious case of medication. — A curious case relating to their medicine is the following, which was related to me by William of Bures [*kilyām dabūr*], the lord of Ṭabarayyah [Tiberias], who was one of the principal chiefs among the Franks. It happened that William had accompanied al-Amīr Mu'īn-al-Dīn[11] (may Allah's mercy rest upon his soul!) from 'Akka to Ṭabarayyah when I was in his company too. On the way William related to us the following story in these words:

We had in our country a highly esteemed knight who was taken ill and was on the point of death. We thereupon came to one of our great priests and said to him, "Come with us and examine so and so, the knight." "I will," he replied, and walked along with us while we were assured in ourselves that if he would only lay his hand on him the patient would recover. When the priest saw the patient, he said, "Bring me

[11] Mu'īn-al-Dīn Anar.

some wax." We fetched him a little wax, which he softened and shaped like the knuckles of fingers, and he stuck one in each nostril. The knight died on the spot. [84] We said to him, "He is dead." "Yes," he replied, "he was suffering great pain, so I closed up his nose that he might die and get relief."

Let this go and let us resume the discussion regarding Harim.[12]

A funny race between two aged women. — We shall now leave the discussion of their treatment of the orifices of the body to something else.

I found myself in Ṭabarayyah at the time the Franks were celebrating one of their feasts. The cavaliers went out to exercise with lances. With them went out two decrepit, aged women whom they stationed at one end of the race course. At the other end of the field they left a pig which they had scalded and laid on a rock. They then made the two aged women run a race while each one of them was accompanied by a detachment of horsemen urging her on. At every step they took, the women would fall down and rise again, while the spectators would laugh. Finally one of them got ahead of the other and won that pig for a prize.

Their judicial trials: A duel. — I attended one day a duel in Nāblus between two Franks. The reason for this was that certain Moslem thieves took by surprise one of the villages of Nāblus. One of the peasants of that village was charged with having acted as guide for the thieves when they fell upon the village So he fled away. The king [13] sent and arrested his children. The peasant thereupon came back to the king and said, "Let justice be done in my case. I challenge to a duel the man who claimed that I guided the thieves to the village." The king then said to the tenant who held the village in fief, "Bring forth someone to fight the duel with him." The tenant went to his village, where a blacksmith lived, took hold of him and ordered him to fight the duel. The tenant became thus sure of the safety of his own peasants, none of whom would be killed and his estate ruined.

I saw this blacksmith. He was a physically strong young man, but his heart failed him. He would walk a few steps and then sit down and ask for a drink. The one who had made the challenge was an old man, but he was strong in spirit and he would rub the

[12] A hemistich quoted from the pre-Islamic poet Zuhayr ibn-abi-Sulma al-Muzani

[13] Fulk of Anjou, king of Jerusalem (1131–42).

nail of his thumb against that of the forefinger in defiance, as if he was not worrying over the duel. Then came the viscount [*al-biskund*], i.e., the seignior of the town, and gave each one of the two contestants a cudgel and a shield and arranged the people in a circle around them.

The two met. The old man would press the blacksmith backward until he would get him as far as the circle, then he would come back to the middle of the arena They went on exchanging blows until they looked like pillars smeared with blood. The contest was prolonged and the viscount began to urge them to hurry, saying, "Hurry on" The fact that the smith was given to the use of the hammer proved now of great advantage to him. The old man was worn out and the smith gave him a blow which made him fall. His cudgel fell under his back The smith knelt down over him and tried to stick his fingers into the eyes of his adversary, but could not do it because of the great quantity of blood flowing out. Then he rose up and hit his head with the cudgel until he killed him They then fastened a rope around the neck of the dead person, dragged him away and hanged him. The lord who brought the smith now came, gave the smith his own mantle, made him mount the horse behind him and rode off with him. This case illustrates the kind of jurisprudence [85] and legal decisions the Franks have — may Allah's curse be upon them!

Ordeal by water. — I once went in the company of al-Amīr Mu'īn-al-Dīn (may Allah's mercy rest upon his soul!) to Jerusalem. We stopped at Nāblus. There a blind man, a Moslem, who was still young and was well dressed, presented himself before al-amīr carrying fruits for him and asked permission to be admitted into his service in Damascus. The amīr consented. I inquired about this man and was informed that his mother had been married to a Frank whom she had killed. Her son used to practice ruses against the Frankish pilgrims and cooperate with his mother in assassinating them. They finally brought charges against him and tried his case according to the Frankish way of procedure.

They installed a huge cask and filled it with water. Across it they set a board of wood. They then bound the arms of the man charged with the act, tied a rope around his shoulders and dropped him into the cask, their idea being that in case he was innocent, he would sink in the water and they would then lift him up with the rope so that he might not die in the water; and in case he was guilty, he would not sink in the water. This man did his best to sink when they dropped him into the water, but he could not do it. So he had to submit to their sentence against him — may Allah's curse be upon them! They pierced his eyeballs with red-hot awls.

Later this same man arrived in Damascus. Al-Amīr Mu'īn-al-Dīn (may Allah's mercy rest upon his soul!) assigned him a stipend large enough to meet all his needs and said to a slave of his, "Conduct him to Burhān-al-Dīn al-Balkhi (may Allah's mercy rest upon his soul!) and ask him on my behalf to order somebody to teach this man the Koran and something of Moslem jurisprudence." Hearing that, the blind man remarked, "May triumph and victory be thine! But this was never my thought" "What didst thou think I was going to do for thee?" asked Mu'īn-al-Dīn. The blind man replied, "I thought thou wouldst give me a horse, a mule and a suit of armor and make me a knight" Mu'īn-al-Dīn then said, "I never thought that a blind man could become a knight."

A Frank domesticated in Syria abstains from eating pork — Among the Franks are those who have become acclimatized and have associated long with the Moslems. These are much better than the recent comers from the Frankish lands. But they constitute the exception and cannot be treated as a rule

Here is an illustration. I dispatched one of my men to Antioch on business There was in Antioch at that time al-Ra'īs Theodoros Sophianos [*tādrus ibn-al-saffi*], to whom I was bound by mutual ties of amity. His influence in Antioch was supreme. One day he said to my man, "I am invited by a friend of mine who is a Frank. Thou shouldst come with me so that thou mayest see their fashions." My man related the story in the following words:

I went along with him and we came to the home of a knight who belonged to the old category of knights who came with the early expeditions of the Franks. He had been by that time stricken off the register and exempted from service, and possessed in Antioch an estate on the income of which he lived. The knight presented an excellent table, with food extraordinarily clean and delicious Seeing me abstaining from food, he said, "Eat, be of good cheer! I never eat Frankish dishes, but I have Egyptian women cooks and never eat except their cooking.

Besides, pork never enters my home." I ate, but guardedly, and after that we departed.

As I was passing in the market place, a Frankish woman all of a sudden hung to my clothes and began to mutter words in their language, and I could not understand what she was saying. This made me immediately the center of a big crowd of Franks. I was convinced that death was at hand. But all of a sudden that same knight approached. On seeing me, he came and said to that woman, "What is the matter between thee and this Moslem?" She replied, "This is he who has killed [86] my brother Hurso [*'urs*]" This Hurso was a knight in Afāmiyah who was killed by someone of the army of Hamāh. The Christian knight shouted at her, saying, "This is a bourgeois [*burjāsi*] (i.e., a merchant) who neither fights nor attends a fight." He also yelled at the people who had assembled, and they all dispersed. Then he took me by the hand and went away. Thus the effect of that meal was my deliverance from certain death.

9. SUNDRY EXPERIENCES AND OBSERVATIONS

Unusual forms of weakness: Usāmah's uncle scared by a mouse. — One of the curious phenomena of the human heart is that a man may wade through the thickest part of combats and face all adventures without feeling the least fear in his heart and yet he may be scared by something of which even boys and women may not be afraid

I have seen my uncle, ‘Izz-al-Dīn abu-al-‘Asākir Sultān (may Allah's mercy rest upon his soul!), — who was one of the bravest among his people, having to his credit a number of well-known stands in combat and worthy lance thrusts — change color on seeing a mouse, feel something like a shudder at the mere sight of it, and leave the place where he saw it.

Among his slaves was a brave man, known for his valor and love of adventure, whose name was Ṣandūq. He was afraid of snakes, to the point of losing his wits. One day my father (may Allah's mercy rest upon his soul!) said to him as he was standing in the presence of my uncle, "O Ṣandūq, thou art a good man, known for thy valor. Art thou not therefore ashamed on account of thy fear of a snake?" He replied, "O my lord, what is there strange about this? In Ḥimṣ there is a valiant man, a real hero, who fears the mouse to the point of death," referring to his master My uncle (may Allah's mercy rest upon his soul!), who heard him, said to him, "May Allah blight thee, thou so and so!"

A hero scared by a snake. — I recall the case of a mameluke of my father (may Allah's mercy rest upon his soul!) named Lu'lu', who was a good man and an adventurer. One night I went out of Shayzar taking with me a large number of mules and other beasts, with the intention of loading them from the mountain with wood which I had cut for a noria [1] which belonged to me. When we started from the environs of Shayzar, we had an idea that dawn was

[1] *nā‘ūrah*, "water wheel," many of which, dating back to the days of the Romans, are still visible today all along the Orontes and particularly in Ḥimṣ, Ḥamāh and Antioch.

approaching, but in fact we arrived in a village called Dubays before it was midnight. I then said to my men, "Dismount. We shall not go into the mountain at night."

No sooner had we dismounted and settled down than we heard the neighing of a horse. We said, "These are the Franks." So we rode on in the dark. I promised myself to pierce one of them with my lance and take his horse while they were seizing our beasts and men. Thereupon I said to Lu'lu' and three other servants, "Go ahead and find out what this neighing is." Accordingly they went ahead at full gallop and met the others, who were in great numbers. Lu'lu' went first of all to them and said, "Speak out, otherwise I shall kill you to the last man," he being an excellent archer. Recognizing his voice, they called out, "Ḥājib [chamberlain] Lu'lu'?" "Yes," said he. And behold! they turned out to be the army of Ḥamāh headed by al-Amīr Sayf-al-Dīn Suwār [2] (may Allah's mercy rest upon his soul!) who had just made a raid on the territory of the Franks [3] and were now on their way back home. Such was the spirit of daring in this man in the face of that huge body of men; and yet if he should see in his house a snake, he would go out in flight, saying to his wife, "It is thy business to kill the snake!" His wife would arise and kill it.

Trifles may lead to serious results: Loose reins. — Sometimes the combatant, though he be a lion in courage, may be ruined and rendered impotent by the least of impediments, as happened to me outside of Ḥimṣ. [87] In a sortie my horse was killed and I received fifty sword blows — through the execution of the divine will, and, in some degree, through the carelessness of my groom in fixing the reins of the bridle. He attached the reins to the rings without letting them go through. So when I pulled the reins, desiring to escape from the midst of the enemy, the reins got loose from the rings and there befell me that which befell me.

No stirrup. — One day the public announcer's [4] voice was heard

[2] Or Sawār, the viceroy of Zanki over Aleppo Ibn-al-Athīr calls him "Aswār" in *Recueil historiens orientaux*, vol. I, pp. 416–17, and so does Kamāl-al-Dīn, *ibid.*, vol III, p. 672.

[3] In 1137

[4] *al-ṣā'iḥ*, which occurs in many places in the text It is difficult to tell whether the term refers to a special person who would send out an alarm cry at the approach of an enemy, or to the general tumult and battle cry of the populace when the enemy is sighted

in Shayzar, coming from the south [*qiblah*]. We instantly put on our armor and got ready. But the announcer proved a liar. My father and uncle (may Allah's mercy rest upon their souls!) departed and I remained behind them. The announcer's cry then came from the north from the side of the Franks. I galloped on my horse towards the announcer and saw our men crossing the ford, one on top of the other and shouting, "The Franks!" I immediately crossed the ford and said to the people, "Fear not. I am already between you and the enemy." Then I went galloping up the hill of the Qarāfitah [5] and behold! the riders were seen advancing in a great mass, preceded by a knight wearing a coat of linked mail and a helmet. He was already close to me. I made for him, taking the opportunity to smite first and then to attack his companions. He faced me, ready for the encounter. The moment I spurred my horse towards him, my stirrup broke. But there was no way then to avoid meeting him. So, with no stirrup, I rushed to attack him. When we were so close together that nothing was left but to wield the lances, he greeted me and offered his services to me. And behold! he turned out to be al-Salār [6] 'Umar, the maternal uncle of al-Salār Zayn-al-Dīn Ismā'īl ibn-'Umar ibn-Bakhtiyār, who had started with the army of Ḥamāh towards the town of Kafartāb. The Franks had made a sortie against them, and so they returned to Shayzar in flight, headed by al-Amīr Suwār (may Allah's mercy rest upon his soul!).

The right course for the combatant to follow, therefore, is to inspect frequently the outfit of his horse, for the least significant and the smallest of things may lead to harm and destruction — all that subject, of course, to the course of fate and destiny.

Usāmah hurt more by a hyena than by lions. — I have taken part in fighting against lions on innumerable occasions, and I have killed many of them single-handed without the cooperation of anybody else — all that without receiving the least injury from a single one of them.

One day I set out with my father (may Allah's mercy rest upon

[5] This word may be a variant of *qarāmiṭah* = "Karmathians," especially in view of the fact that Arabic lexicons make *qarfaṭa* and *qarmaṭa* synonyms, both meaning "to walk heavily, taking short steps."

[6] Persian *sālār* = "commander," is from an older Pahlavi form *sardār* and is synonymous with *serdār* in modern Persian. See *Encyclopaedia of Islam*, art. "Sālār."

his soul!) for the chase in a mountain near our town, desiring to hunt partridges with falcons. Our plan was to have my father, together with ourselves and the falconers, on the mountain, while a few retainers and falconers would be stationed at the foot in order to deliver the quarry from the falcons and determine the hiding places of the birds. All of a sudden a female hyena appeared before us. The hyena entered a cavern in which was a den. Into this the hyena penetrated. I called to a retainer of mine, a groom, named Yūsuf. The latter took off his clothes, clutched a knife and entered the den, while I, lance in hand, stood facing the spot, so I could strike the hyena in case it should come out. My attendant shouted, "Look out! It is going out!" So I smote it with the lance, but missed it, for the hyena is small [88] of body. The attendant then shouted, "Here is by me another hyena." This hyena came out, following the steps of the first one. I arose and stood at the door of the cavern — which was narrow but about two statures high — and looked to see what our companions who were down in the valley might do with the hyenas which had gone down towards them. While my attention was absorbed looking at the first two, a third hyena came out, pushed me and threw me over from the door of the cavern to the ditch below. I came near breaking my backbone. Thus I was hurt by a female hyena, but was never hurt by lions. How mysterious, therefore, are the works of him who determines destinies and brings all things to pass!

One man faints at the sight of gushing blood. — I have witnessed manifestations of some men's weakness of soul and faintness of heart which I did not think possible among women. Here is an illustration.

One day as I was standing at the door of the house of my father (may Allah's mercy rest upon his soul!), not being then more than ten years old, one of my father's retainers, named Muhammad al-'Ajami, hit a boy servant of the house. The latter fled before him and came and clung to my clothes. Muḥammad followed him while he was clinging to my robe and hit him again. I then struck the aggressor with a stick that I had in my hand. He pushed me. Thereupon, I drew a knife from my belt and stabbed him with it. The knife hit his left breast, so he fell. A big attendant of my father named al-Qā'id [leader] Asad came, examined him and saw the wound, out of which flowed blood like bubbles of water every time the wounded man breathed. Asad turned pale, shivered and fell unconscious. He was carried in this condition to his home, which was with us in the castle, and did not regain consciousness until the end of the day. By that time the wounded man was already dead and buried.

Another would faint at the sight of bloodletting. — Something analogous to the above is the following:

There used to visit us in Shayzar a man from Aleppo [Ḥalab] who was meritorious and learned. He could play chess without looking at the board as well as in the ordinary manner.[7] His name was abu-al-Murajja Sālim ibn-Qānit (may Allah's mercy rest upon his soul!). On his visits he used to spend with us a year, more or less. In case he got sick, the physician would prescribe bloodletting, and every time the bloodletter came, Sālim's color would change and he would shiver; and when the bloodletter applied the knife, he would faint and remain unconscious until the cut was bandaged, upon which he would return to consciousness.

Strong spirits: A negro saws his own leg. — Now for a contrary case.

Among our men of the banu-Kinānah was a black man named 'Ali ibn-Faraḥ,[8] in whose foot appeared a pustule. The pustule turned malignant. His toes fell off, and the whole leg began to rot. The surgeon said to him, "There is nothing to do for thy leg but amputation. Otherwise thou art lost." The man procured a saw and sawed his leg[9] until the flow of blood made him faint. On coming back to consciousness he would start sawing it again. This continued until he amputated it at the middle of the leg. After some treatment, it was cured.

This 'Ali (may Allah's mercy rest upon his soul!) was one of the most enduring and powerful of all men. He used to sit his saddle using one stirrup and putting his knee in a strap on the other side, and in this condition take part in combat and exchange lance thrusts with the Franks. I used to see him myself (may Allah's mercy rest upon his soul!) · [89] no man was able to stand a finger

[7] *ṭabaqatan wa-ghā'iban*, of the meaning of which I am not absolutely certain.
[8] Possibly "Faraj"
[9] The pronouns and their antecedents are a little confused in this narrative and may be taken to mean that the surgeon did the sawing.

contest or come to grips with him. With all his strength and courage, he was a jovial and light-hearted fellow.

Early one morning when he and the banu-Kinānah were living in our citadel, the Citadel of the Bridge, he sent a message to certain notables of the banu-Kinānah saying to them, "This is a rainy day and I have left in my house a little wine and some food. Favor me with your presence so that we may drink together." So they assembled in his house. He then sat at the door of the house and said, "Is there any among you who can go out through the door if I oppose him?" (referring to his strength). They replied, "No, by Allah!" He said:

> This is a rainy day and there is left in my house neither flour, bread nor wine. But every one of you has in his home all that he needs for the day Send therefore to your homes and fetch your food and your wine As for the house, I offer that. We shall then get together on this day in order to drink and converse.

They unanimously replied, "What an excellent idea, O abu-al-Ḥasan, is this." They then sent and brought whatever food and drink their homes contained and spent the day with him. Albeit he was a respected man. Exalted is he who made his creatures of different categories! For can the endurance of this man and the strength of his spirit be compared with the faint-heartedness and feebleness of those others we discussed?

One afflicted with dropsy is cured by slashing his abdomen. — The following case is somewhat analogous·

I was told by one of the banu-Kinānah in the Citadel of the Bridge that a man in that citadel, who was afflicted with dropsy, had cut open his abdomen and was cured, returning to his good health as he was before. I said, "I should like to see that man and draw out the information from him." The man who related the story to me was one of the banu-Kinānah named Aḥmad ibn-Ma'bad ibn-Aḥmad. Aḥmad brought that man before me and I questioned him about his condition and the manner in which he treated himself. His answer was this:

> I am a pauper and live all by myself. I was afflicted with dropsy and became so old that I could no more move about and became tired of life. So I took a razor and struck it along my navel across my abdomen and cut it open. About two cooking vessels (meaning two measures) of

water came out. The water continued to ooze out until my abdomen shrunk. I then sewed the cut and treated it until it was healed. The disease has thus gone away.

Saying this, he showed me the place of the cut in his abdomen, which was more than a span in length.

There can be no doubt that this man had still a livelihood on this earth to which he was entitled. Under other circumstances, I have seen people with dropsy whose abdomens physicians cut open and from which water came out just as it did in the case of this man who cut himself, but who nevertheless lost their lives on account of the operation. Fate is an impregnable fortress.

Frankish knights take a part of Shayzar unawares, but are repulsed. — Victory in warfare is from Allah (blessed and exalted is he!) and is not due to organization and planning, nor to the number of troops and supporters.

Whenever my uncle (may Allah's mercy rest upon his soul!) sent me to fight Turks or Franks, I would say to him, "O my lord, instruct me as to how I should conduct myself when [90] I meet the enemy." My uncle would reply, "O my boy, war conducts itself." And he was right.

Once[10] my uncle ordered me to accompany his wife, the lady [*khātūn*], daughter of Tāj-al-Dawlah Tutush,[11] and his children with an escort of troops to Ḥiṣn-Maṣyād,[12] which at that time belonged to my uncle, his idea being to spare them the excessive heat of Shayzar. Accordingly I started on horseback. My father and my uncle (may Allah's mercy rest upon their souls!) rode with us a part of the way and then returned, accompanied only by the young mamelukes who led the extra horses by halter and carried the arms, the troops being all with me. When my uncle and father approached Shayzar, they heard the drum of the Bridge beating, so they said, "Something is wrong at the Bridge." They spurred their horses in the direction of the Bridge. Between us and the Franks (may Allah's curse be upon them!) at that time was a truce. In spite of that, they had dispatched a scout to reconnoitre a ford by which they could cross over to the City of the Bridge

[10] In 1122 or 1123.
[11] The Seljūq king of Aleppo and the brother of Malik-Shāh of Iṣpahān
[12] "Maṣyāth" in the manuscript and so in *al Rawdatayn*, vol I, p 261. Yāqūt, *op. cit.*, vol. IV, p. 556. "Miṣyāb," giving as variant "Miṣyāf."

[*madīnah al-jisr*]. This stood on a peninsula[13] to which no one could cross except over a bridge the arch of which was constructed with stone and lime, and to which the Franks had no access. That scout pointed out to them a ford. So they all rode from Afāmiyah, and the second morning found them on the spot which was pointed out to them. They crossed the water, took possession of the city, pillaged, took captives and killed. Some of the captives and booty they dispatched to Afāmiyah. They took possession of the houses, and each one of them put the sign of the crucifix over one house and planted over it his flag.

When my father and my uncle (may Allah's mercy rest upon their souls!) were within sight of the castle [Shayzar], its inhabitants shouted, "Allah is great!" and howled lustily. Thereby Allah (worthy of admiration is he!) struck terror and helplessness to the hearts of the Franks, and they failed to find the spot at which they crossed. Covered with their coats of mail, they forced their horses, on which they were mounted, into a place in the river where there was no ford. A large number of them were thus drowned. The rider would plunge into the water, fall from his saddle and sink to the bottom, while the horse would get over. Those of them who survived left in disorderly flight with no one of them minding the other. They were a great army, while my father and my uncle had only ten young mamelukes in their company!

My uncle took his abode at the Bridge and my father returned to Shayzar. As for me, I accompanied my uncle's children to Maṣyād and returned on the same day, arriving home early in the morning. Informed about what had taken place, I immediately presented myself before my father (may Allah's mercy rest upon his soul!) and consulted him as to whether I should join my uncle in the Citadel of the Bridge. His reply was: "Thou wilt arrive there in the nighttime while they are asleep. Rather go to them early in the morning."

Early the next morning I started and presented myself before my uncle. We both rode out and stood over the spot where the Franks were drowned. Certain swimmers dived and pulled out a number of their dead cavaliers. I said to my uncle, "My lord, shall we not cut off their heads and dispatch them to Shayzar?"

[13] *jazīrah*, which means "island" but is sometimes used for "peninsula."

Courtesy of Dr. T. Salloum, Hamah, Syria

THE CASTLE OF SHAYZAR

A general view from a hill to the southeast of the castle, showing the Orontes in the foreground.

"Go ahead," said he. So we cut off about twenty heads, out of which blood flowed copiously as if the men had been killed that very moment, although they had been dead for one day and one night. I believe it was the water which preserved the blood in them. Our men carried away as booty from the Franks an assortment of arms, including linked mail, swords, lances, helmets and greaves.

I myself saw one of the peasants of the Bridge [91] come before my uncle with his hand under his clothes. My uncle said to him jokingly, "What hast thou set aside for me from the booty?" The man replied, "I have set aside for thee a horse with its outfit, linked mail, a shield and a sword." Presently he went away and fetched all these. My uncle took the outfit and returned the horse to him, saying, "And what is this in thy hand?" The man replied:

> O my lord, I was in grips with a Frank, having with me neither equipment nor sword, and I felled him to the ground I then began to give him blows with my fist on his face, which was covered with a veil of mail, until I rendered him unconscious Then I took his sword and killed him with it Consequently, the skin on the knuckles of my fingers was torn to shreds, my hand swelled up and since then has been of no use to me.

Saying this he showed us his hand, which was as he had described it: the bones of his fingers were all exposed.

A Moslem captive drowns herself. — In the army of the Bridge was a Kurd named abu-al-Jaysh,[14] who had a daughter named Rafūl, who had been carried away as captive by the Franks. Abu-al-Jaysh was affected by a kind of monomania on account of her, which made him say to everyone he met every day: "Rafūl has been taken captive." The second morning as we were walking on the bank of the river, we saw by the side of the water an object. We said to one of our attendants, "Swim and see what is that thing." The attendant went to it and lo! the object was Rafūl herself, dressed in a blue dress. She had thrown herself from the back of the horse of the Frank who had carried her away and was drowned. Her dress was caught in a willow tree. The anguish of her father, abu-al-Jaysh, was thereby abated.

Thus the howls which scared the Franks, their flight and their destruction were due to the benevolence of Allah (mighty and

[14] Possibly "Ḥabash."

majestic is he!) and not to superior force or army — blessed is Allah, who is potent over whatever he pleases!

The value of stratagem in warfare: A ruse against the army of Damascus. — Inspiring the army with awe is sometimes profitable in warfare. Here is an illustration.

In the year 529,[15] the atābek arrived in Syria with myself in his company and continued on his way to Damascus. When we were encamped at al-Quṭayyifah,[16] Ṣalāḥ-al-Dīn [17] (may Allah's mercy rest upon his soul!) said to me, "Mount and go ahead of us to al-Fustuqah. There station thyself on the road, so that no one of our troops may flee towards Damascus." Accordingly I proceeded [to al-Fustuqah] and stopped there for a while, after which Ṣalāḥ-al-Dīn arrived at the head of a small band of his companions. Thereupon we saw smoke rising in 'Adhrā'. Ṣalāḥ-al-Dīn sent riders to find out what the smoke was, and they discovered it was a detachment of the army of Damascus burning the hay in 'Adhrā'. The latter took to flight. Ṣalāḥ-al-Dīn pursued them, and we escorted him with perhaps thirty or forty horsemen. Arriving at al-Quṣayr we found that the entire army of Damascus was there across from the bridge. We were then near the inn. There we halted, hiding behind the inn. Five or six of our horsemen would now come out at one time, so that the army of Damascus might catch sight of them, and would then return behind the inn, thus making the enemy believe that we had there an ambuscade.

[92] In the meantime, Ṣalāḥ-al-Dīn dispatched a rider to the atābek acquainting him with our critical position. Presently we saw about ten horsemen advancing rapidly towards us while the army behind them formed one continuous procession. When they arrived we found that it was the atābek who led the van, with the army following in his train. The atābek criticized Ṣalāḥ-al-Dīn for his conduct, saying, "Thou hast hastened as far as the gate of Damascus with thirty horsemen in order to be destroyed, O Mūsa!" [18] And he reprimanded him. Both were talking in Turkish and I could not make out what they were saying.

[15] Spring of 1135 The atābek is Zanki

[16] Modern al-Qutayfah, northeast of Damascus on the way to Palmyra. See E Sachau, *Reise in Syrien und Mesopotamien* (Leipzig, 1883), p 24 and map, al-Muqaddasi, *Ahsan al-Taqāsim*, ed de Goeje (Leyden, 1877), p. 190.

[17] Muḥammad ibn-Ayyūb al-Ghisyāni

[18] His name was Muḥammad, but he is here called *Mūsa* = "Moses."

When the vanguard of the army had joined us, I said to Ṣalāḥ-al-Dīn, "By thy command, I shall now lead the troops which have already arrived, cross over to the cavalry of Damascus stationed opposite us and rout them." He replied, "No, thus and thus [19] to him who acts loyally in the service of this man [Zanki]! Didst thou not hear what he has done to me?"

Now had it not been for the grace of Allah (exalted is he!) and then that attempt at terrorizing and playing upon their imagination, they would undoubtedly have routed us.

Usāmah tries a ruse against the army of Kafarṭāb. — A similar case happened to me when I accompanied my uncle (may Allah's mercy rest upon his soul!) from Shayzar going towards Kafartāb. We had with us a crowd of peasants and poor men intent upon pillaging wheat and cotton from the neighborhood of Kafartab. As our men were scattered about pillaging, the cavalry of Kafartāb mounted their horses and stationed themselves near their town while we intervened between them and our men in the wheat and cotton fields. All at once one of our horsemen came galloping from the scouts and said, "The cavalry of Afāmiyah has arrived!" Thereupon my uncle said to me, "Thou shalt remain here to face the cavalry of Kafarṭāb, while I lead the army to encounter the cavalry of Afāmiyah." I took my post at the head of ten horsemen hidden among some olive trees. Of these I made three or four come out from time to time, to create an illusion in the minds of the Franks, and then return behind the olive trees. The Franks, imagining that we were numerous, would assemble, shout and rush their horses until they would get near us and then, finding us unshaken from our position, would turn back. We continued doing this until my uncle returned after the defeat of the Franks who had come from Afāmiyah.

One of the attendants of my uncle then said to him, "O my lord, seest thou what he did (meaning me)? He remained behind and did not accompany thee to meet the cavalry of Afāmiyah " My uncle replied, "Had he not taken a post at the head of ten horsemen opposite the cavalry and infantry of Kafartāb, they would have taken captive this whole crowd." Thus terrorizing

[19] Ar. *kadha wa-kadha*, used by the author as a substitute for the profanity which the author does not think proper to reproduce.

the Franks and playing on their imagination was at that time much more advantageous than fighting them, for we were few in number while they were a numerous detachment.

Disadvantages of excessive audacity: Usāmah recovers stolen calico. — I had a similar experience in Damascus.[20]

One day I was in the company of al-Amīr Mu'īn-al-Dīn (may Allah's mercy rest upon his soul!) when a horseman came and said to him, "The brigands have seized on the hill a caravan carrying calico." Mu'īn-al-Dīn said, "We will ride in their pursuit." I replied, "As thou wishest. Order the sergeants[21] to make the troops mount their horses and go with thee." Mu'īn-al-Dīn said, "But what need have we of the troops?" I replied, "Could there be any harm in their coming with us?" He said again, "We have no need for them."

Now, Mu'īn-al-Dīn was one of the most valiant horsemen; but the strength of the spirit is, under certain circumstances, a weakness and a cause of harm.

We rode out, about twenty horsemen in all. [93] After we got tired of searching, he dispatched two horsemen in one direction, two in another, two in a third direction and one in a fourth direction in order to reconnoitre the roads, while we, a mere handful, went on our way. When the time for the mid-afternoon prayer arrived, Mu'īn-al-Dīn said to an attendant of mine, "O Sūnuj, go up and look out while we pray." Hardly had we repeated the concluding salaam of the prayer when the attendant came running and said, "Behold the men in the valley with the pieces of calico on their heads!" Mu'īn-al-Dīn (may Allah's mercy rest upon his soul!) immediately gave orders to mount. I said to him, "Give us time to put on our jerkins. Then when we meet them we shall hurl our horses at them and smite them with lances, and thus they will not be able to tell whether we are numerous or few." His answer was: "When we get to them we shall put on our jerkins."

He mounted his horse and we all started towards them. We overtook them in Wādi-Ḥalbūn,[22] a very narrow valley where the distance between the two mountains is perhaps five cubits. The mountains on both sides are rugged and steep. The path in

[20] During Usāmah's first visit, 1138–44. [21] Ar. *shāwish*, of Persian origin.
[22] The valley of Ḥalbūn Ḥalbūn is a village north of Damascus noted in antiquity for its wine. Ezekiel XXVII . 18.

the valley is so narrow that not more than one horseman can pass at a time. The brigands were about seventy men armed with bows and arrows.

When we caught up with them, our attendants were still behind, carrying our weapons and unable to reach us. The brigands were partly in the valley and partly on the slope of the mountain. Believing that those in the valley were our friends, peasants from the village who were seeking the brigands, and that those who were on the slope of the mountain were the real brigands, I brandished my sword and charged those who were on the slope. My horse climbed that rugged ascent but almost breathed its last When I got to them with my horse standing still, unable to move, one of them fixed an arrow in his bow [23] to hit me but I yelled at him and threatened him. So he held back. I then turned my horse back and descended, hardly believing that I should escape.

The Amīr Mu'īn-al-Dīn climbed to the summit of the mountain, thinking to find there peasants whom he could arouse to join the combat. He yelled to me from the summit of the mountain, saying, "Leave not the enemy until I return," and disappeared from our sight. I, however, returned, for my place was narrow. The brigands on the mountain withdrew and joined those who were in the valley. I then realized that those too were a part of the brigands and charged them, all single-handed, on account of the narrowness of the place. They took to flight, throwing away whatever calico they had. I also succeeded in wresting from them two animals laden with calico. They climbed to a cavern in the slope of the mountain. We could see them but had no access to them.

The Amīr Mu'īn-al-Dīn (may Allah's mercy rest upon his soul!) returned at the end of the day without finding anyone to arouse for their pursuit. Had only the army been with us, we would have struck off the heads of all the brigands and recovered everything they had.

Usāmah's party loses some of its members through inexperience. — I had a similar experience on another occasion which I attribute to the execution of the divine will as well as to lack of experience in warfare. This is the way it happened.

[23] The manuscript has *qawl*, which I take to be a copyist's mistake for *qaws* = "bow."

We set out with al-Amīr Quṭb-al-Dīn Khusru ibn-Talīl[24] from Ḥamāh desiring to go to Damascus to present ourselves before al-Malik al-'Ādil Nūr-al-Dīn (may Allah's mercy rest upon his soul!) and arrived at Ḥimṣ. Khusru resolved to follow the route of Ba'labakk, so I said to him, "I shall go ahead of thee in order to visit the church of Ta'nīl,[25] [94] where I shall await thy arrival." "Do so," said he.

Accordingly I mounted my horse and went ahead. When I was inside of the church, a horseman came to say to me in the name of Khusru, "A band of brigands on foot have attacked a caravan and captured it. Ride and meet me at the mountain."[26] I rode and met him. When we climbed the mountain we found the brigands in the valley below us, with the mountain on which we stood surrounding that valley on all sides. A companion of Khusru advised him to go down to them, but I said, "Thou shouldst not do it. Let us proceed around the mountain until we are right over their heads, intercepting them on their way towards the west, and then we shall capture them." These brigands were from the territory of the Franks. Another one remarked, "In the time it would take us to ride around the mountain, we could reach them and capture them." Accordingly we went down. But no sooner had the brigands seen us than they climbed the mountain. Khusru said to me, "Climb again to them." I made great effort to climb but could not do so.

There had remained on the mountain six or seven of our horsemen who now dismounted and moved towards the brigands, leading their horses with them. The brigands, who were quite numerous, rushed on our comrades, killed two cavaliers and took possession of their two horses and a third horse whose master escaped. Then they descended from the other side of the mountain carrying their booty. As for us, we returned after two of our horsemen had been killed and three of our horses captured, in addition to the loss of the caravan. This was a case of running a risk through lack of experience in warfare.

[24] A Kurdish amīr, nephew of abu-al-Hayjā' al-Hadbāni, lord of Irbil (Arbela) Ibn-Khallikān, *Dictionary*, vol IV, p 494, ibn-al-Athīr, *Atābeks*, in *Recueil historiens orientaux*, vol II, p 255.

[25] Orthography not clear There is a town today called Ti'nāyil, but that is too far south to suit the narrative, being nearer to Zaḥlah than to Ba'labakk.

[26] Lebanon The road from Ḥimṣ to Damascus via Ba'labakk lies mostly in Coele-Syria (al-Biqā') with Lebanon to the west and Anti-Lebanon to the east

Ambition as the cause of heroic adventure: The case of al-Sawr. — As for running risks in case the adventure is proper, that is not due to loss of interest in life but to the fact that when a man becomes known as an audacious person and is ticketed with the label of courage and that man takes part in a combat, then his ambition requires him to do something noteworthy, above the capacity of others. His soul at the beginning feels so afraid of death and of running the risk that it almost wins over him and checks him from what he desires to accomplish, until he forces it and makes it undertake what it is loath to do. Then he feels a shudder all over his body and undergoes a change in color. But the moment he gets into the actual combat his fear disappears and his emotion subsides.

I took part in the siege of the Castle of al-Sawr [27] with the Malik-al-Umarā' Atābek Zanki (may Allah's mercy rest upon his soul!), of whom I have already made frequent mention. The castle belonged to al-Amīr Fakhr-al-Dīn Qara-Arslān ibn-Dāwūd ibn-Suqmān ibn-Urtuq (may Allah's mercy rest upon his soul!) and was fully manned with arbalesters. Zanki undertook this siege after his defeat [28] at Āmid.

As soon as the tents were pitched, Zanki dispatched one of his men, who yelled right under the castle, "O ye arbalesters, the atābek says to you: 'By the grace of the sultan,[29] in case one of my men is killed by your arrows, I shall verily cut off your hands'" The atābek set against the castle the mangonels, which destroyed a part of it. But the part destroyed was hardly enough to enable us to send our men up through it. One of the bodyguard of the atābek, however, an Aleppine named ibn-al-'Arīq, climbed through that breach and applied [95] his sword to the men there, who, after inflicting several wounds on him, threw him down from the town to the moat. By that time our men at the breach had become too numerous for the defenders to resist, and they took possession of the fortress. The atābek's representatives thereupon went up to the castle and received its keys, which were dispatched to Ḥusām-

[27] In Diyār-Bakr. Yāqūt, *op cit*, vol III, p 435.
[28] In the year 528 = November 1, 1133–October 21, 1134 Al-Dhahabi, *Ta'rīkh al-Islām*, appended to Derenbourg, *Vie d'Ousāma*, p 602, and *Duwal al-Islām* (Ḥayder-ābād, 1337 A H), vol II, p 34
[29] Mughīth-al-Dīn Maḥmūd, the Seljūq sultan of Iṣpahān.

al-Dīn Timurtāsh ibn-Īlghāzi ibn-Urtuq, to whom the atābek ceded the castle.

It happened that an arbalest arrow hit one of the troops from Khurāsān in his knee and cut in two the cap on the knee joint. The man fell instantly dead.

Immediately after taking possession of the castle, the atābek summoned the arbalesters, nine in number, who came with their bows strung around their shoulders. Zanki ordered that their thumbs be cut off from their wrists. Consequently, their hands became weak and useless.

As for ibn-al-'Arīq, he treated his wounds and recovered after having been on the point of death. He was a brave man who ran all kinds of risks.

The case of al-Bāri'ah. — I saw something like that when the atābek came to the siege of al-Bāri'ah [30] Castle. The castle was surrounded by solid rocks on which no tents could be pitched. The atābek therefore camped in the low plain below and intrusted the siege to the amīrs by turn. One day, when it was the turn of al-Amīr abu-Bakr al-Dubaysi, who was not fully equipped for the conflict, the atābek rode to the castle, halted there and said to abu-Bakr, "Advance and fight them" Abu-Bakr marched with his companions who were almost without arms, and the defenders of the castle made a sortie. One of abu-Bakr's men, named Mazyad,[31] who was until then not one of those known for fighting and valor, waged a terrible fight. He applied his sword on them and dispersed their masses, receiving many wounds. I saw him as they carried him back into the camp: he was on the point of breathing his last. Later, however, he recovered, and abu-Bakr al-Dubaysi made him an officer, bestowed on him a robe of honor and appointed him a member of his private bodyguard.

The ferocity of Ṣalāḥ-al-Dīn Muḥammad: He cuts one of his men in two. — The atābek used to say:

I have three retainers, one of whom fears Allah (exalted is he!) but does not fear me (meaning Zayn-al-Dīn 'Ali Kūjak [32] — may Allah's mercy rest upon his soul!), the second fears me but does not fear Allah (exalted is he!) (meaning Nāsir-al-Dīn Sunqur [33] — may Allah's mercy

[30] Or Bārīn, northwest of Ḥims [31] Possibly "Mazīd" or "Marthad."
[32] A minister of Qutb-al-Dīn Mawdūd, the son of Zanki in Mawṣil.
[33] One of Zanki's viziers

rest upon his soul!); and the third fears neither Allah nor me (meaning Ṣalāḥ-al-Dīn Muḥammad ibn-Ayyūb al-Ghisyāni — may Allah's mercy rest upon his soul!).

I have witnessed something which Ṣalāḥ-al-Dīn (may Allah pass by his excesses!) did and which corroborates the statement of the atābek. It is this. One day we marched against Ḥimṣ. The night before, so much rain had fallen that our horses could not move because of the thick layer of mud on the ground, while our infantry were already engaged in a skirmish. Ṣalāḥ-al-Dīn was standing still and I was with him, while we could both see the infantry right before our eyes. Presently, one of our footmen ran to the infantry of Ḥimṣ and joined them while Ṣalāḥ-al-Dīn was looking at him. Ṣalāḥ-al-Dīn thereupon said to one of his companions, "Fetch that man who was beside the one who deserted" The companion went and fetched him. Ṣalāḥ-al-Dīn asked, "Who was that man who fled away from thy side and entered Ḥimṣ?" The man replied, "By Allah, I know him not." Ṣalāḥ-al-Dīn ordered that he be chopped in two at the middle. I then said, "O my lord, [96] imprison him and investigate the case of the man who deserted. If this man knows or is related to him, then wouldst thou strike off his head. Otherwise, thou shalt treat him as thou seest fit." Ṣalāḥ-al-Dīn looked as though he had leaned in the direction of my counsel. But an attendant who stood behind him said, "When one deserts, the one next to him is seized and either his head is struck off, or he is chopped in two at the middle." This remark aroused the anger of Ṣalāḥ-al-Dīn, who ordered that the attendant himself be halved. Accordingly they bound him according to the usage in such cases and cut him in two at the middle — although he had committed no crime except that he was insistent and feared not the punishment of Allah (exalted is he!).

Another is halved. — I was also present at another affair of Ṣalāḥ-al-Dīn. That was after our return from the battle of Baghdād [34] when the atābek, anxious to show endurance and strength, had ordered Ṣalāḥ-al-Dīn to march against al-Amīr Qafjāq [35] and

---

[34] Evidently in the year 1133, for al-Dhahabi, *Ta'rīkh al-Islām*, loc cit, p. 602, mentions a battle between Zanki and Caliph al-Mustarshid in 527 = 1132-33.

[35] Qıfjāq or Qıbjāq was a Turkoman chief whom abu-al-Fıda, *Annales Muslemici*, vol III, p 482 *Ta'rikh* (Constantinople, 1286 A H), vol III, p 16, makes the son of Alp-Arslān-Shāh, and ibn-al-Athīr, *al-Kāmıl* (ed. Tornberg), vol. XI, p. 50, the son of Arslān-Tāsh.

take him unawares. Accordingly we marched from al-Mawṣil, a distance of six days, while we were extremely weak. When we got to the encampment of Qafjāq, we found that he had climbed the mountains of Kūhistān to an inaccessible spot. We then descended to a castle named Māsurra and encamped around it at sunrise. Presently a woman appeared on the castle and said, "Have ye calico?" We replied, "What a fine time is this for selling and buying!" She said, "We need the calico so that we may shroud you with it in your coffins. In five days at most ye'll all be dead." She meant by that that the place was infested with disease.[36]

Ṣalāḥ-al-Dīn dismounted and planned out an early attack on the castle. He ordered the sappers to penetrate under one of the towers, the castle being constructed wholly of clay and manned entirely with peasants. In the meantime we marched up the hill on which the castle stood. The troops from Khurāsān undermined the tower, which toppled over with two men on it. One of the two was killed, but the other was taken captive by our men, who brought him before Ṣalāḥ-al-Dīn. "Cut him in two at the middle," ordered Ṣalāḥ-al-Dīn "O my lord," I remarked, "we are in the month of Ramaḍān and this man is a Moslem whose killing constitutes a sin which we should not bear." "Cut him in two," said Ṣalāḥ-al-Dīn, "so that they may deliver the castle " I said, "O my lord, the castle thou shalt instantly possess." "Cut him in two," repeated Ṣalāh-al-Dīn and insisted on doing it quickly. Accordingly they cut him in two, and immediately we captured the castle.

He cuts the beard of an old man. — Ṣalāḥ-al-Dīn after that came to the door, desiring to leave the castle, accompanied by the crowd and the victors. He intrusted the castle to a band of his men and went down to his tent, where he stayed a moment — long enough to have the army that was with him dispersed. He then mounted and said to me, "Ride." So we rode up to the castle. There he took a seat and ordered brought before him the watchman of the castle that he might learn from him its contents. He also had brought before him the women and young men who were Christian and Jew.

[36] *wakhim*, literally "foul" or "dirty," but used by Arab writers to designate places infested with disease or pestilence, probably malaria in this case.

An aged Kurdish woman presented herself and said to the watchman, "Hast thou seen my son, so and so?" The watchman replied, "He was killed. An arrow hit him." She then said, "And my son, so and so?" The watchman replied, "The amīr has cut him in two." The woman shrieked and uncovered her head, the hair of which was like carded cotton. The watchman said to her, "Be still, because of the amīr" She replied, "And what thing is left which the amīr can do with me? I had two sons, both of whom he has killed." They pushed her away.

The watchman then went and produced a very aged sheikh, walking on two canes, whose white hair looked beautiful on him. The old man greeted Ṣalāḥ-al-Dīn, who inquired, "What is this sheikh?" The watchman replied, "He is the imām of the castle." Ṣalāḥ-al-Dīn said, "Come forward, O sheikh, come forward," until the man sat in front of him. Then he stretched out his hand, seized the beard of the old man, drew a knife which was fastened to the belt of his robe, and cut off the beard to the very chin He held it in his hand like the tail of a sea cow.[37] [97] The sheikh said to him, "O my lord, what thing have I done which made me deserve this treatment at thy hand?" Ṣalāḥ-al-Dīn replied, "Thou hast rebelled against the sultan"[38] "By Allah," said the old man, "I knew nothing about thy arrival until this very moment when the watchman told me and summoned me."

He takes captive people of the covenant. — After that we departed and encamped before another castle belonging to al-Amīr Qafjāq, called al-Karkhīni,[39] of which we took possession. There we found a closet full of calico clothes which had been prepared for use as alms for the poor of Mecca. Ṣalāḥ-al-Dīn took captive all the Christians and Jews in the castle, who were included among the people of the covenant, and pillaged all of the two castles as if they were Byzantines May Allah (worthy of admiration is he!) pass by his excesses!

I shall now stop at this point in this chapter, applying to the case a verse of my own composition:

[37] Ar *barjam* is Persian *parcham*, meaning "tail of the sea cow," which they hung around the necks of horses, and is not related to Ar *barājim*, pl of *burjumah*, meaning "knuckle of a finger"

[38] Mughīth-al-Dīn Maḥmūd

[39] Not far from Irbil Yāqūt, *op. cit*, vol IV, p. 257.

Stop now the account of those who were killed by passion; for
Their story among us makes the hair of the newborn turn white.

The Ismā'īlites in Shayzar. — I now return to the account of something which happened to us while the Ismā'īlites were in the Castle of Shayzar.

On that day,[40] a cousin of mine named abu-'Abdallāh ibn-Hāshim (may Allah's mercy rest upon his soul!) saw, as he was passing by, a Bātinite, armed with sword and shield, in a tower of the house of my uncle. The door was open. Outside stood a great crowd of people but none dared to go in. My cousin said to one of them standing outside, "Go in to him." And he went in. The Bāṭinite, losing no time, struck him and wounded him. So he came out wounded My cousin said to another, "Go in to him," and he went in. The Bāṭinite struck him and wounded him. So he came out as his predecessor had done. My cousin then said, "O Ra'īs [chief] Jawād, go in to him." The Bāṭinite said to my cousin, "O thou keeping behind, why dost thou not come in? Thou makest people come in to me while thou standest still! Come in and I'll show thee." The Ra'īs Jawād went in and killed him. This Jawād was a master of the duel. He himself was a man of valor and an expert in the use of the sword Only a few years after that, in the year 534,[41] I saw him in Damascus. He had become a dealer in fodder and was selling barley and hay He was old and looked like a worn-out water bag, too weak even to keep the mice away from his fodder — much less the men. I could not but feel surprised at the condition of his early days, as I considered his state in his later days and the changes which longevity wrought in his condition.

Reflections by Usāmah on old age. — Little did I realize at that time that the disease of senility is universal, infecting everyone whom death has neglected. But now that I have climbed to the summit of my ninetieth year, worn out by the succession of days and years, I have become myself like Jawād, the fodder dealer, and not like the generous man [*al-jawād*] who can dissipate his money. Feebleness has bent me down to the ground, and old age has made one part of my body enter through another, so much so

[40] About 1135. [41] August 28, 1139–August 16, 1140.

that I can now hardly recognize myself, and I continually bemoan my past. Here is what I have said in describing my own condition:

When I attained in life a high stage
For which I had always yearned, I wished for death.
Longevity has left me no energy
By which I could meet the vicissitudes of time when hostile to me.
[98] My strength has been rendered weakness, and my two confidants,
My sight and my hearing, have betrayed me, since I attained this height.
When I rise, I feel as if laden
With a mountain, and when I walk, as though I were bound with chains.
I creep with a cane in my hand which was wont
To carry in warfare a lance and a sword.
My nights I spend in my soft bed, unable to sleep
And wide awake as though I lay on solid rock.
Man is reversed[42] in life. the moment
He attains perfection and completion, then he reverts to the condition from which he started.

I also composed the following verses in Cairo, condemning a life of inaction and ease (and how quickly has life waned and passed by!):

Behold the vicissitudes of time, how they taught me new habits,
Since my hair turned gray, different from my former habits,
And in the changes of time is a lesson to learn by example —
And is there any state which the succession of days does not change?
I have always been the firebrand of battle: every time it abated
I lit it again with the spark struck by applying the sword to the heads of the enemy.
My whole ambition was to engage in combat with my rivals, whom I always took
For prey. They therefore were in constant trembling on account of me.
More terrible in warfare than nighttime, more impetuous in assault
Than a torrent, and more adventurous on the battlefield than destiny!
But now I have become like an idle maid who lies
On stuffed cushions behind screens and curtains.
I have almost become rotten from lying still so long, just as
The sword of Indian steel becomes rusty when kept long in its sheath.
After being dressed with coats of mail, I now dress in robes
Of Dabīqi[43] fabric. Woe unto me and unto the fabrics!

[42] *yunkas*, a Koranic word XXI 66, XXXVI · 68, here means, when man becomes old he goes back to his childhood state.

[43] See *supra*, p. 35, n. 25.

Luxury has never been my idea nor my desired goal;
Comfort is not my affair nor my business.
I would never consent to attain glory through ease,
Nor supreme rank, without breaking swords and lances.

There was a time in which I thought that the newness of life was never to be worn out and its strength was never to be rendered weak. I thought that when I should return to Syria I would find my days there as I knew them to be — with no change that time had wrought since my departure. But when I did return, the promises of my ambition proved false and my former thoughts turned out to be a bright mirage.

O Allah, forgive me for this digression! I have inserted, in my account above, a parenthetical statement. It was a sigh of anguish which gave me relief in the utterance.

And now I return to a discussion of what is more important, without deviating again into paths in the dark night.[44]

The duration of life is predetermined: The case of a Shayzar man cut by an Ismā'īlite. — If hearts could be purified from the evil of sins, and intrusted to him who knows unseen things, then men would realize that to be exposed to dangers of wars does not diminish the period of life inscribed beforehand.

On the day on which we were engaged in combat with the Ismā'īlites in the Castle of Shayzar, I witnessed an object lesson which makes it clear to the intelligent brave man, as well as to the ignorant coward, that the duration of the life of a man is fixed and predetermined, that its end can neither be advanced nor retarded. This is how it happened.

After we were done with fighting that day, a man yelled from the other side of the castle: "The enemies!" I had with me [99] a band of comrades all equipped with their weapons. So we hastened to the man who yelled and asked him, "What is the matter with thee?" He replied, "The noise of the enemy is right here." We went together to a vacant, dark stable and on entering therein we found two armed men, whom we immediately put to death. We found there also one of our men lying dead upon something. Lifting

[44] In the original Arabic these reflections on old age, exclusive of the verse, are rhymed prose in which there is no metrical form but a recurrent rhyme It is difficult to do justice to them in a translation In them the author, Usāmah, deviates from the simple, unaffected style he followed throughout the book.

the body we found under it a Bāṭinite who, wrapped up in a shroud, lay flat and held the corpse on his chest. We carried away our man and put to death the one who was under him. We placed the body of our comrade, all covered with deep wounds, in an adjacent mosque. We never doubted that he was dead; he neither moved nor breathed. I, myself, by Allah, pushed his head on the paved floor of the mosque with my foot, for we never doubted that he was dead.[45] The poor fellow was passing by that stable when he heard a noise. As he stuck his head in to find out whence it came, one of the Bāṭinites dragged him inside, and they stabbed him with their knives until they took him for dead But Allah (worthy of admiration is he!) decreed differently. The wounds in his neck and over his body were stitched and he recovered. He regained his normal health as he was before. Blessed therefore be Allah who fixes destinies and determines the lengths of ages!

Another survives a deep gash in his face. — I was an eyewitness to something else similar to that. It was at the time the Franks (may Allah's curse be upon them!) made a raid against us in the last third of the night. We mounted our horses, intent upon their pursuit. But my uncle, 'Izz-al-Dīn (may Allah's mercy rest upon his soul!), forbade us, saying, "This is a ruse." Some of our infantry, however, left the upper town, pursuing them without our knowledge. On their way back, the Franks fell upon them and killed them, with the exception of a few who escaped.

The second morning, as I was standing in Bandar-Qanīn, a village near Shayzar, I saw three persons advancing, two of whom looked like human beings, but the middle man had a face different from the faces of human beings. When they came near us, behold! the middle man had had his face struck by the sword of a Frank in the middle of his nose and cut as far back as the ears. One half of his face was so loose that it hung over his chest. Between the two halves was an opening almost the width of a span. With all that, he was walking between two men. In this condition he entered Shayzar. The surgeon sewed his face and treated it. The sides of the cut stuck together, the man recovered and returned to his previous condition and finally died a natural death on his own bed. He used to deal in beasts of burden and was nicknamed

[45] This last phrase may have been repeated through a copyist's mistake

ibn-Ghāzi al-Mashṭūb. His nickname al-Mashṭūb [the gashed one] he acquired as a result of that cut.

The burden of old age. — Let no one therefore assume for a moment that the hour of death is advanced by exposing one's self to danger, or retarded by over-cautiousness. In the fact that I have myself survived is an object lesson,[46] for how many terrors have I braved, and how many horrors and dangers have I risked! How many horsemen have I faced, and how many lions have I killed! How many sword cuts and lance thrusts have I received! How many wounds with darts [100] and arbalest stones have been inflicted on me! All this while I was with regard to death in an impregnable fortress until I have now attained the completion of my ninetieth year And now I view health and existence in the same light as the Prophet (may Allah's blessing and peace rest upon him!) when he said, "Health sufficeth as a malady." In fact, my survival from all those horrors has resulted for me in something even more arduous than fighting and killing. To me, death at the head of an army would have been easier than the troubles of later life For my life has been so prolonged that the revolving days have taken from me all the objects of pleasure. The turbidity of misery has marred the clearness of happy living. I am in the position described in my own words as follows:

When, at eighty, time plays havoc with my power of endurance,
I am chagrined at the feebleness of my foot and the trembling of my hand.
While I write, my writing looks crooked,
Like the writing of one whose hands have shivers and tremors.
What a surprise it is that my hand be too feeble to carry a pen,
After it had been strong enough to break a lance in a lion's breast.
And when I walk, cane in hand, I feel heaviness
In my foot as though I were trudging through mud on a plain.
Say, therefore, to him who seeks prolonged existence:
Behold the consequences of long life and agedness.[47]

My energy has subsided and weakened, the joy of living has come to an end. Long life has reversed me: all light starts from darkness and reverts to darkness. I have become as I said:

[46] *mu'tabar* from the same stem as *i'tibār*, the word which occurs in the title of the book.
[47] Cf. *al-Rawḍatayn*, vol. I, p. 114.

Destiny seems to have forgotten me, so that now I am like
An exhausted camel left by the caravan in the desert.
My eighty years have left no energy in me.
When I want to rise up, I feel as though I had a broken leg.
I recite my prayer sitting; for kneeling,
If I attempt it, is difficult.
This condition has forewarned me that
The time of my departure on the long journey has drawn nigh.[48]

Enfeebled by years, I have been rendered incapable of performing service for the sultans. So I no more frequent their doors and no longer depend upon them for my livelihood. I have resigned from their service and have returned to them such favors as they had rendered, for I realize that the feebleness of old age cannot stand the exacting duties of service, and the merchandise of the very old man cannot be sold to an amīr. I have now confined myself to my own house, therefore, taking obscurity for my motto.

A eulogy of Saladin.[49] — My soul was once satisfied by isolation in strange lands and by leaving home and country until quieted down . . .[50] I have exercised the patience of a captive with his chains, and of a thirsty man held back from the water . . . our lord al-Malik al-Nāṣir Ṣalāḥ-al-Dunya w-al-Dīn,[51] the sultan [101] of Islam and the Moslems, the unifier of the creed of faith, the vanquisher of the worshipers of the cross, the raiser of the banner of justice and benevolence, the resuscitator of the dynasty of the commander of the believers,[52] abu-al-Muẓaffar Yūsuf ibn-Ayyūb. May Allah embellish Islam and the Moslems by his long existence, and give them victory through his sharp swords and counsels, and spread wide around them his protecting shadow, just as he [Allah] has rendered pure to them the sources of his [Saladin's] benefaction! May Allah render effective throughout the whole

[48] These verses are quoted by 'Imād-al-Dīn, *Kharīdah al-Qaṣr* (ed Derenbourg), p 142.

[49] The style of this eulogy stands in conspicuous contrast to the style of the narrative in the book It is rhymed prose, marked with affectation, and is not easy to render into English.

[50] About four words in the manuscript are effaced here and four others in the following sentence.

[51] The famous Saladin. The reference is probably to the summons which Usāmah received from Saladin in 1174 Usāmah, after the death of his patron Fakhr-al-Dīn Qara-Arslān (1167), remained in Ḥiṣn-Kayfa at Diyār-Bakr and was treated with indifference by the son and successor of his patron, Nūr-al-Dīn Muḥammad

[52] This is an allusion to the destruction of the Fāṭimite caliphate in Egypt by Saladin and the recognition of the 'Abbāsid Caliph al-Mustaḍī' in Baghdād.

world his high orders and prohibitions and set up his swords in power over the necks of his enemies! For his mercy has searched for me throughout the land, as I was beyond the mountains and plains in a lost corner of the world,[53] having no possessions and no family.

Suddenly he extricated me from the very teeth of calamities through his good will, transported me to his Sublime Porte[54] through his abundant benevolence, set right all that time had inflicted upon me, and through his generosity put me in commission after I had been considered of no use by all on account of my old age. He surrounded me with his astonishing favors, and made me, through his benefaction, the object of the most pleasing gifts, so much so that by his overflowing generosity he has paid me back what I had loaned in terms of service to others[55] before him. He counts those services and takes them into consideration as though he had witnessed them himself. His gifts knock at my door while I am sleeping, and make their way unto me while I am retired without employment. Every day his munificence to me is on the increase. He honors me the same way as he honors a member of his family, though I be one of his humblest slaves. His good opinion of me has made me safe from all calamities, and his munificence has made up for me what time has deprived me of through its horrible disasters. The lightest supererogatory gifts he bestowed on me, after having bestowed all which duty and law require, were indeed heavier than any shoulders could carry His generosity left no desire in me which I wish to fulfill. I, therefore, spend my life, its day and its night, praying for him.

He is the mercy by which Allah has brought relief to the people and by the blessings of which he has renovated the whole land; the sultan who resuscitated the tradition of the orthodox caliphs,[56] and reinstalled the pillar of the state and of the faith, the source whose water is not exhausted by the great number of drinkers; the bountiful one whose bounty does not cease, no matter how numerous are the recipients.

May our nation remain as it is, in an impregnable defense, thanks to his swords; and in a flourishing spring season, thanks to

[53] In Ḥiṣn-Kayfa [54] In Damascus
[55] Particularly Nūr-al-Dīn Muḥammad of Ḥiṣn-Kayfa
[56] The four immediate successors of the Prophet.

his liberality; and in an illumination that disperses the darkness of oppression and withholds the stretched arm of the violent transgressor, thanks to his justice; and in a thick shadow of protection, thanks to his victorious government; and in an uninterrupted state of felicity in which one fresh bliss follows in the steps of an old bliss, as long as night and day succeed each other, and the celestial globe rotates!

> I prayed, and the two guardian angels[57] said, "Amen";
> And the one on the throne[58] is nigh unto him who calls him.
> The praiseworthy himself has said to his worshipers,
> "Invoke me, for I am the hearing, the answering one "[59]

And praise be to Allah, the lord of the worlds! May Allah's blessing be upon our lord Muhammad and upon all the members of his family. Allah is sufficient unto us, and he is the best of guardians[60]

[57] Koran VI 61, LXXXII 10 [58] Allah [59] Cf. Koran XI 64

[60] Koran III 167 These last pious phrases are probably glosses from the copyist This whole passage in praise of Saladin, in which the writer states that the sultan by his munificence has left no desire unfulfilled, is in marked and rather amusing contrast with his complaints on old age just preceding.

SECTION II

RARE ANECDOTES

SECTION II

RARE ANECDOTES

[102] "And whatsoever good fortune is yours, it is assuredly from Allah." [1]

CHAPTER [2]

Said Usāmah ibn-Murshid ibn-'Ali ibn-Muqallad ibn-Nasr ibn-Munqidh (may Allah forgive him his sins as well as the sins of his two parents and all Moslems)

Here are rare anecdotes in some of which I figured myself, the others having been related to me by people in whom I trust. These anecdotes I have added as a supplement to this book because they do not form a part of what I intended to treat in the preceding pages.

[1] Koran XVI 55 This pious phrase is probably a gloss from the copyist.
[2] This is the only heading in the manuscript. No number follows it.

1. STORIES OF HOLY MEN

Al-Baṣri's clairvoyance. — I shall put first among the anecdotes, stories of the holy men — may Allah bestow on all of them his favor!

It was related to me by the Sheikh al-Imām al-Khaṭīb [the preacher] Sirāj-al-Dīn abu-Ṭāhir Ibrāhīm ibn-al-Ḥusayn ibn-Ibrāhīm, the preacher of the City of Is'ird,[3] when I was in that city, in dhu-al-Qa'dah, year 562,[4] on the authority of abu-al-Faraj al-Baghdādi,[5] who said.

I once attended in Baghdād a meeting conducted by the Sheikh al-Imām abu-'Abdallāh Muhammad al-Baṣri, when a woman came in. The woman said to him, "O my master, thou wert one of the witnesses in the certificate of my marriage. I have now lost the certificate specifying my dowry. I ask thee to favor me by coming to the tribunal and testifying in my favor." The sheikh replied, "I shall not do so unless thou bringest me first some sweets." The woman hesitated, believing that he was joking. But he repeated, "Let not matters drag. I shall not go with thee unless thou bringest me first some sweets." Accordingly, she went out and then returned pulling out from her pocket underneath her wrapper [*izār*] a piece of paper in which were wrapped some dry sweets The friends of the old man were all amazed at his request for sweets, with all his asceticism and abstinence. But he took the paper and opened it, throwing away the sweets, one piece after the other, until the paper was empty. Then he examined the paper, and lo! it was itself the dowry certificate of the woman which she had lost. Then he said to her, "Take thy certificate. Here it is!" Those who were present deemed the affair extraordinary but he remarked, "Subsist only on what is lawful[6] and then ye can do the same, if not more."

A man in Kūfah hears a voice from Ḥamāh. — The following was related to me by the Sheikh abu-al-Qasam al-Khiḍr ibn-Muslim ibn-Qāsim[7] al-Ḥamawi when I was in Ḥamāh, on Monday, the

[3] In the region of Diyār-Bakr. "Is'irt" in Yāqūt, *op. cit.*, vol. II, pp. 341, 380, etc.

[4] August 19–September 17, 1167

[5] Jamāl-al-Dīn abu-al-Faraj 'Abd-al-Raḥmān ibn-al-Jawzi, the well-known historical writer who died in Baghdād in 1201 A.D. Ibn-Khallikān, *Ta'rīkh*, vol. I, pp. 500–501 = *Biographical Dictionary*, vol. II, pp 96–98

[6] Koran II 163, V 90, VIII · 70

[7] "Qusaym" below.

last day of dhu-al-Ḥijjah, in the year 570.[8] He said, "There came to me once a descendant of the Prophet [*sharīf*] who lived in al-Kūfah and who related to us the following anecdote on the authority of his father, who said:

I used to visit the Qādi-al-Qudāh [the chief judge] al-Shāmi al-Hamawi [the Syrian from Hamāh], who always received me with special honor and respect. One day he said to me, "I like the people of al-Kūfah because of one man among them When I was young I was in Hamāh at the time of the death of 'Abdallāh ibn-Maymūn al-Hamawi (may Allah's mercy rest upon his soul!) When they asked him to make his will, he replied, 'When I die and ye are done with preparing my body for interment, take me to the desert and let one of you climb the hill overlooking the cemetery and call out: "O 'Abdallāh ibn-al-Qubays! 'Abdallāh ibn-Maymūn is dead. Come and pray over him"' When ibn-Maymūn died, they executed his will All of a sudden there appeared a man dressed in a robe of calico and a mantle of wool, coming from the direction from which the announcement had been made He came and prayed over the dead body while everyone stood dumfounded, without addressing a word to him The prayer over, he returned in the same direction from which he had come The people present began then to blame each other for not holding him and questioning him They ran [103] after him, but he escaped them without saying a word to them."

The wish of a dying sheikh granted. — I witnessed an analogous experience in Ḥiṣn-Kayfa.

There was in the mosque of al-Khidr [9] a man known by the name of Muḥammad al-Sammā' [al-Shammā'?] who occupied a cell [10] by the side of the mosque. He would go out to the mosque at the time of the community prayer, pray with the people and return to his cell He was a saint. His hour of death approached when he was near my home, and he said, "I wish from Allah (exalted is he!) that he would bring me my sheikh, Muhammad al-Busti!" No sooner had the preparations for his washing and shrouding been made than his sheikh, Muḥammad al-Busti, was at his side. He presided over the washing of the body and walked behind it, leading the funeral procession and praying over it.

With that done, al-Busti retired to the cell of al-Sammā', where

[8] August 1, 1174.

[9] Or al-Khaḍir = "the green man," a Moslem saint supposed to be everliving, whose story in the Koran, XVIII 59–81, may be traced back to three main sources the Gilgamesh epic, the Alexander romance and the Jewish legends of Elijah

[10] *zāwiyah*, used for the domicile of a ṣūfi, and corresponding to a Christian monastery.

he sojourned for a short time, during which he and I exchanged a number of visits. This sheikh (may Allah have mercy upon his soul!) was a learned ascetic, the like of whom I have never seen nor heard of. He would fast daily, drink no water, eat no bread and no kind of cereals. His fast he would break with two pomegranates or a bunch of grapes or two apples. Once or twice a month he would eat a few mouthfuls of fried meat. One day I asked him, "O Sheikh abu-'Abdallāh, how couldst thou get to the point where thou eatest no bread and drinkest no water while thou art always fasting?" He replied:

I first fasted and suffered from hunger But I found that I could stand the suffering. I then suffered hunger for three days, saying to myself, "I will let my food be dead animals,[11] which are allowed only in case of necessity after three days of fasting." I found myself able to stand that. Then I gave up regular eating and drinking. Now my system is accustomed to it and does not resist its practice. Since then I have continued to do it.

A notable of Ḥiṣn-Kayfa built for the sheikh a cell in a garden, which he put at his disposal. The sheikh called on me the first day of Ramaḍān and said, "I have come to bid thee farewell" "And how about the cell which has been prepared for thee with the garden?" I asked. "O my brother," he replied, "I have no use for them. I shall not stay." He then bade me farewell and departed — may Allah's mercy rest upon his soul! That was in the year 570.[12]

A man at Ma'arrah is conscious of the death of one at Mecca. — It was related to me by the Sheikh abu-al-Qasam al-Khiḍr ibn-Muslim ibn-Qusaym[13] al-Ḥamawi, in Ḥamāh, in the aforementioned year,[14] that a man who was one day working in the garden of Muḥammad ibn-Mis'ar (may Allah's mercy rest upon his soul!) came to the family of the latter while they were sitting at the doors of their homes at al-Ma'arrah and said to them, "I have this very moment heard something astonishing." They asked, "What is it?" He replied:

A man passed by me carrying a jar, in which he asked me to put water. I did so and he went through his ablutions. I offered him two

[11] Koran II . 168.
[12] August 1, 1174–July 21, 1175.
[13] "Qāsim" above.
[14] 570 A.H. = 1174–75.

cucumbers, but he refused to take them. So I said to him, "This garden is owned one half by me by the right of my labor in it, and the other half by Muhammad ibn-Mis'ar by the right of proprietorship." "Did Muhammad go on the holy pilgrimage?" asked the passer-by. "Yes," said I. "Yesterday," said he, "after we had made the station,[15] he died and we prayed for him."

The relatives of Muḥammad ran after the strange man to interrogate him, but they saw that he was so far away that they could not overtake him. So they returned home and recorded the conversation with the dates. Matters turned out just as he had said.

Dreams come true: 'Ali removes a tumor from a custodian of one of his mosques. — The most glorious Shihāb-al-Dīn abu-al-Fath al-Muẓaffar ibn-As'ad ibn-Mas'ūd ibn-Bakhtakīn ibn-Sabuktakīn (Sabuktakīn was formerly a freedman of Mu'izz-al-Dawlah ibn-Buwayh) related to me in al-Mawṣil, on the eighteenth of Ramaḍān, 565,[16] the following account [104] in these words.

The Commander of the Believers al-Muqtafi li-Amr-Allāh[17] (may Allah have mercy upon his soul!) visited the mosque [*masjid*] of Sandūdiya[18] in the environs of al-Anbār on the western Euphrates, accompanied by his vizier. I was present at the time. The caliph entered the mosque known by the name of the Commander of the Believers 'Ali (may Allah's favor rest upon him!), dressed in a Dimyāti[19] robe and girded with a sword with an iron handle. No one could tell that he was the commander of the believers unless he knew him personally. The custodian of the mosque began to invoke Allah's blessings upon the vizier, who said to him, "Woe to thee! Invoke blessings on the commander of the believers." Hearing that, al-Muqtafi (may Allah's mercy rest upon his soul!) said to the vizier, "Ask him something useful Find out from him what became of the malady in his face, for I have seen him in the days of our lord al-Mustazhir[20] (may Allah's mercy rest upon his soul!) with a malady in his face. His face was almost all covered with a tumor such that when he wanted to eat he used to cover it with a handkerchief in order to enable the food to get to his mouth" To this the custodian replied, "I used, as is well known, to frequent this mosque from my home in al-Anbār. One day a man met me and said, 'If thou wert to frequent so and so (meaning the governor of al-Anbār) as thou frequentest that mosque, he would certainly have

15 *al-waqfah* = the halting of Moslem pilgrims at Mt 'Arafāt for prayer.
16 June 5, 1170
17 "bi-Amr-Allāh" in the manuscript 'Abbāsid caliph, d 1160 A D
18 This town is mentioned by Arab geographers under the form "Ṣandawdā'."
19 Fabricated in Dimyāṭ See *supra*, p. 35, n. 26.
20 'Abbāsid caliph, d. in 1118 A.D.

summoned a physician to remove this malady from thy face.' I felt something in my heart as a result of these words, which made me greatly depressed. That night as I was sleeping I saw the Commander of the Believers 'Ali ibn-abi-Tālib (may Allah's favor rest upon him!) in the mosque. He said to me, 'What is this building material?' (referring to some building material on the floor of the mosque). I took advantage of the opportunity and complained to him about the cause of my distress. He turned away from me. I once more approached him and reported to him the remark which that man had passed on me. His reply was, 'Thou art one of those who seek the satisfaction of this world.'[21] Then I awoke. The tumor was cast to my side and all the ailment was gone."

Hearing that story, al-Muqtafi (may Allah's mercy rest upon his soul!) remarked, "He told the truth." Then he said to me,[22] "Talk to him and find out what he wants. Draw up a document to that effect and let me have it to sign." Accordingly I talked to him, and he said, "I am the head of a family of many daughters. I want every month three dīnārs." This I recorded in a statement, at the top of which the servant wrote, "the custodian of Masjid [mosque] 'Ali." The caliph signed it, thus granting his request. He then said to me, "Go and register it in the bureau of stipends." I took it there without reading it over except for the words, "Let this be executed." The official procedure was to have the beneficiary of the ordinance receive a copy and to have the original document bearing the handwriting of the caliph taken away from him. When, therefore, the scribe opened it in order to make a copy he found written under the words, "the custodian of Masjid 'Ali": "Written by al-Muqtafi, the Commander of the Believers" (may Allah's blessing be upon him!). Had the custodian demanded more, al-Muqtafi would have sanctioned it for him.

The Prophet sends a poor man to Malik-Shāh. — The Qāḍi al-Imām Majd-al-Dīn abu-Sulaymān Dāwūd ibn-Muḥammad ibn-al-Ḥasan ibn-Khālid al-Khālidi (may Allah's mercy rest upon his soul!) related to me in a suburb of Ḥiṣn-Kayfa, on Thursday, the twenty-second of Rabī' I, of the year 566,[23] on the authority of those who had told him, the following:

An old man [*sheikh*] asked for an audience with the Khawāja Buzurk[24] (may Allah's mercy rest upon his soul!). When he was admitted, Buzurk saw that he was an old man, respectable and radiant-looking, and asked him, "Where is the sheikh from?" The latter

[21] Koran XVII 19
[22] The narrator, i.e., Shihāb-al-Dīn abu-al-Fatḥ al-Muẓaffar.
[23] December 3, 1170
[24] Or "Buzruk" from Persian *khwāja buzurg* = "prime minister," a title assumed by Niẓām-al-Mulk, the vizier of Malik-Shāh. In *Kitāb al-'Aṣa* in *Vie d'Ousāma* by Derenbourg, p. 504, Usāmah mentions "Khawāja Buzurk Niẓām-al-Dīn."

replied, "From a foreign land."[25] Buzurk asked, "Is there anything that thou needest?" He replied, "I am the messenger of the Messenger of Allah (may Allah's blessing and peace be upon him!) [105] to Malik-Shāh." Buzurk said, "What kind of talk is this?" The old man replied, "If thou dost present me before him, I shall deliver the message, otherwise I shall stay here until I meet him and deliver to him what I have." Khawāja Buzurk went in to the sultan and reported what the sheikh had said. The sultan ordered that he be admitted. When the sheikh was admitted, he offered the sultan a toothpick and a comb, saying, "I am the father of many girls but, being poor, am unable to provide them with the necessary trousseaux for their marriage I therefore pray Allah (exalted is he!) every night that he may provide me with the necessary means for securing their trousseaux. On Thursday night of such and such a month, I went to sleep praying for succor in their behalf. I saw in a dream the Messenger of Allah, who said to me, 'Is it thou who art praying Allah (exalted is he!) to grant him what is necessary for preparing trousseaux for his daughters?' I answered, 'Yes, O Messenger of Allah.' He said, 'Go to so and so (giving the name of 'Izz[26] Malik-Shāh, meaning the sultan) and tell him that the Messenger of Allah (may Allah's blessing and peace be upon him!) asks him to buy the necessary trousseaux for thy daughters.' I said, 'O Messenger of Allah, if he asks me for a sign, what shall I say to him?' He replied, 'Say to him that the sign is that he recites every night before sleep sūrah *tabāraka*.'"[27]

Hearing that, the sultan said, "This is a true sign, for none has ever known it but Allah (blessed and exalted is he!) My preceptor ordered me to read it every night at bedtime and I still do it." The sultan thereupon gave orders that the sheikh be given everything he demanded for securing the trousseaux of his daughters. Besides, he bestowed on him rich presents before dismissing him.

The Prophet sends a father of three daughters to the caliph's vizier.—The above story is similar to something I heard regarding abu-'Abdallāh Muhammad ibn-Fātik al-Muqri',[28] who said:

I was one day studying the Koran under abu-Bakr ibn-Mujāhid (may Allah's mercy rest upon his soul!) al-Muqri' in Baghdād when there came to him an old man wearing a worn-out turban with a green robe and torn clothes. Ibn-Mujāhid, who knew the old man, asked him, "What is the story of the little girl?" The old man replied, "O abu-Bakr, yesterday a third girl was born to me. The women of my house-

[25] *ghurbah*, which in the absence of diacritical marks may read *ghaznah* = "Ghaznah"

[26] Orthography ambiguous

[27] Sūrah LXVII, which begins with the word *tabāraka* = "blessed be."

[28] One whose profession is the teaching of the Koran.

hold asked me for a *dāniq*[29] with which to buy ghee butter [*samn*] and honey to rub her mouth with, but I did not have it. I therefore went to sleep worried and saw in my dream the Prophet (may Allah's blessing and peace be upon him!), who said to me, 'Grieve not and feel not sad. When the morning comes, go to 'Ali ibn-'Īsa the caliph's[30] vizier, salute him in my behalf and say to him, "The sign being that thou hast prayed for me[31] at my [the Prophet's] tomb four thousand times, pay me one hundred dīnārs in gold."'"

Hearing this, abu-Bakr ibn-Mujāhid said to me, "Abu-'Abdallāh, this is something of special value" Saying this, he interrupted the reading, seized the hand of the old man and conducted him to 'Ali ibn-'Īsa. Seeing with ibn-Mujāhid an old man whom he did not know, 'Ali ibn-'Īsa said, "Where didst thou get this man from?" Ibn-Mujāhid replied, "Let the vizier call him near and hear his words from him." The vizier called him near and said, "What is thy trouble, O sheikh?" The sheikh replied, "Abu-Bakr ibn-Mujāhid knows that I have two daughters, and yesterday a third daughter was born to me. The women of my household asked me for a *dāniq* with which to buy honey and ghee butter for rubbing her mouth, but I did not have it. I therefore went to sleep yesterday greatly worried. [106] I saw the Prophet (may Allah's blessing and peace be upon him!) in my sleep who said to me, 'Grieve not and feel not sad. When the morning comes, go to 'Ali ibn-'Īsa, salute him in my behalf and say to him, "The sign being that thou hast prayed for me at my tomb four thousand times, pay me one thousand dīnārs in gold."'"

Ibn-Mujāhid continued thus: "Tears flowed down from the eyes of 'Ali-ibn-'Īsa Then the latter said, 'Allah and his Messenger have said the truth, and so hast thou said the truth, O man For this is something about which none knew anything but Allah himself (exalted is he!) and his Messenger (may Allah's blessing and peace be upon him!). Attendant, fetch the bag!' The attendant brought the bag 'Ali put his hand in and took out of it one hundred dīnārs, saying, 'This is the hundred about which the Messenger of Allah (may Allah's blessing and peace be upon him!) spoke to thee. This is another hundred for the good news that thou hast announced to me. And here is a third hundred, a present from us to thee.' The old man went out from his presence with three hundred dīnārs in his sleeve."

A paralyzed man miraculously healed by 'Ali.—The following was related to me by al-Qā'id[32] al-Ḥājj [the pilgrim] abu-'Ali

[29] Or *dānaq*, one-sixth of a *dirham* or dīnār, is the Arabicized form of Persian *dānak* = "grain"

[30] The 'Abbāsid al-Muqtadir-Billāh, 908–32 A D

[31] That is, repeated the formula, "May Allah's blessing and peace be upon him!"

[32] One in command of one hundred soldiers, al-Ṭabari, *Ta'rīkh*, vol III, p 1799.

in the month of Ramaḍān, year 568[33] in Ḥiṣn-Kayfa. These are his words:

I was in al-Mawsil in the shop of Muhammad ibn-'Ali ibn-Muhammad ibn-Māmah when a brewer with huge body and thick legs passed by. Muhammad called him and said, "O 'Abd-'Ali,[34] I conjure thee by Allah, tell so and so thy story." The man said, "I am a dealer in *fuqqā'*[35] as thou seest. One Tuesday night I went to sleep whole and sound, but I awoke to find my body broken at the waist, unable to move. My legs dried up and became so thin that they were reduced to skin and bone. The way I walked after that was to creep backwards, for my legs would not follow me and had no mobility in them at all. Once I sat across the path of Zayn-al-Dīn 'Ali Kūjak (may Allah's mercy rest upon his soul!), and he ordered me carried to his house. I was carried there, and he called physicians and said to them, 'I want you to heal this man.' The physicians said, 'Yes, we will heal him, if it pleases Allah.' They then took a nail and, after heating it red hot, they cauterized my leg. But I felt nothing. So they said to Zayn-al-Dīn, 'We cannot cure this man; he is hopeless.' Zayn-al-Dīn then presented me with two dīnārs and a donkey. The donkey remained in my possession for about a month and died. Again I sat across the path of Zayn-al-Dīn, and he gave me another donkey. And it died too. He gave me a third donkey, which died also. I once more implored him for help, upon which he said to one of his companions, 'Take this man away and throw him in the ditch.' I said to Zayn-al-Dīn, 'By Allah, throw me on my hip, for I shall then feel nothing when I am thrown.' But he replied, 'I shall not throw thee except on thy head.' After I was taken out, a man sent by Zayn-al-Dīn (may Allah's mercy rest upon his soul!) came to me and took me back to him, for what he had said regarding throwing me was said as a joke. When I was admitted into his presence, he gave me four dīnārs and a donkey.

"Such was my condition until one night I saw in my dream as if a man stood by me and said, 'Arise.' I asked, 'Who art thou?' He replied, 'I am 'Ali ibn-abi-Tālib.' Accordingly I arose and awoke my wife, saying to her, 'May Allah have mercy on thee, I have had such and such a vision.' She replied, 'Why, thou art already on thy feet!' So I walked on my feet, my ailment gone, and returned to the condition in which thou seest me.

"I then went to Zayn-al-Dīn al-Amīr 'Ali Kūjak (may Allah's mercy rest upon his soul!) and related to him the story of my dream. He saw [107] that the ailment which was in me had gone and gave me ten dīnārs."

33 April 16–May 15, 1173

34 "Servant of 'Ali" The man must have been a Shī'ite

35 A beer-like drink, so called because of the bubbles, *faqāqī'*, on its surface.

Worthy of admiration is the Healer, the Restorer to health!

Prayer answered: A reward for honesty. — The following story was related to me by al-Sheikh al-Ḥāfiẓ[36] abu-al-Khaṭṭāb 'Umar ibn-Muḥammad ibn-'Abdallāh ibn-Ma'mar al-'Ulaymi, in Damascus in the early part of the year 572,[37] on the authority of a man who told it to him in Baghdād on the authority of al-Qāḍi abu-Bakr Muḥammad ibn-'Abd-al-Bāqi ibn-Muḥammad al-Anṣāri al-Furḍi, surnamed Qāḍi-al-Māristān [the judge of the hospital], who said:

In the course of my pilgrimage as I was making the tour of the Ka'bah I found, all unexpectedly, a pearl necklace, which I tied to the end of my pilgrim's robe. An hour later, I heard a man seeking its recovery by making inquiries in the sanctuary [*haram*] and offering twenty dīnārs to him who would restore it I asked him for a sign proving that the lost article was his, and he gave it to me. So I delivered the necklace to him. Receiving it, he said to me, "Accompany me to my house so that I may pay thee the reward I had promised to pay." To this I replied, "I have no use for that reward, nor have I given the necklace back to thee for the sake of the prize. For, thanks to Allah, I live in great bounty." He asked, "Thou hast not then returned it except for the sake of Allah (mighty and majestic is he!)?" "Yes," I replied. "Let us, therefore, turn our faces," said he, "towards the Ka'bah and thou shouldst say 'Amen!' to my prayer." Accordingly, we turned our faces towards the Ka'bah and he prayed, "O Lord, forgive him [and me] our sins and grant me means to repay him!" Then he bade me farewell and departed.

It happened that later I undertook a journey from Mecca to the land of Egypt and took a boat to al-Maghrib [Mauretania]. Our boat fell into the hands of the Byzantines and I, among others, was taken captive. My lot fell to one of the priests, in whose service I remained until the hour of his death approached, upon which he willed that I be set free.

Consequently I left the land of the Byzantines and made my way into a certain region of al-Maghrib, where I was employed as a clerk in a baker's shop. Among the baker's customers was one of the great landowners of the town. At the beginning of the new month, a servant of that landowner came to the baker and said, "My master calls thee to make the account with him." The baker asked me to accompany him, and we went together to the landowner, who settled the account according to his bills. Impressed by my knowledge of arithmetic and my beautiful handwriting, he demanded me from the baker. The landowner changed my clothes and intrusted to me the collection of the

[36] One who knew the Koran by heart.

[37] This year began July 10, 1176.

levies from his estate, he being the proprietor of a vast piece of land. In the meantime, he vacated for me a special apartment on one side of his mansion.

After the lapse of a short period of time, he said to me, "Abu-Bakr, what thinkest thou of marriage?" I replied, "My master, I cannot stand the expense of my own living, how can I stand the expense of a wife?" He said, "I shall provide in thy behalf the dowry, the dwelling place, the clothing and everything else that thou needest." I said, "Thy order is done." Then he said, "My boy, here is a wife who has a great number of defects," and he did not leave a possible physical defect from her head to her foot which he did not enumerate, while I replied, "I am satisfied." In fact, I felt satisfied internally as I claimed I was externally. Then he continued, "That wife is my daughter " He called a group of people and the contract was closed

A few days later he said to me, "Prepare thyself to enter thy home " He ordered for me superb clothes, and I entered into a house luxuriously furnished [108] and equipped with the best outfit. I was placed on a high seat and the bride was brought covered with a colored woolen mantle. I immediately arose to meet her, and, pulling aside the cover, found a countenance prettier than which I never saw in this world. I fled out of the house. The old man met me and asked me about the reason for my flight, to which I replied, "This wife is not the one thou hast described to me as having the defects which thou hast enumerated." Hearing this, he smiled and said, "Yes, my boy, she is thy wife, and I have no other child but her. But I described her the way I did to thee so that thou mayest not be disappointed on seeing her." And the proper ceremony of unveiling the bride was conducted in my presence.[38]

The second morning, as I was admiring the jewels and precious gems she wore, I saw, among other things on her, the necklace which I once found in Mecca. I was amazed at that and was absorbed in the thought of it. As I was leaving the bedroom my father-in-law called me and asked me about my condition, repeating the verse, "Legitimate enjoyment has mutilated the nose of jealousy." [39] I thanked him for what he had done for me and then felt possessed with the thought of the necklace and how it got to him. Noticing that, he asked me, "What art thou thinking of?" I replied, "Of such and such a necklace. For in such and such a year I made a pilgrimage and found it itself in the sanctuary, or found some other necklace very similar to it." The man exclaimed, "Art thou the man who returned my lost necklace?" "Yes," said I, "I am he." He said, "Rejoice at the good news, for Allah has forgiven me and thee,

[38] *juliyat 'alayya.* This ceremony, still practiced in Syria as the climax of the wedding festival, consists of placing the bride, dressed in her bridal clothes and looking her best, at the head of a procession of maidens singing her charms and praising her beauty

[39] Meaning, I can now ask you without arousing jealousy, as she has become your legitimate wife.

for I, at that moment, prayed Allah (worthy of admiration is he!) to forgive me and thee our sins and to grant me means to repay thee. And here now I have delivered into thy hands my possessions and my child. And I have no doubt that my end is near at hand."

He later drew his will in my favor, and after a short period, he died — may Allah's mercy rest upon his soul!

2. NOTEWORTHY CURES

A carbuncle removed by supping a raw egg. — The Amīr Sayf-al-Dawlah Zanki ibn-Qarāja (may Allah have mercy upon his soul!) related to me the following story. He said:

Shāhanshāh invited us once in Aleppo (he was the husband of Zanki's sister), and as we met in his home, he sent word to a companion of ours, with whom we had often associated and drunk, and who was light-hearted and of delightful company, calling him to join us. So he did. We offered him a drink, but he said, "I am prohibited from its use. The physician has ordered me to diet for a few days until this carbuncle opens" There was on the back of his neck a large carbuncle. We replied, "Join us today and let prohibition begin tomorrow." So he did and drank with us until the end of the day. We then asked Shāhanshāh for something to eat and he said, "I have nothing." But we insisted so much that he agreed to bring us some eggs to fry on the brazier. The eggs were produced, together with a plate. We broke the eggs, turning the contents over into the plate. We placed the frying pan on the brazier, that it might become hot. I then beckoned to the man who had the carbuncle on his neck to sup the raw eggs. As he lifted the plate to his mouth in order to take in some of it, all its contents flowed down his throat. We then said to the master of the house, "Replace those eggs for us," but he replied, "By Allah, I shall not do it." So we drank together and then separated

At the dawn of the second morning, as I was still in bed, a knock was heard at the door. The maid went out to see who was at the door and lo! it was that same friend of ours So I said, [109] "Bring him in." He came in while I was still in bed and said, "O my lord, that carbuncle which was on my neck has disappeared, leaving no trace." I looked at the place where it was and found it like any other place on his neck. So I asked, "What was it that made it disappear?" He replied, "Allah (worthy of admiration is he!). For so far as I know I have never used anything which I did not use before, unless it be the supping of those raw eggs."

How mysterious are the deeds of the Almighty, who afflicts with disease and gives the cure!

Hernia cured by eating ravens. — We had with us in Shayzar two brothers, natives of Kafarṭāb, the name of the elder of whom was Muẓaffar and the younger Mālik ibn-'Ayyāḍ. In their capacity as traders they used to travel to Baghdād and other places. Muẓaffar was afflicted with a dreadful scrotal hernia, which made him feel always tired. As he was once in a caravan crossing al-Samāwah[1] to Baghdād, the caravan encamped with a clan of Arabs, who prepared and cooked birds for them as guests. After supper they went to sleep. Muẓaffar awoke in the nighttime, roused his comrade, who was sleeping by his side, and said to him, "Am I sleeping or awake?" The other replied, "Awake. If thou wert sleeping, thou wouldst not discourse." Muẓaffar said, "That hernia is all gone and has left no trace." His neighbor examined it and found that Muẓaffar had returned to normal health like any other man.

When they got up in the morning they asked the Arabs who were their hosts regarding the food they had given them for supper, to which the Arabs replied, "Ye encamped in our quarters at a time when our animals were in a distant pasturage. So we went out, seized young ravens [*ghirbān*] and cooked them for you."

On their arrival in Baghdād they went to the hospital and related the story to the director in charge. The director sent and procured young ravens and fed those suffering with the same disease on them, but the ravens did the patients no good and had no effect whatsoever on them. So the director said, "The father of the bird which Muẓaffar ate must have fed that bird on vipers. That is why it did him good."

Dropsy cured by vipers in vinegar. — A similar case is that of one who came to Yūḥanna ibn-Buṭlān,[2] the physician celebrated for his knowledge, science and leadership in the art of medicine, when the latter was in his shop in Aleppo, and complained to him about a disease which he had. The physician saw that he was suffering from chronic dropsy, his abdomen was inflated, his neck had become thin and his whole appearance changed. The physician said, "My boy, by Allah, there is nothing that I can do to help thee; and medicine can no more be of any avail to thee." The man departed.

[1] The Syrian desert.

[2] A Christian physician of Baghdād who also practiced in Aleppo and Antioch. His full name was abu-al-Ḥasan al-Mukhtār ibn-al-Ḥasan, and his biography was sketched by ibn-abi-Uṣaybi'ah, *Tabaqāt al-Aṭibbā'* (Cairo, 1882), vol. I, pp. 241–43, and al-Qifṭi, *Akhbār al-Ḥukamā'* (Cairo, 1326 A H), pp. 192–208.

After a while this same man passed by the physician's shop entirely cured from his disease, with his abdomen drawn back to its original position, and his condition satisfactory. Ibn-Buṭlān called him and said, "Art thou not the one who came to me some time ago suffering from dropsy, with an inflated abdomen and thin neck, and I told thee that there wasn't a thing I could do for thee?" "Certainly," replied the man. The physician asked, "With what didst thou then treat thyself that thy ailment has disappeared?" The man replied, "By Allah, I treated myself with nothing. I am a pauper, possessing nothing whatsoever. I have nobody to take care of me except my mother, an aged and feeble woman. She had in two small casks some vinegar on which she fed me every day with bread." Ibn-Buṭlān asked him, [110] "Is there anything left of that vinegar?" "Yes," he replied. The physician said, "Come with me and show me the cask in which the vinegar is kept." So he walked ahead of him to his house and showed him the cask of vinegar. On emptying the vinegar that was in it, ibn-Buṭlān discovered at the bottom of the cask two vipers which had become rotten. Then he said to the man, "My son, no one could have treated thee with vinegar having two vipers until thou wert healed but Allah — mighty and majestic is he!"

Marvelous cures by ibn-Buṭlān — This ibn-Buṭlān made marvelous cures in medicine. Here is an illustration:

There came to him in his shop in Aleppo a man who had lost the faculty of speech and whose words could hardly be understood when he tried to utter them. Ibn-Butlān asked him, "What is thy profession?" The man replied, "I am a sifter " The physician said, "Bring me half a rotl of sharp vinegar." The man did so. The physician said to him, "Drink it " So he drank it and took his seat for an instant, after which he felt nauseated and began to vomit clay in abundance, mixed with the vinegar which he had drunk. Consequently his throat became open again and his speech normal. Then, turning to his son and students, ibn-Buṭlān said to them, "Treat not with this medicine anybody, for ye may kill him. In this case a great quantity of dust from sifting had been deposited in the œsophagus and nothing could clean it out except the vinegar."

Ibn-Buṭlān was for some time attached to the service of my great-grandfather, abu-al-Mutawwaj Muqallad ibn-Naṣr ibn-Munqidh.[3] There appeared on my grandfather, abu-al-Ḥasan 'Ali ibn-Muqallad ibn-Naṣr ibn-Munqidh (may Allah's mercy rest upon his soul!), who was then still a young boy, some white spots which greatly disturbed his father for fear that the malady might be leprosy. So he summoned ibn-Buṭlān and said to him, "See what has appeared on the body of 'Ali." The physician looked it over and said, "I demand five hundred dīnārs to treat his malady and cause it to disappear." My grandfather said to him, "If thou hadst treated 'Ali, I would not have been satisfied with five hundred dīnārs for thee." Seeing that my grandfather was angry, ibn-Buṭlān said:

> I am thy servant and thy slave, living on thy benevolence I did not say what I said except jokingly. As for those things on 'Ali, they are nothing but skin eruptions caused by youth. As soon as he is fully adolescent, they will disappear. Worry not, therefore, about it, and listen not to someone else who might say that he would cure him and thereby make money from thee. All this will disappear with the maturity of the young man.

And things turned out just as he had said.

There lived in Aleppo a woman, one of the notable women of the city, named Barrah. She was afflicted with a bad cold in the head. She would wrap her head up with old cotton, a hood, a piece of velvet and some napkins until she looked as though she wore a huge turban on her head, and she would still appeal for relief against the cold. She called ibn-Butlān and complained to him about her malady. He said to her, "Procure for me early tomorrow fifty *mithqāls*[4] of camphor with a strong smell, which thou canst either borrow or rent from some perfumer with the understanding that it will be returned to him intact." She procured the camphor for him. In the morning, the physician removed all that she had on her head and stuffed her hair with the camphor. Then he put back the wraps she had on her head. All that while she was appealing for relief against the cold. After sleeping for a short time, she woke up [111] complaining of the heat and the tiresome weight on her head. The physician began to remove one piece at a time

[3] Ibn-al-Athīr, *al-Kāmil*, ed Tornberg, vol IX, p 343, mentions him under the name "al-Muqallad ibn-Munqidh al-Kinānī al-Kafarṭābī."

[4] One *mithqāl* = 1⅘ drams.

from her head until nothing was left but one veil. Then he shook off the camphor from her hair and all her cold disappeared. After that, she was contented with one veil for her head.

Usāmah's cold cured by Indian melon. — Something similar to that I myself experienced while in Shayzar. I felt great cold and had chills with no fever, although I wore heavy clothes and furs. Every time I stirred as I was sitting, I would shiver, my hair would stand on end and I would feel all my muscles contracting. I called al-Sheikh abu-al-Wafā' Tamīm, the physician, and complained to him about my case. He said, "Procure for me an Indian melon." When it was procured, he broke it up and said to me, "Eat whatever thou canst of it." I said, "O doctor, I am cold to death and the pomegranate [5] is cold. How can I therefore eat this cold thing?" He repeated, "Eat as I say to thee." I ate. And no sooner had I finished eating it than I began to perspire and the cold which I felt disappeared The physician then remarked, "What thou wert suffering from was due to over-biliousness, and not to real cold."

Colic cured by a dream. — I have given above some accounts of extraordinary dreams. In my book entitled *Kitāb al-Nawm w-al-Aḥlām* [book on sleep and dreams] I have also given various accounts of sleep and dreams, mentioned what other writers had to say regarding them, discussed the time of visions and the opinions of the learned relative to them, quoting appropriate verses from Arab poetry, and have gone into details fully covering the whole subject. It is not therefore necessary to mention anything of that here. But there is one anecdote mentioned there which especially interested me. I am therefore repeating it.

My grandfather, Sadīd-al-Mulk abu-al-Ḥasan 'Ali ibn-Muqallad ibn-Naṣr ibn-Munqidh (may Allah's mercy rest upon his soul!), had a maid named Lu'lu'ah, who brought up my father, Majd-al-Dīn abu-Salāmah Murshid ibn-'Ali (may Allah's mercy rest upon his soul!). When my father grew old enough, he left the home of his father, and the maid left with him. When I was born, that same old woman brought me up until I became old enough to marry and leave the home of my father (may Allah's mercy rest upon his soul!), and she left with me. When my children were born, she brought them up. She was (may Allah's mercy rest

[5] The Indian melon (*baṭṭīkh hindi*) looks like the pomegranate.

upon her soul!) one of the pious women, who spent her days fasting and her nights praying.

From time to time Lu'lu'ah suffered from colic. One day she had such a violent attack that she became unconscious and was given up for lost. For two days and two nights she remained in that condition; then she awoke and said, "There is no God but Allah! How marvelous is the state through which I have just passed! I met all our dead ones and they related to me extraordinary things. Among other things they said to me, 'This colic shall never again come back to thee.'" In fact, she lived after that for a long time and the colic never attacked her. She lived until she was almost a hundred years old, observing regularly her prayers — may Allah's mercy rest upon her soul!

I once went in to see her in an apartment which I had reserved for her use in my house and found in front of her a basin in which she was washing a napkin for use in prayer. I asked her, "What is this, mother?" She replied, "O my dear son, someone has handled this napkin with hands soiled with cheese, and the more I wash it the more it emits [112] the odor of cheese." I said to her, "Show me the soap with which thou art washing it." She pulled out the soap from the napkin and lo! it was a piece of cheese which she took for soap. And the more she rubbed that napkin with the cheese, the worse the smell became. I said to her, "O mother, this is a piece of cheese and not a cake of soap!" She looked at it and said, "Thou art right, my dear son. I never thought it was anything but soap."

Blessed be Allah the most truthful of sayers, who says: "Him whose days we lengthen, we reverse his exterior form." [6]

To go on relating such events at large results in boredom, for accidents and misfortunes are too numerous to be counted.

My supplication I submit to Allah (mighty and majestic is he!) for his protection and for continued health during the remaining days of life, and for mercy and favor at the hour of death. For he (worthy of praise is he!) is the most gracious of all who receive supplications, and the nearest of all those around whom hopes center.

Praise be to Allah alone, and may his benedictions and peace be upon our lord Muḥammad and upon his family!

[6] Koran XXXVI : 68.

SECTION III

USĀMAH'S HUNTING EXPERIENCES

SECTION III

USĀMAH'S HUNTING EXPERIENCES

[113] I put my trust in Allah (exalted is he!) [1]

To Allah belongs one phase of my life which I shall never neglect,
And to sports and leisure belongs the other phase.

I have in the above given those accounts of warfare, and those experiences I had in battles, fights and adventures which I could remember and which time with its rolling years did not make me forget. For my life has been prolonged, and I have for some time now been living in isolation and seclusion. Besides, oblivion is a heritage the antiquity of which goes back to our father Adam (peace be upon him!)

I shall now devote a chapter to what I have witnessed and partaken of in the field of hunting, be it the chase or falconry.

Some of these experiences I had in Shayzar when I was still in the early part of life, others I had in the company of the Malik-al-Umarā' Atābek Zanki ibn-Āqsunqur (may Allah's mercy rest upon his soul!), others I had in Damascus in the company of Shihāb-al-Dīn Mahmūd ibn-Tāj-al-Mulūk (may Allah's mercy rest upon his soul!); others I had in Egypt; others I had with al-Malik al-'Ādil Nūr-al-Dīn abu-al-Muẓaffar Mahmūd ibn-Atābek Zanki (may Allah's mercy rest upon his soul!), and still others I had in Diyār-Bakr with al-Amīr Fakhr-al-Dīn Qara-Arslān ibn-Dāwūd ibn-Urtuq (may Allah's mercy rest upon his soul!).

[1] This pious formula, Koran X . 72, is probably a gloss from the copyist.

1. HUNTING IN SYRIA, MESOPOTAMIA AND EGYPT

Usāmah's father as a hunter. — As for my hunting experiences in Shayzar, they were in the company of my father (may Allah's mercy rest upon his soul!) who was extremely fond of the chase, always talking about it and about collecting birds of prey, considering no amount of expense too great for the satisfaction of his curiosity in this sport. This was his only distraction, he had no other business but combat and holy war against the Franks, and copying the Book of Allah (mighty and majestic is he!) after having attended to the business of his friends. All this my father did while he (may Allah's mercy rest upon his soul!) observed a daily fast, and persevered in the recital of the Koran. To him the chase was in accordance with the following traditional saying: "Air ye your hearts so that they can better retain the word of Allah!" In fact, I never saw anything like his hunting and his ability to organize parties for it.

Hunting with Zanki. — I have witnessed hunting scenes of the Malik-al-Umarā' Atābek Zanki (may Allah's mercy rest upon his soul!). He possessed a great number of birds of prey. This was his method of procedure as we would be marching along the banks of the rivers. The falconers would proceed ahead of us with the falcons which would be flown at the waterfowl. The drums would be beaten in accordance with the prevailing custom. The falcons would catch whatever birds they could, and would miss the rest. The mountain [2] shahins would be on the wrists of the falconers behind. These are then loosed upon the waterfowl which had been missed by the falcons and which had now flown quite a distance and had perched on an elevated place. The shahins would follow and clutch them. The shahins are next loosed upon the partridges which they pursue and clutch as they climb up the slopes of the mountain. For shahins are characterized by marvelous swiftness in flight.

[2] *kūhiyyah,* from Persian *kūh* = "mountain." *Falco peregrinus peregrinator.* See W. T. Blanford, *The Fauna of British India* (London, 1895), vol. III, p. 415.

One day I accompanied the atābek to al-Maghraqah[3] in the environs of al-Mawṣil, where we had to walk across a field planted with eggplants. Ahead of the atābek walked a falconer carrying a sparrow hawk [*bāshiq*]. A male francolin started to fly. The falconer flew the sparrow hawk at the francolin, which it clutched, and then it descended. When they struck the ground, the francolin escaped from its talons and took the air again. As it soared high, the hawk[4] darted from the ground, seized it and descended holding it tight in its claws.

I have also seen the atābek [114] take part in chasing wild beasts on various occasions. As soon as the hunting party had drawn up in circular formation, with the beasts within, then nobody could get inside of the circle. And the moment a beast came out they would shoot their arrows at it. The atābek was himself one of the best archers. Whenever a gazelle came near he would shoot his arrow at it, the gazelle would appear to stumble, and would drop to the ground. It would then be slaughtered. It was his custom to send to me by one of his attendants the first gazelle brought down in every hunting expedition on which I accompanied him.

I was once with him when the circle was drawn in the region of Nasībīn [Nisibis] on the banks of al-Hirmās.[5] Our tents were pitched when the beasts came to them. The attendants attacked them with sticks and poles and struck down a large number of them. A wolf, caught in the circle, pounced upon a gazelle in the center of it and, having seized it, crouched down upon it, and was killed while in that position.

I was with the atābek in Sinjār when a horseman from among his companions came and said to him, "Here is a female hyena sleeping." The atābek started at our head to a neighboring valley, on one side of which the hyena lay on a rock. The atābek dismounted and advanced on foot until he stood opposite to it. He then struck it with his arrow so that it dropped to the bottom of the valley. The attendants descended and brought it dead before him.

I also saw the atābek in a suburb of Sinjār when a hare was

[3] A place so heavily irrigated that one would sink in it

[4] The author uses here *al-bāz* = "falcon" The sparrow hawk is the *Accipiter nisus*. See A. Newton, *A Dictionary of Birds* (London, 1893–96), p. 898.

[5] A tributary of the Khābūr, which empties into the Euphrates.

roused from its form. By his orders, the horsemen made a circuit around the hare. He then ordered an attendant carrying a lynx [*washaq*] behind him, after the manner in which a cheetah is carried, to come forward and send the lynx against the hare, which doubled back among the legs of the horses and escaped. Never before did I see a lynx used in the chase.

Hunting in Damascus. — In Damascus I took part, during the days of Shihāb-al-Dīn Maḥmūd ibn-Tāj-al-Mulūk, in the chase of birds, gazelles, wild asses and roes. One day I saw him as we went out together to the forest of Bāniyās, where the ground was thickly covered with grass. After killing a number of roe deer, we pitched our tents in the form of a circle and encamped. A roe deer which was sleeping in the grass now appeared in the midst of the enclosure. It was seized among the tents.

As we were returning, I saw a man who, noticing a squirrel in a tree, told Shihāb-al-Dīn about it. Shihāb-al-Dīn came, halted under it and shot at it two or three arrows, all of which missed. So he departed on his way somewhat vexed for having missed it. Then I saw a Turk come and shoot at it. The arrow cut it in the middle; its forelegs dangled inert; but it remained suspended by its hind legs, with the arrow nailing it to the tree, until the tree was shaken. Then it dropped. If that arrow had hit a human being, he would undoubtedly have been killed on the spot. But worthy of admiration is the Creator of all creatures!

Chase in Egypt. — I have also witnessed the chase in Egypt.[6] Al-Ḥāfiẓ li-Dīn-Allāh 'Abd-al-Majīd abu-al-Maymūn (may Allah's mercy rest upon his soul!) possessed a large number of birds of prey, including falcons, sakers and river [*baḥriyyah*] shahins. These birds were in charge of a master huntsman who used to take them out twice a week, most of them perching on the hands of falconers on foot. [115] I made it a point on their day of outing to mount my horse and enjoy the sight of them in action.

The master huntsman, noticing me, went to al-Ḥāfiẓ and said to him, "Thy guest, so and so, goes out regularly with us," seeking to find out his opinion in the matter. Al-Ḥāfiẓ replied, "Let him go out with thee and enjoy the sight of the birds."

One day as we went out together one of the falconers was carry-

[6] Between 1144 and 1154.

ing a red-eyed falcon which was intermewed.[7] We saw cranes. The master said to that falconer, "Go ahead. Hurl at them the red-eyed falcon." So he proceeded and hurled it. The cranes took the air. The falcon overtook one of them at some distance and brought it down. I said to one of my attendants on an excellent horse, "Gallop the horse towards the falcon, dismount and thrust the bill of the crane in the ground. Hold it thus and keep its legs under thine until we overtake thee." The man went and did as I commanded. When the falconer arrived, he slew the crane and fed the falcon to the point of satisfaction.[8]

When the master huntsman returned, he reported to al-Ḥāfiẓ what had happened and what I had said to my attendant, adding, "O my lord, he talks the way a true sportsman would talk." Al-Ḥāfiẓ replied, "And what other business has this man but to fight and to hunt?"

The falconers had sakers which they would loose upon herons[9] while on the wing. As soon as a heron sees a falcon, it circles upwards to a great height. The saker makes circles in another quarter of the sky until it has attained a higher pitch than the heron and then it swoops down upon it and clutches it.

In that country are birds called *al-bujj*,[10] similar to the flamingo,[11] which they also hunt. The waterfowl are easy to hunt at the fords of the Nile. The gazelle is rare in Egypt, but there live in that land the "cows of the children of Israel."[12] These are yellow cows whose horns are like those of the ordinary cow, but they are smaller in body than the latter and can run very fast.

The Nile brings forth to the people an animal called hippopotamus,[13] which resembles a small cow and has small eyes. Its skin, however, is hairless, like the skin of the buffalo. In its lower jaw it has long teeth. In its upper jaw it has holes through which the

[7] *muqarnaṣ bayt* Arab writers inform us that when a bird of prey began to shed its feathers its master would keep it in confinement where dust, smoke, wind and noise could not reach it, and would surround the place of confinement with willow leaves For "intermewed" and other technical terms used in hawking, see article on "Falconry" in *Encyclopædia of Sport* and in *Encyclopædia Britannica*.

[8] Cf Walter Scott, *The Betrothed* (Edinburgh, 1894), p 220

[9] *balshūb*, a variant of *balshūn* or *balshūm*, of Coptic origin

[10] An aquatic bird mentioned by Yāqūt, *op cit*, vol I, p 885

[11] *nuhām*, defined in the lexicons as a red bird that looks like the goose

[12] *baqarāt bani-isrā'īl* Cf Koran II 64–67 and al-Damīrī, *Ḥayāt al-Ḥayawān* (Cairo, 1313 A H), vol I, p. 134 = Jayakar's translation (London, 1906), vol. I, p. 329.

[13] *faras al-bahr* = the mare of the river.

roots of the teeth issue from underneath the eyes. It grunts like a hog, and cannot live except in a pool of water. Its food is bread, grass and barley.

Hunting in 'Akka. — When I went in the company of al-Amīr Mu'īn-al-Dīn [14] (may Allah's mercy rest upon his soul!) to 'Akka [Acre] to the king of the Franks, Fulk, son of Fulk, we saw a Genoese who had just landed from the country of the Franks. He brought with him a large molted falcon, which hunted cranes, and a young bitch. Whenever the falcon was flown at the cranes, the bitch would run right below the falcon, so that the moment the falcon clutched a crane and brought it down, the hound would grab the crane in its teeth, which could not then escape. That Genoese said to us, "In our country, if the falcon has thirteen feathers in its tail, it can hunt cranes." As we counted the feathers in that falcon's tail, they turned out to be exactly so.

Al-Amīr Mu'īn-al-Dīn (may Allah's mercy rest upon his soul!) asked the king to give him that falcon. The king took it with the bitch from the Genoese and gave them to al-Amīr Mu'īn-al-Dīn. I saw the falcon, which accompanied [116] us on the way, pounce on gazelles as though they were pieces of meat. After its arrival in Damascus, the falcon's life was brief; death overtook it before it had hunted.

Hunting in Ḥiṣn-Kayfa. — I have also taken part in the hunt at Ḥiṣn-Kayfa in the company of al-Amīr Fakhr-al-Dīn Qara-Arslān ibn-Dāwūd (may Allah's mercy rest upon his soul!). In that region partridges and sand grouse abound, and so do francolins. As for the waterfowl, they can be found on the banks of the river, [15] which is so wide that the falcon finds it difficult to get hold of them. Most of the quarry there consists of mountain goats, male and female. Hunters make nets for them which they spread in the valleys and into which they drive the female mountain goats [*arāwi*] until they are finally trapped. The female mountain goats abound in that region and are easy to hunt. The same thing is true of the hares.

The hunt with Nūr-al-Dīn. — I have likewise taken part in hunting expeditions with al-Malik al-'Ādil Nūr-al-Dīn (may Allah's mercy rest upon his soul!). I was in his company in the land of

[14] Mu'īn-al-Dīn Anar, about 1140.

[15] *al-shaṭṭ*, i.e., the Tigris.

Ḥamāh when our men started a hare. Nūr-al-Dīn shot a jagged arrow at it. The hare leaped, outstripped pursuit and escaped into its burrow. We all ran after it, and Nūr-al-Dīn stood watching for it. The Sharīf al-Sayyid [16] Bahā'-al-Dīn (may Allah's mercy rest upon his soul!) handed me its leg, which the arrow had cut off above the hamstring. The abdomen was cut open by a corner of the arrowhead, and the uterus had fallen out. Despite that, it beat us all running and entered its burrow. By Nūr-al-Dīn's order, one of his pages descended, took off his sandals and went in behind it, but could not reach it. I said to the man carrying the uterus, which had two leverets in it, "Cut it open and cover the young ones in soil." This he did, and the animals stirred about and lived.

It was also in my presence that Nūr-al-Dīn set a bitch on a fox near Qara-Ḥiṣār [17] in the region of Aleppo. Nūr-al-Dīn galloped behind the fox and I galloped with him. The bitch overtook the fox and seized it by the tail. Turning its head back, the fox bit the bitch on its nose. The bitch began to yelp, while Nūr-al-Dīn (may Allah's mercy rest upon his soul!) laughed. The fox then let go and dodged into its hole, escaping us entirely.

One day as we were riding together under the walls of the Castle of Aleppo [Qal'ah-Ḥalab] on the north side of the city, Nūr-al-Dīn was given a falcon. He thereupon said to Najm-al-Dīn abu-Ṭālib ibn-'Ali-Kurd [18] (may Allah's mercy rest upon his soul!), "Let so and so (meaning me) take this falcon and amuse himself with it." Najm-al-Dīn asked me to do so and I replied, "I do not know how." Nūr-al-Dīn remarked, "Ye are incessantly in the chase and ye know not how to train a falcon?" I said, "My lord, we never train falcons ourselves. We have falconers and attendants who train them and go before us using them for the chase." And I did not take the falcon.

[16] "The lord descended from the Prophet." [17] Yāqūt, *op cit*, vol IV, p 44.
[18] The son of 'Alam-al-Dīn 'Ali-Kurd, the lord of Ḥamāh mentioned above.

2. USĀMAH'S FATHER AS A HUNTER

I have taken such a great part in the hunting parties of these great personages that I have no time to do justice to it in detail. They had all facilities to get their game, being fully equipped with hunting outfits and other necessities. But I never saw a hunt comparable to that of my father (may Allah's mercy rest upon his soul!). I know not whether this was due to the fact that I was viewing him with the eye of love, as the poet has said:

> And whatever the beloved does is lovely,

or whether my opinion of him was based on reality. I shall at all events relate something concerning his hunting, leaving it to the reader to judge for himself.

My father (may Allah's mercy rest upon his soul!) employed all his time [117] reading the Koran, fasting and hunting during the day, and copying the Book of Allah (exalted is he!) at night. In all he transcribed forty-six complete copies in his own handwriting (may Allah's mercy rest upon his soul!), two complete copies of which were written in gold from beginning to end. He was wont to ride for the hunt one day and rest the next day and fast incessantly.

In Shayzar we had two hunting fields, one for partridges and hares, in the mountain to the south of the town; and another for waterfowl, francolins, hares and gazelles, on the bank of the river in the cane fields to the west of the town.

My father took special pains to dispatch men from among his followers to distant lands to buy falcons. He even sent messengers to Constantinople to secure falcons for him. His retainers brought back with them what they considered a sufficient number of pigeons to feed the falcons they had, but owing to the rough seas the voyage was prolonged until all provisions for the falcons were exhausted. They were then forced to feed the falcons on the meat of the fish, which so affected their wings that it made their feathers brittle and easy to break. Shayzar certainly possessed rare specimens of falcons when his emissaries returned!

There was at that time in the service of my father a falconer, named Ghanā'im, who was an expert in training and treating falcons. He imped the broken parts of the wings and used the birds for hunting. Some of them molted in his house. Most of the falcons Ghanā'im would order and buy from Wādi [valley]-ibn-al-Aḥmar, and would pay exorbitant prices for them. So he called together some of the inhabitants of the mountain[1] adjoining Shayzar, in the villages of Bashīla, Yasmālikh and Ḥillah-'Āra, and discussed with them the possibility of establishing in their villages stations for trapping falcons. He bestowed presents on them and gave them clothes. They built trapping stations and caught many falcons — some young, others molted and still others white hawks. These they brought to my father and said, "O our lord, we have given up our means of livelihood and our work of agriculture in thy service. It is our desire that thou buyest from us everything we catch and fix for us a price which we shall know and which will not be subject to bargaining." Accordingly, my father fixed the price of a young falcon at fifteen dīnārs, a young white hawk [*zurraq*] at half as much, a falcon that had already molted at ten dīnārs, and a white hawk which had molted at half as much.

Thus a new means opened up before the mountaineers for making money without much effort or fatigue. All that was necessary was to have a stone house built to the height of a man. It would then be covered with branches concealed under hay and grass, with an opening. The trapper would then secure a pigeon, perch it on a stick, binding its two legs tightly to the stick, and display the pigeon from an opening, as a lure. As he moves the stick up and down the pigeon flutters its wings. Seeing it, the falcon turns down and pounces on it to seize it. As soon as the hunter feels the falcon, he pulls the stick back to the opening, stretches out his hand and seizes the two legs of the falcon while it is still binding the pigeon. He would then bring it down and seel its eyes.[2] Early the next morning he would fetch it to us and receive its price. After two days he would return home.

[1] The Nusayriyyah mountain

[2] The same method of trapping hawks is still used in the Nuṣayriyyah mountain in Syria and is described by 'Īsa Iskandar al-Ma'lūf in *al-Āthār*, vol IX (Zaḥlah, Lebanon, 1927), p 477 Hawking is still practiced by al-Mū'i family in that region, al-Kīlāni and al-Nawwāb families in Baghdād and by others in Antioch and Cilicia. In Syria the sparrow hawk is almost exclusively used.

Consequently, the number of trappers multiplied, and the number of falcons increased so much that they were as thick as hens about our house. Some of them were good for hunting purposes, others would die on the perch on account of overcrowding.

The service of my father (may Allah's mercy rest upon his soul!) comprised falconers, saker trainers and masters of hounds. He taught some of his mamelukes how to breed falcons, and they became experts at it. He used [118] to go out to the chase, with us, his four children, accompanying him, and taking with us our attendants, our extra horses led by our side and our weapons. For we never felt secure on account of the Franks, whose territory was adjacent to ours. We would also take with us many falcons, as many as ten or more. My father would take along two saker men, two cheetah keepers and two masters of hounds. One of the last mentioned would have slugis [3] and the other braches [*zaghārī*].

On the day on which he would start for the mountain to hunt partridges, while he was en route towards the mountain but still at some distance from it, he would say to us, "Disperse. Every one of you who has not yet recited his task in the Koran will do it now." We, his children, knew the Koran by heart. We would then disperse and recite our tasks until we got to the hunting field. He would thereupon order someone to summon us and would question each one of us as to how much he had read. After listening to us, he would say, "I have myself recited a hundred texts" or some number near a hundred. My father (may Allah's mercy rest upon his soul!) could recite the Koran exactly as it was revealed.

When we got to the hunting field, he would order the attendants to disperse and some of them to join the falconers. In whatever direction the partridge took the air, there was sure to be in that spot a falcon ready to be flown at it. His accompanying mamelukes and comrades, forty mounted men in all, since they were the most experienced hunters, were sure to get any bird that rose or any hare or gazelle that was started. We would reach the top of the mountain in our chase, remaining there until the late afternoon. Then we would return, after we had fed the falcons and allowed them to drink and bathe themselves in the mountain pools,

[3] *sulūqi*, an Arab breed of dogs indigenous to the Near East. See A. Goodrich-Freer, *Arabs in Tent and Town* (London, 1924), p. 234.

arriving in town at dusk. That was a care-free day for us when we mounted our horses and went to hunt waterfowl and francolins. We would start for the hunt from the gate of the lower town, then go to the marshy canebrakes [*azwār*]. The cheetahs and sakers would be kept outside the field while we would go into the brakes with the falcons. If a francolin rose, the falcon would strike it. If a hare jumped, we would throw off a falcon upon it. If the falcon seized it, well and good; otherwise as soon as the hare got beyond the canebrakes, the cheetahs would be loosed upon it. If a gazelle was started, it was allowed to run until it got beyond the brake, when a cheetah would be loosed upon it; if the cheetah seized it, well and good; otherwise the sakers would be thrown off upon it. Thus hardly a single specimen of game could escape us unless by a special dispensation of fate.

In the marshy canebrakes the wild boar abounded. We would gallop after it and kill it, rejoicing more in killing it than in killing any other game.[4]

My father had a way of organizing the hunting party as though it were a battle array or a very serious affair No one was supposed to engage in conversation with his companion, and everybody was expected to have one concern only, scanning the ground to spy out a hare in its form or a bird in its nest.

Between my father and the two sons of Rūbāl — Tarūs and Lāwūn,[5] the Armenian lords of al-Maṣṣīṣah, Anṭartūs, Adhanah and the Durūb [6] — mutual relations of friendship and correspondence existed, chiefly caused by his desire for the acquisition of falcons. These lords used to forward to my father every year about ten falcons or so in care of Armenian falconers, who would come on foot. They would also send to him a number of braches. My father, on his part, would dispatch to them horses, perfumes and Egyptian-made apparel. Thus we used to get from them excellent falcons of rare quality. We had accumulated [119] in a certain year a large collection of falcons from al-Durūb, including a young one which was as large as an eagle and other smaller ones. The collection was augmented by additional falcons from the

[4] The boar, like the pig, is unclean according to the Koran V 4.
[5] Reuben, Theodoros and Leon.
[6] Near the famous Cilician gates leading across the Taurus mountains from northern Syria to Asia Minor.

mountain, including one which was young and broad like a saker, but which could not keep up with the other falcons in flight, yet the falconer Ghanā'im used to say, "Among all the falcons there is none the like of this young one, named al-Yaḥshūr. It will let no game escape it." We could not at first believe him. But after he had trained the falcon, it turned out to be as he had expected, one of the strongest, swiftest and cleverest of all falcons. It molted in our house and became after the molting superior to what it was before. That falcon lived long and molted in our house during thirteen years, so that it became almost a member of the family. It would hunt for the service of its master, not following the usage of other birds of prey which hunt for themselves.

Al-Yaḥshūr. — Al-Yaḥshūr's roost was near my father (may Allah's mercy rest upon his soul!), who would not leave it with the falconer, for the falconer would carry the falcon around during the night and would starve it in order to get a better hunt out of it. But this falcon would satisfy its hunger by itself and still carry out all that was expected of it. As we went out to hunt partridges, with many falcons in the party, my father would give this particular falcon to one of the falconers and say to him, "Stand aside with it and let it not go with the rest of the falcons as they attack. Rather hide thyself somewhere in the mountain." Once isolated from the rest of the party, if a partridge was seen clinging to a tree and was reported to my father, he would say, "Fetch al-Yahshūr." And the moment my father would raise his hand, al-Yaḥshūr, without any further call, would instantly fly from the wrist [*yad*] of the falconer and perch on my father's wrist and raise erect its head and neck. My father would draw near the sleeping partridge and throw at it a stick from his hand. The moment the partridge was flushed he would throw off al-Yahshūr, who would seize it within a range of ten cubits [*dhirā'*]. The falconer would then descend to it, slay the bird [7] held in its claws and take al-Yaḥshūr away.

My father would again say, "Stand aside with it." And whenever they saw another partridge hugging a branch of a tree, he would do the same thing, until five or six partridges had been caught, each one within a range of ten cubits.

[7] Moslems are forbidden to eat "that which dieth of itself . . . or is killed by a blow, unless ye make it clean by giving the death stroke yourselves." Koran V . 4.

My father would then say to the falconer, "Feed the falcon." The falconer would reply, "Dost thou not want to let it alone so that we may hunt some more with it?" But my father would remark, "My son, we have ten other falcons which we can employ in the hunt. This one has already done enough. Much coursing would shorten its life." Then the falconer would feed it and hold it away.

The hunt over, we would feed our falcons and put them on the water to drink and bathe. When, with al-Yaḥshūr on the falconer's wrist, we approached the town from the mountain, on our homeward way, my father would say, "Let me now have al-Yaḥshūr." He would then proceed with it on his wrist. In case a partridge flew in front of my father, he would throw off upon it al-Yaḥshūr, which might fly ten or more courses on the way, according to the number of partridges which rose. And because it would then be satiated, al-Yaḥshūr would not put its beak to a partridge's throat nor would it taste its blood.

When we entered the house, my father would say, "Fetch me a bowl of water." They would fetch him one and he would offer it to the falcon while it was still on his wrist (may Allah's mercy rest upon his soul!). The falcon would drink [120] from it. In case it wanted a bath, it would shake its beak in the water — which would indicate that it wanted to bathe. My father would then order that a big basin full of water be brought and would offer it to the falcon. The falcon would flutter down into it. It would then beat its wings in the water until it had a sufficient bath, when it would get out of the water. My father would put it on a large wooden perch especially made for it and would bring near it a brazier of live coal; and after it was combed and rubbed with oil until it was dry, a folded piece of fur would be placed by it. The falcon would go down to it and sleep. It would remain among us sleeping on the fur until late in the night, at which time my father would want to retire into the harem's apartment. He would then say to one of us, "Carry the falcon." And the falcon would be carried as it lay sleeping on the fur until it was placed near the bed of my father (may Allah's mercy rest upon his soul!).

Of the marvelous traits of this falcon, and it certainly had many of them, I shall only recount the few which I still remember, for a long time has passed since then and the years have made me forget many of its habits. In my father's house were pigeons, green waterfowl with their females, and starlings [8] of the kind kept among the cattle to catch flies and rid the yard of them. My father would enter the house, with this falcon on his wrist, sit on a platform in the courtyard, placing the falcon on a perch beside him. The falcon would seek none of those birds, nor would it pounce upon any of them, just as if they were not of the kind which it was in the habit of hunting.

In wintertime, so much water would accumulate around Shayzar that outside of the city wall swamps, that were more like pools of water, were formed, to which birds would gather. My father would then order the falconer and an attendant with him to approach those birds. He would himself take al-Yaḥshūr on his wrist and stand with it on the citadel and point out to it the quarry. My father would be on the east side, the birds on the west side of the town. As soon as the falcon saw them, my father would throw it off and, flying low, it would leave the town behind in its flight towards the birds. The falconer would thereupon beat the drum, the birds would be flushed and the falcon would catch some of them, though the distance from the place where it was thrown off was considerable.

We used to go out hunting waterfowl and francolins and return after dusk. On the way back we might hear the sound of birds in the big streams around Shayzar, upon which my father would say, "Let me have al-Yaḥshūr." He would take al-Yaḥshūr, crop-filled, and advance towards the birds, with the drum beating until the birds were flushed. He would then throw off the falcon upon them. If its chase proved successful, it would drop back to us; the falconer would go down to it, slay the bird held in its claws, and lift it up. If it proved unsuccessful, it would drop into some cavern of the river without our seeing or knowing where it alighted. We would then leave it to itself and enter the city. At the dawn of the next morning the falconer would go out to it and bring it back to my father (may Allah's mercy rest upon his soul!) in the citadel, saying, "My lord, this frost has so sharpened the back part

[8] *bayḍāniyyāt*, the reading of which is uncertain because of lack of diacritical marks. I cannot find such a word in Arabic, but *zarāzir*, starlings, can still be seen in the barber shops of Beirūt hunting flies.

of its neck that it can now cut steel. Mount, therefore, and see what it will do today!"

From quails to salamander geese [9] and hares, no game could escape this falcon. The falconer was always anxious to hunt cranes [121] and argalas [10] with it, but my father would not allow him, saying, "The cranes and argalas should be hunted with the sakers."

One year the customary ability of this falcon seemed to have failed it so much that whenever it was flown at a quarry and missed it would not respond to the lure. It became weak and would not bathe. We did not know what was wrong with it. But finally it recovered its strength and was once more good for the chase.

One day after it had bathed, the falconer lifted it up from the water and saw on its side, which was exposed on account of the wet feathers, a carbuncle the size of an almond. The falconer brought it before my father, saying, "O my lord, this is the thing that has weakened the falcon and came near causing its death." Saying this, he held the falcon and squeezed the carbuncle, which came out like a dry almond. The spot where it grew closed up, and al-Yaḥshūr returned to its customary attacks on birds with its sword and blood sack.[11]

Shihāb-al-Dīn Maḥmūd ibn-Qarāja, the lord of Ḥamāh at that time, used to send every year for al-Yaḥshūr, which, accompanied by the falconer, would go and spend twenty days with him, serving him in the hunt. The falconer would carry it there and return with it. Finally al-Yaḥshūr died in Shayzar.

It happened that as I was paying a visit to Shihāb-al-Dīn in Ḥamāh, I arose one morning to find the Koran readers, the "Allah is great" chanters [*mukabbirūn*], and a large crowd of the inhabitants of the town assembled. On asking, "Who is dead?" I was told that it was a daughter of Shihāb-al-Dīn. So I desired to walk in the funeral procession, but Shihāb-al-Dīn began to argue with me and prevented me. The dead body was carried and interred in Tell-Ṣaqrūn. On their return, Shihāb-al-Dīn said to me, "Knowest thou who was the dead one?" I replied, "I was told that it was

[9] *al-wazz al-samand*, which I can neither find in any zoological lexicon nor identify.

[10] *harjal* = "Indian stork," "adjutant," *Leptoptilus dubius*. See Newton, *op. cit.*, p. 2.

[11] *naṭ'*, the sack in which the executioner receives the blood of the one whom he decapitates. It is used here with "sword" figuratively to indicate the ferocity of this bird in catching its prey.

a child of thine." He said, "No, by Allah. It was rather the falcon, al-Yaḥshūr. Hearing that it died, I sent and had it brought hither. Then I made for it a coffin, arranged a special funeral and interred it. For it surely deserved as much."

A remarkable cheetah. — My father (may Allah's mercy rest upon his soul!) had a female cheetah [*fahdah*] which was among cheetahs what al-Yaḥshūr was among falcons. This animal, one of the largest of cheetahs, was captured in a wild state. The cheetah trainer took it, made an incision in the skin of its nose and tamed it. It seemed at first to have given up the idea of hunting, but afterwards it was willing to be carried to, but not to take part in the hunt. It was subject to attacks of epilepsy, similar to the attacks which afflict a madman, during which it would froth at the mouth, and when a young deer was offered, it would not seek it and would show no desire for it but would only smell and bite it. This condition lasted for a long time — about a year.

One day we went to the marshy canebrakes. Our horsemen entered the brakes while I stopped at the entrance, with the cheetah trainer and the cheetah close by me. A gazelle rose from the brake and came out towards me. I galloped the horse under me, which was a horse of one of the best breeds, in an effort to turn the gazelle in the direction of the cheetah, but the horse proved too quick for the gazelle and hit it in the chest, making it fall. At once the cheetah jumped and caught the gazelle, as though it had suddenly been awakened from a sleep and said, [122] "Receive now all the game ye desire!" After this, any gazelle that appeared, it would seize at once. The cheetah keeper could no longer control it. It would drag him and throw him down and would not halt as cheetahs ordinarily do in their chase. In fact every time its keeper thought it had stopped, it would start again at a run and seize the gazelle.

In Shayzar we used to hunt the admi, a large species of gazelle. Whenever we took this cheetah to al-'Alāh [12] and the land to the east of the town, in which the white gazelles abounded, we would not allow the cheetah keeper to run with the cheetah lest it drag him and throw him down. It would attack those gazelles as though they were gazelle fawns, for the ordinary white gazelles are very small.

[12] The rocky region.

This was the only cheetah among all of them which was allowed to stay in the house of my father (may Allah's mercy rest upon his soul!). He had a special maid who served it. In one side of the courtyard she had a velvet quilt folded, with dry grass beneath. In the wall was an iron staple. After the hunt, the cheetah trainer would bring it to the door of the house in which its couching place lay, and leave it there. It would then enter the house and go to that place, where its bed was spread, and sleep. The maid would come and tie it to the staple fastened in the wall.

In that same house were, by Allah, twenty admi and white gazelles, rams, goats and fawns born in the yard; yet the cheetah would neither seek them nor frighten them. It would never leave its place. Though left by itself, it would enter the yard without even looking at the gazelles.

I watched the maid in charge of the cheetah dress its skin with a comb, while the cheetah neither objected nor tried to get away One day after the cheetah had urinated over the quilt spread for it, I saw the maid shake it violently and hit it because it had urinated on the couch, without the cheetah growling at the maid or striking back at her.

On another day I saw it when two hares started right in front of the trainer. It overtook one and seized it, biting it with its teeth. It then followed the other and, on overtaking it, began to hit it with its two front paws, while its mouth was occupied with the first hare. After giving it a few blows with its paws, the cheetah let it go and the hare went its way.

Among those who joined us on hunting expeditions was the learned Sheikh abu-'Abdallāh al-Ṭulayṭuli,[13] the grammarian (may Allah's mercy rest upon his soul!), who was in grammar the Sībawayhi[14] of his age. I studied grammar under him for about ten years. Previous to that he was in charge of the Academy of Learning [*dār al-'ilm*] in Tripoli,[15] and when the Franks captured that city,[16] my father and uncle (may Allah's mercy rest upon their souls!) sent and procured this al-Sheikh abu-'Abdallāh, together

[13] Of Toledo, Spain
[14] Considered the greatest Arab grammarian, died in 796 A D
[15] Ibn-al-Athīr in *Recueil historiens orientaux*, vol I, p 274; ibn-Khallikān, *Ta'rīkh*, vol III, p 8 = *Biographical Dictionary*, vol III, p. 455.
[16] July 12, 1109.

with Yānis, the copyist. The latter's system of calligraphy was very much like the system of ibn-al-Bawwāb.[17] He lived with us in Shayzar for some time and copied for my father (may Allah's mercy rest upon his soul!) two complete Korans. [123] After that he changed his residence to Egypt, where he died.

I witnessed something marvelous in al-Sheikh abu-'Abdallāh. As I entered his room one day in order to study under him and found lying before him the principal textbooks on grammar — the *Kitāb Sībawayhi*, *al-Khaṣā'iṣ* by ibn-Jinni,[18] *al-Īḍāḥ* by abu-'Ali al-Fārisi,[19] *al-Luma'* [20] and *al-Jumal* [21] — I said to him, "O Sheikh abu-'Abdallāh, hast thou read all these books?" "Read them?" he replied. "No, by Allah, I have rather inscribed them on the tablet [of my heart] and memorized them all. If thou wishest to ascertain that, take any section, open it and read from the top of the page just one line." Accordingly, I took a section, opened it and read one line of it. He continued repeating by heart the whole page and so he could do with all the other sections. Thus I witnessed in the case of this man a remarkable phenomenon which is beyond human power.

The above is a parenthetical paragraph which was inserted in the course of a narrative to which it does not really belong.

I saw this Sheikh abu-'Abdallāh when he joined us on a hunting expedition in which our remarkable cheetah took part. He was riding on horseback and had his feet covered with rags. The ground was rich in thistles, many of which stuck into his feet and made them bleed. But as he was absorbed watching the cheetah hunt, he felt no pain in his feet; for all his attention was directed to the sight of the cheetah, which crept slyly towards the gazelles, bounded after them, and succeeded in catching them.

The red-eyed falcon. — My father (may Allah's mercy rest upon his soul!) was very fortunate in having exceptional and clever birds of prey, because he possessed so many of them and could

[17] Abu-al-Ḥasan 'Ali ibn-Hilāl, one of the most renowned Arab calligraphers, died in Baghdād in 1022 or 1032 A D

[18] "The Peculiarities of Speech," by abu-al-Fatḥ 'Uthmān ibn-Jinni, d. 1002.

[19] "The Explanation," by abu-'Ali al-Ḥasan al-Fasawi al-Fārisi, d 987.

[20] "The Salient Features," by ibn-Jinni

[21] "The Sentences," either by abu-al-Qāsim 'Abd-al-Raḥmān al-Zajjāji, d 950, or by 'Abd-al-Qāhir al-Jurjāni, d 1081. See Ḥāji Khalfah, *Lexicon bibliographicum* (Leipzig, 1837), vol. II, pp. 624–25.

select from among them the cleverest and most rapacious. On a certain year he had a red-eyed falcon that was intermewed and was one of the cleverest of falcons. He received a letter from my uncle, Tāj-al-Umarā' [the crown of amīrs] abu-al-Mutawwaj Muqallad (may Allah's mercy rest upon his soul!), in Cairo, where he had taken his abode in the service of al-Āmir bi-Aḥkām-Allāh, saying, "In the audience chamber of al-Afḍal I heard the red-eyed falcon mentioned and heard al-Afḍal questioning his informant about it and about its methods of chase." Thereupon, my father (may Allah's mercy rest upon his soul!) sent the falcon with a falconer to al-Afḍal. When the falconer presented himself before al-Afdal, the latter said, "Is this the red-eyed falcon?" The falconer replied, "Yes, my lord." He asked him, "What does it chase?" The falconer replied, "Quails, argalas and other kinds of birds included between these two varieties." This falcon remained in Egypt for some time, after which it escaped and disappeared. After it had spent a year in the wilderness among the sycamore trees where it molted, they succeeded in catching it again. A letter was then received from my uncle (may Allah's mercy rest upon his soul!) saying, "The red-eyed falcon was lost and molted among the sycamore trees. But they succeeded in catching it again and are now using it for the chase. It is proving once more to be a great calamity for the birds."

A Frankish falcon. — One day as we were with my father (may Allah's mercy rest upon his soul!) one of the peasants of Ma'arrah-al-Nu'mān came to him with a molted falcon the size of a big eagle, whose wings and tail had broken feathers. I never saw a falcon like it. [124] The man said, "O my lord, I was laying snares[22] for wood pigeons [*dalamah*] when this falcon struck a wood pigeon caught in the snare. So I seized it and brought it to thee." My father took the falcon and gave generously to the man who offered it to him as a present. The falconer imped its feathers, carried it along and tried to train it. The falcon, however, turned out to be a hunting falcon, habituated to the chase, that had first molted in confinement but had since escaped from the Franks and molted in the mountain of al-Ma'arrah. It proved to be one of the nimblest and cleverest of all birds of prey.

[22] *naddāf* = "carder's bow."

A young shahin. — One day when I was on a hunting expedition with my father (may Allah's mercy rest upon his soul!), we saw at a distance a man coming towards us carrying something which we could not identify. When he approached us, behold! it was a young shahin, that was one of the largest and best of its kind. It had scratched the hands of its carrier, and therefore he turned it upside down and seized its fetters and its legs while the shahin was hanging down with its wings spread. When he met us he said, "O my lord, I have caught in the chase this bird and brought it to thee." My father delivered it to the falconer, who put it in good shape and imped the parts of its feathers that were broken. But its deeds did not prove as good as its appearance, for evidently the hunter had spoiled it by the way he treated it. A shahin, like the scales of the balance, is spoiled and rendered useless by the slightest bit of ill treatment. As for this falconer, he was very skilled in the handling of shahins.

When we used to go for the chase from the lower town gate, we used to take with us all the outfit for the chase, even nets, hatchets, shovels and grapnels for the game which went to earth. We would also take with us the hunting animals, falcons, sakers, shahins, cheetahs and hounds. Soon after leaving the town, my father would let two shahins circle around, and they would continue to circle around the procession. In case one of them raked out, all the falconer would do would be to cough lightly and point with his hand in the direction in which he desired the falcon to go. The shahin would, by Allah, instantly turn back in that direction.

I once saw my father turn a shahin against a flock of wild pigeons [*ṣulṣulah*] which had alighted in a meadow. When the shahin had made its point, the drum was beaten and the pigeons were flushed. The shahin then swooped on them and struck the head of a pigeon, which it cut off. Then he bound the pigeon and went down. We went around, by Allah, in all directions looking for that head but could not find it. Its traces showed that it had fallen at a distance in the water, for we were close by the river.

A retainer of my father, named Aḥmad ibn-Mujīr, who was not among those who rode with us on hunting expeditions, said one day to my father, "O my lord, I am so anxious to see a hunt." My father said, "Offer Aḥmad a mare, so that he may ride with us." We were then going out to hunt francolins. A male francolin rose, fluttering its wings as was its custom. My father (may Allah's mercy rest upon his soul!) was carrying on his wrist al-Yaḥshūr, which he now threw off upon the francolin. Al-Yaḥshūr flew close to the ground, grazing the tops of the grass with its breast. Meanwhile the francolin had risen [125] to a great height. Seeing that, Aḥmad said to my father, "By thy life, the falcon is playing a game with the francolin." Finally the falcon seized its prey.

Hunting dogs. — My father used to receive from the land of the Byzantines braches [*zaghāri*], which are hounds of excellent breed, male and female. These hounds would multiply in our possession. To them, bird chasing was an instinct.

I once saw a female puppy which followed the other hounds as the master of hounds took them to the chase. The master sent a falcon after a francolin which had darted into covert within a thicket of brambles on the banks of the river. The dogs were then set loose on the thicket in order to flush the francolin. The puppy was standing on the bank of the river. As soon as the francolin rose, the puppy leaped after it from the bank and fell into the river, although it did not know how to hunt and had never hunted before.

I once saw one of these braches penetrate into a thicket of henbane after a female partridge which had sought covert in that impassable thicket on the mountain side. The dog was slow in coming out. We heard a violent noise inside of the thicket My father (may Allah's mercy rest upon his soul!) said, "There must be a wild beast in there which has killed the dog." After an hour the dog issued, pulling by the leg a jackal which had been in the thicket and which it had killed and was dragging out to us.

Previous to this my father (may Allah's mercy rest upon his soul!) had gone on a trip [23] to Iṣpahān to the court of the Sultan Malik-Shāh (may Allah's mercy rest upon his soul!). On his return he related to me the following in his own words:

When I finished my business with the sultan [24] and desired to return home, I wished to bring back in my company some bird of prey with

[23] About 1085

[24] His business evidently was to secure the intervention of Malik-Shāh against the Seljūq amīr of Asia Minor, Sulaymān ibn-Qutlumish, who in the early part of 1085 had taken possession of Ma'arrah-al-Nu'mān and Kafarṭāb and was threatening Shayzar.

which I could amuse myself en route. Accordingly, they brought me some falcons and a ferret which was trained to chase birds out of the henbane bushes. I chose, however, sakers, which chase hares and bustards, because I considered it difficult to handle falcons on that long and tiresome road.

My father (may Allah's mercy rest upon his soul!) also had in his possession certain slugis of the finest breed. One day he set the sakers loose on the gazelles while the ground was still covered with thick mud after a heavy rain. I was in his company as a young boy, riding on a hackney of my own. The horses of the other members of the party were stuck in the mud unable to run; but my hackney, thanks to my light weight, triumphed over the mud. The sakers and dogs knocked down the gazelle. My father said to me, "O Usāmah, follow the gazelle, alight and hold it by its legs until we get to thee." I did so. When he arrived (may Allah's mercy rest upon his soul!) he slew the gazelle.

As he slew the gazelle, there stood by him his bitch of yellow skin and good breed, called al-Ḥamawiyyah,[25] which was the one that knocked the gazelle down. All at once the herd of gazelles from among which we had separated this one came back, passing by us. My father (may Allah's mercy rest upon his soul!) immediately seized the collar of al-Ḥamawiyyah and ran swiftly with it until it caught sight of the gazelles. He then set it loose after them and it caught another gazelle.

Despite his heavy body and advanced years, my father (may Allah's mercy rest upon his soul!), who was always fasting, would gallop all day long, and he would never go hunting except on a fine hunter or a fleet pack horse, and would feel neither weak, [126] worn out nor tired; although we, his four children, while with him, would feel fatigued and exhausted. Nor might any servant, any groom holding an extra horse by halter or any carrier of arms lag behind in the chase after the game.

I had an attendant named Yūsuf, who carried my lance and my leather shield and who held the halter of my extra horse, but who would neither run after the game nor follow it. My father felt angry with this attendant; he felt so time after time. The attendant finally said to him:

[25] "Coming from Ḥamāh."

O my lord, of all the members of thy party none is of as much use to thee (and in Allah we seek refuge!) as this, thy son. Let me, therefore, keep behind him with his led horse and weapons. Whenever thou hast need of him, thou shalt find him. As for me, consider that I am not in the company at all.

After that, my father never blamed him nor showed him disapproval for not running after the game.

A hunting trip interrupted by the return of the Franks. — The lord of Antioch [26] camped against us and, after a combat, departed without concluding peace. Before the rear guard of the Franks had gone any distance from the upper town [Shayzar], my father (may Allah's mercy rest upon his soul!) was already on horseback going out for a hunt. Our horsemen pursued the enemy, who now turned against them. As for my father he was by that time at quite a distance from the town. The Franks went back until they got to the town. In the meantime, my father had climbed Tell-Sikkīn in order to watch them as they stood between him and the town. He remained standing on that Tell [hill] until they departed from the town. He then resumed his route for the chase.

An Arab mare contrasted with a hackney. — My father (may Allah's mercy rest upon his soul!) used to chase the roes [*yaḥāmīr*] in the land around the Citadel of the Bridge.[27] Riding on a black mare of his, called the Khurji [28] mare after the name of the man from whom my father had bought it for three hundred and twenty dīnārs, he knocked down five or six roebucks. As he was chasing the last of them, the front leg of the mare went into a pitfall dug for the wild boar. The mare tumbled over him and broke his collar bone. Then it jumped up and galloped for about twenty cubits, while he was still lying flat, after which it returned and stood right over his head moaning and neighing until he arose. The attendants then came and helped him to mount. Such is the way Arab horses behave!

I went out with my father (may Allah's mercy rest upon his soul!) in the direction of the mountain to hunt partridges. An attendant of his, named Lu'lu' (may Allah's mercy rest upon his soul!), descended from the mountain for some personal affair of

[26] Tancred, in 1110. [27] Ḥiṣn al-Jisr, in Shayzar.
[28] *khurji* = "maker of saddlebags."

his, while we were still near the town, and when it was yet early in the morning. Under him was a hackney [*birdhawn*]. The hackney, seeing the shadow of its rider's quiver, was startled, threw him off and ran away loose. I galloped, by Allah, to catch it, together with an attendant of mine, and kept pursuing it from the morning till late in the afternoon, until we succeeded in forcing it to take refuge among a flock of animals [29] pasturing in the marshy canebrakes. Those who tended the flock stretched a rope for the hackney and trapped it, as the wild beast is trapped. I then got hold of it and took it back. All this, while my father (may Allah's mercy rest upon his soul!) was standing outside the town waiting for me, neither hunting nor resting in his home. Thus you see that hackneys are more like wild beasts than horses.

A teacher's scruples against killing birds. — My father (may Allah's mercy rest upon his soul!) related to me the following in his own words:

I used to go out to the hunt accompanied by al-Ra'īs abu-Turāb Haydarah ibn-Qaṭrmatar [30] (may Allah's mercy rest upon his soul!), who was my father's sheikh and under whom my father memorized the Koran and studied Arabic. When we arrived at the hunting field, Abu-Turāb would dismount from his mare, sit on a rock and read the Koran while we would be hunting around him. With the chase done, he would ride along with us.

Abu-Turāb related to me the following: "Sir, as I was sitting once on a rock [127] a small partridge came all of a sudden trotting heavily along, because of exhaustion, towards the rock on which I was sitting. As soon as it took cover underneath the rock, a falcon appeared, coming after it, but was still at some distance from it. The falcon alighted opposite me while Lu'lu' was screaming, 'Look out! Look out, O our master!' He then came galloping, while I was praying, 'O Allah, conceal the partridge so that he may not see it,' and said, 'Our master, where is the partridge?' I replied, 'I did not see anything. It did not come here.' He then dismounted from his mare and went around the rock looking underneath it. There he saw the partridge and said, 'I thought the partridge was here, but thou dost insist that it is not.' He took it, sir, broke its legs and threw it to the falcon, as my heart was breaking for it."

Hunting hares. — This Lu'lu' (may Allah's mercy rest upon his soul!) was of all men the most experienced hunter. I was with him

[29] *jushar* = cattle which pasture in the fields and do not return to their folds during the night.

[30] Derenbourg, *Autobiographie*, p. 206, reads "Qaṭrama."

one day on a hunt when a number of hares came from the wilderness and ran freely around us. We used to go out and hunt a large number of these hares. They were small, red hares. One day I saw Lu'lu' rouse ten of them, nine of which he hit with a pike[31] and killed. As he was rousing a tenth hare, my father (may Allah's mercy rest upon his soul!) said to him, "Let it alone. The dogs will chase it, while we shall be amused by watching them" Accordingly, they let the hare run and let the dogs loose after it. But the hare beat them all running, and escaped Lu'lu' said to my father, "If thou hadst only left me free, I would have pierced and killed it!"

One day I saw a hare which we roused from its earth and on which we set loose the dogs. It entered a cave in the land of al-Ḥubaybah[32] and was pursued therein by a black bitch. Presently the bitch came out yelping and fell dead Before we left it, its skin had already cracked and it lay dead and rotten. The reason was that a viper had bitten it in the cave

A starling caught by a falcon. — One of the marvelous things I witnessed in the chase with falcons was the following·

I set out with my father (may Allah's mercy rest upon his soul!) after a period of successive rains which had prevented us for days from riding out. As soon as the rain ceased, we went out with the falcons, seeking waterfowl. We saw birds lying in a meadow at the foot of a hill. My father advanced and threw off upon them a falcon which was intermewed. The falcon attacked the birds, footed one of them and alighted. But we could see no game with it. We dismounted where it was and found to our surprise that what it had caught was a starling, on which it had closed its talons without wounding or hurting it. The falconer went down and extricated the bird, which was safe and sound.

Hunting geese and bustards. — I have witnessed among the salamander geese [?] fortitude and courage similar to the fortitude and courage of men. Here is an illustration

We sent out our sakers against a flock of geese and beat our drums until they were flushed. The sakers chased the geese, seized one of them and pulled it down to the ground from among the other geese. We were still at some distance from it. That

[31] *al-bālah*, a staff with a pointed iron at the end, used by hunters, who throw it at the game

[32] Uncertain readıng.

goose began to scream, and five or six other geese rushed to its assistance and began to beat the sakers with their wings. Had we not been quick, they would have saved the goose and cut the wings of the sakers with their beaks.

[128] The courage of the bustard takes quite a different form. Whenever the saker approaches, it goes down to the ground; and in whichever way the saker circles around it, the bustard opposes its tail. When the saker is close by, the bustard squirts on it its excrement, wetting its feathers and filling its eyes, and makes its escape. But in case the bustard misses the saker as it does this, the saker gets hold of it.

The ʻaymah. — One of the most extraordinary hunts made by a falcon owned by my father (may Allah's mercy rest upon his soul!) took place as follows:

My father had on his wrist an excellent falcon which was still young. On a stream of water was a *ʻaymah*, which is a big bird of the same color as the heron, but bigger than a crane, measuring from the extremity of one wing to the extremity of the other about fourteen spans. The falcon began to seek the *ʻaymah*, so my father threw it off upon it and beat the drum for the *ʻaymah* until it arose. The falcon, striking among the feathers of the *ʻaymah*, managed to bind. Both fell into the water. In fact, this was the reason for the falcon's escape, for the *ʻaymah* would have otherwise killed it with its beak. Thereupon one of the attendants threw himself into the water with his clothes and outfit, seized the *ʻaymah* and lifted it up. When it got on the ground, the falcon looked at it, screamed and flew away without interfering at all with it. Save this one, I never saw a falcon attack a *ʻaymah*, because the *ʻaymah* is in the same position as the griffon, about which abu-al-ʻAlā ibn-Sulaymān[33] has said:

> I consider the griffon too big to be caught in a chase.

A lion scared by a falcon. — My father (may Allah's mercy rest upon his soul!) used to go to the Citadel of the Bridge, in the vicinity of which game was plentiful, and spend there a few days. We would be with him hunting partridges, francolins, waterfowl, roebucks, gazelles and hares. One day my father went there and we mounted

[33] The famous al-Maʻarri, 973–1057 A.D.

our horses to chase the francolins. He flew at a francolin a falcon which was carried and trained by a mameluke, named Niqūla [Nicholas]. Niqūla himself went galloping behind the falcon. The francolin put in within a thicket of brambles All of a sudden the screams of Niqūla filled our ears and he himself came back galloping. We asked him, "What is the matter with thee?" He replied, "A lion has issued from the bush where the francolin fell. So I left the falcon and took to flight." And lo! the lion also was scared like Niqūla. When it heard the sound of the flight of the falcon, it rushed out of the thicket and bounded towards the forest.

Watching the fishermen. — Hunting over, we used to return and sit on the banks of Būshamīr, a small stream near the citadel. We would then call the fishermen and see the marvelous things which they did One of them would hold a reed having at its end a spearhead with a cavity into which the reed fits like a pike Out of the cavity spring three hooks of iron, each hook being a cubit in length. At the extremity of the reed there is a long string which the fisherman ties to his hand. The fisherman would stand at the bank of the river, which was rather narrow, and as he saw a fish he would dart at it the reed with the iron. Nor would he miss it. He would then drag the reed towards himself with the string until it came out of the water loaded with the fish. Another fisherman would have a stick as thick as a fist, having at one end an iron grapnel and at the other a string tied to his hand. This fisherman would go down and swim in the water, and as he saw a fish he would snatch it with the grapnel and hold it. He would then come out of the water and, with the string, draw the stick, thus pulling out the grapnel and the fish. [129] A third fisherman would go into the water and swim, and as he swam he would pass his hand under the willow trees on the banks, feeling for a fish until his fingers entered into the gills of one in such a way that the fish could neither move nor escape. He would then take it and leave the water. Thus the amusement we got out of watching the fishermen was no less than the amusement we got out of hunting with falcons.

Ghanā'im, the falconer. — We had successive rain and wind for many days as we were in the Citadel of the Bridge. Then the rain stopped for a time, in the course of which Ghanā'im, the falconer, came and said to my father, "The falcons are hungry and in good shape for the chase. The weather has become fine and the rain has ceased. Dost thou not desire to mount and go out?" "Why, yes," replied my father. So we rode out. But we had scarcely got out as far as the desert when the gates of heaven were open with rain. We said to Ghanā'im, "Thou didst claim that the weather had become good and that all rain had ceased. And so thou hast brought us out in this rain." Ghanā'im replied, "Did ye not have eyes to see the clouds and the signs of rain? Ye could have said to me, 'Thou liest in thy beard. Neither has the weather become better, nor is it going to cease raining'"

This Ghanā'im was an expert in the dressing of shahins and falcons, well versed in matters pertaining to birds of prey, interesting in conversation and of delightful company. He had seen of the birds of prey what was known and what was not known.

One day as we were going out from the Castle of Shayzar for the chase, we saw something near al-Jalāli Mill which turned out to be a crane squatting on the ground. An attendant dismounted and turned it over to find that it was dead. But it was still warm and had not yet become rigid. On seeing it Ghanā'im said, "This must have been the victim of a *luzzayq*. Search under its wing" The side of the crane was found pierced and its heart eaten out. Ghanā'im remarked, "The *luzzayq* is a bird of prey similar to the *'awsaq*.[34] It chases the crane, sticks under its wing and then pierces its ribs and eats its heart."

By the decree of Allah (praise be to him!) I became attached to the service of Atābek Zanki [35] (may Allah's mercy rest upon his soul!). While I was there, he received a bird of prey similar to the *'awsaq*, red of beak and foot and of red eyelashes. It was one of the most excellent birds of prey. They told us it was a *luzzayq*. But it stayed with Zanki only a few days, for it tore the straps with its beak and flew away.

Hunting wild asses. — My father (may Allah's mercy rest upon his soul!) went out one day to hunt gazelles, and I was in his company as a young lad. When he got to Wādi-al-Qanāṭir [the valley of arches] he suddenly came upon some negro vagabonds carrying on highway robbery. My father laid hold on them, pinioned their

[34] *luzzayq* and *'awsaq* are local names for varieties of falcons which stick to (*lazaqa*, *'asaqa*) their prey, and which I cannot find in any dictionaries or books on zoölogy.
[35] About 1130.

arms behind their backs and delivered them to a band of his attendants with orders to take them to the jail in Shayzar. As for me, I took a pike from one of them, and we proceeded to the hunt.

All of a sudden, a herd of wild asses appeared. I said to my father, "My lord, I never before saw wild asses. By thy permission I shall gallop and look at them." My father replied, "Do so." Under me was a chestnut mare of the best breed. I galloped, holding in my hand the pike which I had taken from the vagabonds When I got in the midst of the herd, I isolated one of them and began to stab it with the pike without leaving the least impression on the animal [130] on account of the weakness of my arm and the dullness of the spearhead. I turned and chased the ass back as far as my companions, who laid hold on it My father and those with him greatly admired the way my mare ran its course

By the decree of Allah (worthy of admiration is he!) I went out one day to amuse myself by the sight of the river of Shayzar.[36] That same mare was under me. In my company was a teacher of the Koran who would sometimes recite poetry, sometimes sing I dismounted under a tree and turned my mare over to the attendant, who shackled it on the border of the river. The mare took fright and fell into the river on its side. Every time it tried to rise, it would fall again into the water, and that because of the shackle. The attendant was too young to be able to save it, and we were entirely unaware of what was going on. Seeing that the mare was on the point of death, he yelled to us. So we came and found it dying We immediately cut the shackle and took it out of the water, but it died, although the water in which it was drowned was not deep enough to reach the upper part of its leg. It was rather the shackle that killed it

Someone afraid the falcon would drown — One day [37] my father (may Allah's mercy rest upon his soul!) went out for the chase accompanied by an amīr called al-Ṣamṣām, who was a comrade in arms of Fakhr-al-Mulk ibn-'Ammār, the lord of Tripoli, having been in his service. He was a man of little experience in the chase. My father having sent a falcon after certain birds of prey, the falcon clutched one of them and dropped into the middle of the river. Al-Ṣamṣām began to beat one hand against the other, saying,

[36] The Orontes [37] About 1109.

"There is no power and no strength except in Allah![38] Why did I go out today?" I said to him, "O Ṣamṣām, art thou afraid that the falcon will drown?" "Certainly," said he. "It is already drowned. Is the falcon a duck that could fall in the water and not drown?" I laughed and said, "It will be up in a minute." The falcon seized the bird by its head and swam with it until they both got out of the water. Al-Ṣamṣām was for a long time after this amazed at the action of the falcon, repeating, "Praise be to Allah!" (worthy of admiration is he!), "Glory be to Allah!" for the safety of the falcon.

Birds have their fates, too. — Animals meet their deaths in various manners. My father once set loose a white hawk on a francolin. The francolin fell in a thicket of brambles and the white hawk went in with it. In the thicket was a jackal, which seized the hawk and bit off its head. That hawk was one of the best and most skilful birds of prey.

I have seen other cases of death among birds of prey. One day I rode out having in front of me an attendant carrying a sparrow hawk. The attendant hurled the hawk against a group of small birds and it caught one of them. The attendant came and killed the bird held in the claws of the hawk. The hawk shook its head, vomited blood and fell dead, as the little bird lay slain in its claws. Worthy of praise, therefore, is he who fixes the lengths of lives!

One day I passed through a door, which we had opened in the citadel leading to an adjoining building, carrying a pea-shooter. I saw a small bird[39] on a wall at the foot of which I was standing, and I shot at it. The ball missed the bird, which flew away. My eyes followed [131] the ball, which, going down the wall, hit the head of another small bird, which had just stuck its head out of a hole in that wall, and killed it. The bird dropped right in front of me and I slit its throat. I neither intended nor desired to shoot this bird.

My father (may Allah's mercy rest upon his soul!) flew one day his falcon at a hare which rose before us in a marshy canebrake which was full of thorns. The falcon seized the hare, but it got loose again and escaped. The falcon dropped to the ground, and

[38] Cf. Koran XVIII 37.

[39] *'uṣfūr*, commonly used for any small bird, but more particularly for the house sparrow. See Tristram, *op cit*, p. 67.

the hare ran off. I immediately galloped on a black mare of excellent breed which was under me, in order to turn the hare back. The front leg of the mare struck a hole and the mare tumbled over me, covering my hands and face with thorns. The hind leg of the mare was dislocated. As for the falcon, after the hare had gone some distance, it flew from the ground, pursued the hare and clutched it, as though it had no other object but to destroy my mare and to cause me mischief by falling among the thorns

Hunting the wild boar. — Early one morning, the first day of Rajab, when we were fasting, I said to my father (may Allah's mercy rest upon his soul!), "I wish I could go out hunting in order to keep my mind away from the fast." My father replied, "Go." So I set out with my brother, Bahā'-al-Dawlah abu-al-Mughīth Munqidh (may Allah's mercy rest upon his soul!), towards the canebrakes, carrying with us a few falcons. As we penetrated among certain licorice trees, a wild boar rose before us. My brother struck it with the lance and wounded it. The boar ran in among those licorice trees. My brother said, "In a minute the wound will begin to hurt and it will come out again. I shall then face, strike and kill it." I said to him, "Do not so, for it may strike thy mare and kill it." As we were thus conversing, the boar came out, seeking another brake. My brother encountered the boar and struck it on the hump of its back, inside of which the lance with which he struck broke. The boar charged under the chestnut mare of my brother, which was pregnant and had three white legs and a white tail, struck it and tumbled it over. The mare had its thigh dislocated and it perished; as for its rider, his little finger was disjointed and his ring broken.

I galloped behind the boar, which entered a field covered with luxuriant licorice trees and asphodel, in which lay a herd of cattle which I could not see on account of the thickness of the growth. One bull attacked my horse, striking it in the chest and overthrowing it. Both I and the horse, whose bridle broke, fell to the ground. I got up, took the lance, mounted again and pursued the bull. It dashed into the river. I stood at the bank and threw my lance at it. The lance hit it and broke at a length of two cubits. The point and the broken part remained in its body. Still it swam to the other side of the river. We called out to some people who were on that side and who were beating brick to build houses in the village belonging to my uncle. They came and kept watch on the bull as it tried in vain to climb a steep part of the bank. They then threw big stones at it until they killed it. In the meantime, I said [132] to one of my grooms, "Go down to it." He immediately took off his outfit, unclothed, and, sword in hand, swam to and finished it. Then he dragged it by the leg and brought it, saying, "May Allah bestow upon you the blessings of the fast of Rajab, which we have inaugurated by the impurity of swine." [40]

If the boar had claws and teeth like the lion, it would be even more deadly than the lion.

I once saw a wild sow which we roused from its farrow. One of the young began to strike with its snout the hoof of the horse of one of my attendants. It was the size of a kitten. Taking from his quiver an arrow, my attendant inclined towards it, pierced it and lifted it with the arrow. I could not but admire its fighting spirit and its striking the hoof of a horse, while it was small enough to be carried by a mere arrow.

An indefatigable mameluke. — One of the marvels of the chase took place when we used to go out to the mountain to hunt partridges, having with us ten falcons with which we used to carry on the chase all day long. The falcons would be scattered all over the mountain. Each one of them would have with him two or three mameluke horsemen. We would also have two masters of hounds, one of whom was named Buṭrus [Peter] and the other Zarzūr Bādiyah. Every time the falconer flew a falcon at a partridge and the partridge took the air, they would shout, "O Buṭrus!" Buṭrus would make in to them as swiftly as a dromedary. All day long Buṭrus would run in this manner from one mountain to another, both he and his companion. After feeding the falcons full and on our way back home, Buṭrus would take a stone, run after one of the mamelukes and hit him with it. The mameluke would in turn take a stone and hit Buṭrus with it. Thus Buṭrus would not cease chasing the attendants, who would be riding while he was on foot, and exchanging with them missiles from the mountain until they got to the lower town gate — as though he had not been all day long running from one mountain to another.

[40] Swine are unclean according to the Koran V : 4.

Playing chess on a bitch. — One of the strange things about the braches is that they do not eat birds. The only parts they eat are the birds' heads and feet, which have no flesh on them, as well as the bones, the flesh from which had been eaten by the falcons. My father (may Allah's mercy rest upon his soul!) had a black bitch of this breed on the head of which the servants would put in the nighttime a lamp, beside which they would sit and play chess while the bitch would not stir. It would keep its position until its eyes became blear. My father (may Allah's mercy rest upon his soul!) would feel vexed with the servants and say, "Ye have blinded this bitch," but they would not refrain.

Al-Amīr Shihāb-al-Dīn Mālik ibn-Sālim ibn-Mālik, the lord of al-Qal'ah,[41] sent to my father a bitch distinguished for its intelligence, which could be sent below the sakers against the gazelles. From this bitch we saw marvelous things

Hunting according to a system — Hunting by sakers follows a certain system. At first should be sent [133] the leader [*al-muqaddam*] which, striking a gazelle, binds on its ear. The auxiliary [*al-'awn*] is sent after the leader, and it hits another gazelle. The second auxiliary is then flown and it does likewise. The fourth saker is then flown under like conditions Thus each saker hits a different gazelle. The leader, now clutching its gazelle by its ear, isolates it from the herd. Thereupon all the other sakers leave the gazelles which they had been binding and join the leader. In the meantime the bitch would be below the sakers, paying no attention to any of the gazelles except those particular ones on which the sakers were. It sometimes happens that an eagle appears at this juncture. The sakers would then let go the gazelle, the gazelle would run away and the sakers would begin to fly around in a circle. At the same time, we would see the bitch letting alone the gazelles, simultaneously with the sakers, and turning around in a circle on the ground below the sakers, as the sakers were circling in the air. The bitch would continue to run around below them until they came down in response to the lure. It would then stop and start walking behind the horses.

Hunting gazelles and francolins. — Between Shihāb-al-Dīn Mālik and my father (may Allah's mercy rest upon his soul!) were

[41] The Castle of Ja'bar.

special bonds of amity. They communicated by correspondence and by messengers. One day the former sent word to my father, saying, "I have been on a gazelle hunting expedition in the course of which we caught three thousand fawns, all in one day."

The explanation is that gazelles abound in the region of al-Qal'ah. They choose the period in which the gazelles give birth to their young. They then go out on horseback and on foot and seize of the young such as were born that same night, the preceding night and two or three nights before. They collect them in the same way that wood or grass is collected.

Francolins abound in the marshy canebrakes on the banks of the Euphrates. If a francolin is cut open, drawn and then stuffed with hair, its odor does not change for many days.

One day I saw a francolin the body of which had been cut open and the crop also taken out. In the crop was a snake, about one span in length, which the francolin had eaten up.

As we were once hunting, we killed a snake from the belly of which came out another snake which the first snake had swallowed whole and which was just a little smaller than the other.

It is thus the nature of all animals for the strong to prey upon the weak.

> Injustice is a characteristic of all souls. If thou therefore findest
> Someone who does not practice it, then there must be a special reason
> for it.

Epilogue

To encompass all the accounts of the chase, which I practiced for seventy years of my life, is neither feasible nor possible. And to lose one's time in relating fables is one of the worst calamities that may befall a person. As for me, [134] I would seek the pardon of Allah (exalted is he!) if I were to waste the little that remains of my life in other than obedience to his will and preparation for final reward and recompense. And Allah (blessed and exalted is he!) forgives sins and lavishes bounties from his own mercy. He is the generous one who does not disappoint the man who sets his hope on him and from whom the seeker is never turned away.

THE END OF THE BOOK

Praise be to Allah, the lord of the universe.
And may Allah's grace rest upon our master,
Muhammad, his prophet, and upon his holy
family, and may he give them peace!
And in Allah is our sufficiency
and he is the best to trust.[1]

At the end of the book[2] the following words occurred:

I have read this book from beginning to end in a number of sessions under the direction of my lord, my grandfather, the most eminent amīr, the meritorious savant, the perfect leader, 'Adud-al-Dīn,[3] the companion of kings and sultans, the great authority among the Arabs, the confidant of the commander of the believers — may Allah perpetuate his happiness! And I have asked him to give me a certificate authorizing me to transmit the contents of this book to others, which he did, inscribing the certificate with his own noble hand. And that was on Thursday, the thirteenth of Safar, in the year 610.[4]

"I certify that this is true.

Signed by his grandfather,
Murhaf ibn-Usāmah ibn-Munqidh,
Praising Allah and imploring his blessing."

[1] This paragraph is presumably added by some copyist, as is the following one

[2] The book from which the copyist of this manuscript made his copy

[3] "The upper arm of faith," one of the titles of Murhaf, the favorite son of Usāmah, and the grandfather of the one who owned the original manuscript from which this one is copied.

[4] July 4, 1213.

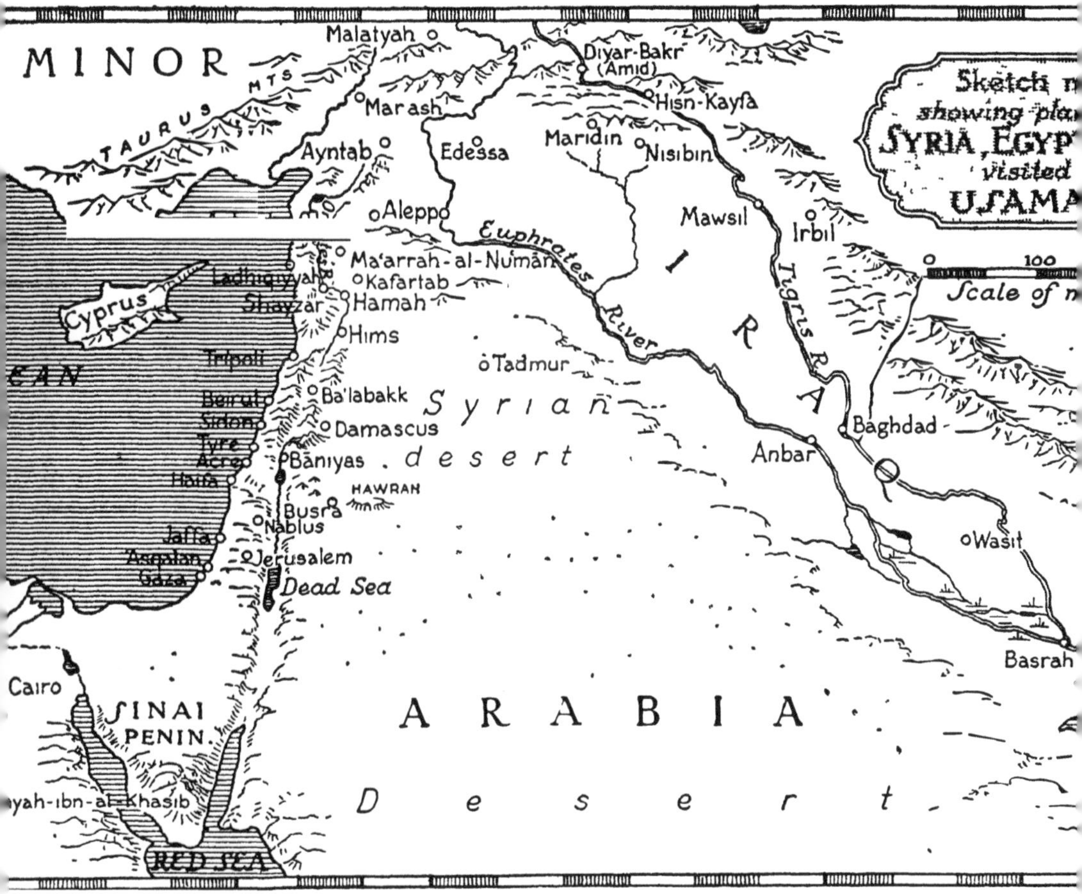

MINOR
TAURUS MTS
Malatyah
Marash
Ayntab
Edessa
Diyar-Bakr (Amid)
Hisn-Kayfa
Maridin
Nisibin
Sketch
showing pla
SYRIA, EGYP
visited
USAMA
Aleppo
Mawsil
Irbil
0 100
Scale of
Euphrates River
Tigris R.
IRAQ
Ma'arrah-al-Numan
Kafartab
Hamah
Ladhiqiyyah
Shayzar
Cyprus
Hims
Tripoli
Tadmur
EAN
Beirut
Ba'labakk
Sidon
Damascus
Syrian desert
Tyre
Acre
Baniyas
Haifa
Baghdad
Anbar
HAWRAN
Busra
Nablus
Jaffa
Wasit
'Asqalan
Jerusalem
Gaza
Dead Sea
Basrah
Cairo
SINAI PENIN.
ARABIA
Desert
yah-ibn-al-Khasib
RED SEA

INDEX

ibn-'Abbās, *see* Nāsır-al-Dīn Naṣr
'Abbās, *see* Rukn-al-Dīn
'Abd-al-Raḥmān al-Ḥalḥūlı, 124
'Abdallāh al-Mushrıf, 123
abu-'Abdallāh al-Ṭulaytulı, 237, 238
'Abdallāh ıbn-al-Qubays, 203
abu-'Abdallāh ıbn-Hāshım, 190
'Abdallāh ıbn-Maymūn al-Ḥamawı, 203
abu-'Abdallāh Muḥammad al-Basrı, 202
abu-'Abdallāh Muḥammad al-Bustı, 203, 204
abu-'Abdallāh Muḥammad ıbn-Fātık, 207, 208
abu-'Abdallāh Muḥammad ıbn-Yūsuf, 114
'Abs, 66
Abyssınıans, 60
Academy of Learnıng, 237
Adam, 62, 108, 221
Adam, Sır, 140
Adhanah, 231
'Adhrā', 180
'Aḍud-al-Dīn Murhaf ıbn-Usāmah, 54, 255
Afāmıyah, 67, 69, 74, 75, 80, 86, 87, 96, 97, 117, 120, 149, 158, 161, 170, 181
al-Afḍal, son of Amīr-al-Juyūsh, 30
al-Afḍal Rıḍwān, *see* Rıḍwān
Aḥmad ıbn-Ma'bad ıbn-Aḥmad, 176
Aḥmad ıbn-Mujīr, 240, 241
ıbn-al-Aḥmar ıbn-Kınānah, 113
'Akka [Acre], 61, 111, 166, 226
abu-al-'Alā' ıbn-Sulaymān al-Ma'arrı, 246
al-'Alāh, 78, 236
'Alam-al-Dīn 'Alı-Kurd, 107
Aleppo [Ḥalab], 57, 82, 105, 106, 122, 175, 213–216, 227
Alexandrıa, 50
Alexandrıans, 30
abu- Alı, al-Qā'ıd, 208
'Alı 'Abd ibn-abı-al-Raydā', 156–158
abu-'Alı al-Fārısı, 238
'Ali ibn-abi-Ṭālıb, 205, 206, 209
'Ali ıbn-al-Dūdawayhı, 73
'Ali ıbn-Faraḥ, 175
'Ali ibn-'Īsa, 208
'Alı ıbn-Maḥbūb, 152
'Alı ıbn-Salām, 65
'Alı ıbn-Shams-al-Dawlah Sālim ibn-Mālık, 128
'Allān ıbn-Fārıs, 126
'Alwān al-'Irāqı, 131, 132
'Alwān ıbn-Ḥarrār, 153
Āmıd, 112, 113, 185
Amīn-al-Dawlah Kumushtakīn, 58
Amīn-al-Mulk, 47
al-Amīr al-Sayyıd al-Sharīf, 104, 105
al-Āmır bı-Aḥkām-Allāh, 239
al-Anbār, 101, 205
'Annāz the Kurd, 146
Ansārs, 77
'Antar (or 'Anbar) al-Kabīr, 50, 51
'Antarah (or 'Antar) ıbn-Shaddād, 66
Antartūs, 231
Antıoch, 67, 70, 85, 90, 92–99, 105, 117, 126, 144, 145, 148–151, 169, 243
'Aqabah al-Mandah, 138
al-'Aqīqı Mansıon, 57
al-Aqmar Mosque, 59
al-Aqṣa Mosque, 163
Arab horses, 243
Arabs, 35, 36, 55, 64, 67, 80, 214
ıbn-al-'Arīq, 185, 186
Armenıans, 133, 136, 231
Asad, al-Qā'ıd, 174, 175
Asad-al-Dīn Shīrkūh, 39
Asfūna, 125
'Asqalān [Ascalon], 34, 35, 40–42, 158
Atābek, *see* 'Imād-al-Dīn Zankı, also Ṭughdakīn
'Attāb, 70
al-Awḥad ıbn-al-Walakhshı, 56
'Ayn-al-Dawlah al-Yārūqı, 39

Bāb-al-Nasr, 51
Badı al-Ṣulayḥı, 158
Badı ıbn-Talīl al-Qushayri, 70
Badlīs, 118, 119
Badr the Kurd, 146
Badrān, son of Shıhāb-al-Dīn, 159
Badrhawa, 97
Baghdād, 187, 202, 207, 210, 214
Bahā'-al-Dawlah abu-al-Mughīth Munqıdh, 131, 134, 136, 251

Bahā'-al-Dīn, al-Sharīf al-Sayyid, 227
abu-Bakr al-Dubaysi, 186
abu-Bakr al-Ṣiddīq, 64
abu-Bakr ibn-Mujāhid, 207, 208
abu-Bakr Muḥammad ibn-'Abd-al-Bāqi, 210
Baktimur, 102
Ba'labakk, 56, 108, 129, 184
al-Balāt, 67
Balātunus, 149
Baldwin (II), 110, 133, 148–150
Bandar-Qanīn, 92, 193
Bāniyās, 93, 94, 116, 224
abu-al-Baqa, 47
Baqiyyah ibn-al-Usayfir, 152
Barāq al-Zubaydi, 40
al-Bāri'ah Castle, 186
al-Barqiyyah, 48
Barrah, 216
Barshak, 39
Bashīla, 229
Bastakīn Gharzah, 155
Bātinites, 154, 193
ibn-al-Bawwāb, 238
Bayt-Jibrīl, 41, 109
Bedouin, 109, 110
Bedouins, 32
Bernard, knight, 162
Bilbīs, 43, 52
ibn-Bishr, 25
Bohemond (I), 94
Bohemond (II), 93, 150, 151
Book of Allah, *see* Koran
Bridge, the, *see* al-Jisr
Buraykah, slave, 152
Burhān-al-Dīn al-Balkhi, 169
Burj Khuraybah Musfān, 76
Bursuq ibn-Bursuq, al-Isbāslār, 102, 104–106, 120, 149
Būshamīr, river, 247
Busra, 39
Butrus, mameluke, 252
Buzurk, Khawāja, 206, 207
Byzantines, 26, 122, 124, 143, 189, 211, 241

Cairo, 30–32, 43, 44, 47, 48, 58, 191, 239
Cairo Gate, 44, 51
Castle of abu-Qubays, **147**, 148
Castle of Aleppo, 227
Castle of al-Khirbah, 107, 108
Castle of al-Ṣawr, 185
Castle of Bāsahra, 89
Castle of Ja'bar, al-Qal'ah, 119, 159, 160, 253, 254
Castle of Shayzar, *see* Shayzar
Children of Israel, 38, 225
Christ, 164
Citadel of the Bridge, 113, 120, 176, 178, 243, 246, 247
City of the Bridge, 177
Constantinople, 122, 228
Count of Cerdagne, 78

Dabīqi clothes, 35, 191
Dalās, 32
Damascus, 28, 37, 39, 41, 50, 54, 57, 58, 93, 98, 99, 108, 111, 123, 124, 127, 129, 137, 144, 145, 149, 168, 169, 180, 181, 190, 210, 221, 224
Dānīth, 105, 106, 148
ibn-al-Daqīq, 25
Dārayya, 129
Darmā', 50
Dhakhīrah-al-Dawlah abu-al-Qana Khitām, 88
Dimyāt, 61
Dimyāṭi, fabric, 35, 205
Diyār-Bakr, 118, 221
Dome of the Rock, 164
Dubays, 172
Dumayr, 130
al-Durūb, 231

Egypt, 28, 31, 42, 48, 49, 55, 56, 58–60, 109, 123, 158, 210, 221, 224, 225, 238, 239
Egyptian dīnārs, 54
Euphrates, 57, 81, 120, 205, 254

Faḍl ibn-abi-al-Hayjā', 117
Fakhr-al-Dīn abu-Kāmil Shāfi', 158
Fakhr-al-Dīn Qara-Arslān ibn-Dāwūd, *see* Fakhr-al-Dīn Qara-Arslān ibn-Suqmān
Fakhr-al-Dīn Qara-Arslān ibn-Suqmān ibn-Urtuq, 112, 185, 221, 226
Fakhr-al-Mulk ibn-'Ammār, 125
Faraḥiyyah, 30
abu-al-Faraj al-Baghdādi, 202
Fāris al-Kurdi, 124–126
Fāris ibn-Zimām, 66
abu-al-Fatḥ, artisan, 163
al-Find al-Zimmāni, 78
al-Findalāwi, 124
Franks, 25, 26, 34, 35, 37, 39–43, 53–55, 60, 67–76, 78, 79, 84, 85, 87–91, 93, 95–98, 100, 102, 103, 106, 109, 114–116,

120–125, 133, 140, 141, 144–149, 151, 152, 157–170, 172, 173, 175, 177, 179, 181, 182, 226, 230, 237, 239, 243
banu-Fuhayd, 53, 54
Fulk, son of Fulk, 93, 110, 161, 226
Funūn, 154
al-Fustuqah, 180

Ghanā'im, falconer, 229, 232, 247, 248
ibn-Ghāzi al-Mashṭūb, 194
Ghāzi al-Talli, 91, 92, 127, 128
Ghazzah, 34, 42, 54
Ghazzi saddle, 54
Ghunaym, 88–90
Greater Bairam, 37

al-Ḥadīqah, 77
Ḥaḍr-al-Ṭūt, 91, 92
al-Ḥāfiẓ li-Dīn-Allāh, 30, 31, 47, 55, 56, 58, 59, 109, 224, 225
Ḥaifa, 141
Ḥamadāt, 77–79
Ḥamāh, 63, 66, 72, 73, 76, 91, 107, 108, 115, 120, 127, 128, 130, 131, 145, 146, 170, 172, 173, 184, 202–204, 227, 235
al-Ḥamawiyyah, dog, 242
Hammām al-Ḥājj, 146
banu-Ḥanīfah, 64
Harim, 167
Ḥārithah al-Numayri, 75, 96
abu-al-Ḥasan 'Ali, *see* Sadīd-al-Mulk
Ḥasan al-Zāhid, 122
Ḥasanūn the Kurd, 94, 95
abu-Hāshim Muḥammad ibn-Muḥammad ibn-Ẓafar, 142
al-Ḥawf, 31, 32
abu-al-Hayjā', 117
Ḥayzān, 123
Ḥillah-'Ārah, 229
Ḥims, 72, 127, 131, 133, 171, 172, 184, 187
al-Hirmās, river, 223
Ḥisma, 36
Ḥiṣn-Kayfa, 203, 204, 206, 209, 226
Ḥiṣn-Masyād, 177, 178
al-Ḥubaybah, 245
Ḥunāk, 140, 141
Hurso [*'urs*], 170
Ḥusām-al-Dawlah ibn-Dilmāj, 118, 119
Ḥusām-al-Dawlah Musāfir, 71
Ḥusām-al-Dīn Timurtāsh ibn-Īlghāzi, 133, 150, 185–186
Ḥusām-al-Mulk, son of Rukn-al-Dīn 'Abbās, *see* Ḥusām-al-Mulk ibn-'Abbās
Ḥusām-al-Mulk ibn-'Abbās, 53, 55

al-Īḍāh, 238
Iftikhār-al-Dawlah abu-al-Futūḥ ibn-'Amrūn, 147, 148
'Imād-al-Dīn Zanki, Atābek, 25, 26, 28, 56, 73, 74, 88, 108, 119, 129, 134, 180, 185–187, 221–223, 248
Irbil, 117
'Īsa, al-Ḥājib, 107
al-Isbāslār, *see* Bursuq ibn-Bursuq, also Mawdūd
Is'ird, 202
Ismā'īl al-Bakji, 102
Ismā'īlites, 107, 108, 146, 153, 190, 192
Ispahān, 77, 79, 241
'Izz-al-Dawlah abu-al-Ḥasan 'Ali, 41, 42, 127
'Izz-al-Dawlah abu-al-Murhaf Nasr, 81–83, 138
'Izz-al-Dīn abu-al-'Asākir Sultān, 67, 77, 82, 94, 100, 130, 138, 148, 155, 158, 171, 193

Jabalah, 125
Ja'far, 50
al-Jafr, 35, 36
al-Jalāli Mill, 91, 92, 248
Jamāl-al-Dīn Muḥammad ibn-Tāj-al-Mulūk Būri, 110, 129
Jāmi', groom, 147
Jawād, Ra'īs, 190
abu-al-Jaysh the Kurd, 179
Jazziyyah, 37
Jerusalem, 117, 148, 150, 158, 163, 168
Jibrīl, son of al-Ḥāfiẓ, 47
ibn-Jinni, 238
al-Jisr (the Bridge), 134, 177–179
al-Jīzah (Gīzah), 58
Joscelin (*jūslīn*), 119, 120
Judhām, 50
Jum'ah al-Numayri, 63, 64, 75, 86–88, 90–93, 96, 97
al-Jumal, 238
Juyūshiyyah, 30, 31

Ka'bah, 210
Kafarnabūdha, 113
Kafarṭāb, 73, 80, 87, 102, 105, 106, 113, 127, 144, 145, 157, 173, 181, 213
al-Kahf, 39
Kamāl-al-Dīn 'Ali ibn-Nīsān, 113

Kāmil al-Mashṭūb, 95, 126, 127
Kar'ah [Lar'ah?], 74
ibn-Kardūs, 122, 123
al-Karkhīnī, 189
Kaysūn, 61
Khafājah, horse, 95
Khalaf ibn-Mulā'ib, *see* Sayf-al-Dawlah
al-Khaṣā'iṣ, 238
abu-al-Khaṭṭāb 'Umar ibn-Muḥammad, 210
Khilāt, 118, 119
Khīrkhān ibn-Qarāja, 131, 133
Khurāsān, 102, 103, 188
Khurji mare, 243
Khutlukh, al-Isbāslār, 91
Khutlukh, mameluke, 143
banu-Kinānah, 175-176
Kitāb al-Nawm w-al-Aḥlām, 217
Kitāb Sībawayhi, 238
Koran, 45, 50, 64, 81, 85, 156, 222, 228, 230, 235, 238, 244, 249
al-Kūfah, 203
Kūhistān, 188
Kūm-Ashfīn, 51
Kundughadi, 102
Kurds, 64, 75, 146

al-Lādhiqiyyah [Laodicea], 125, 138
Lakrūn, 31
Lawātah, 32, 50, 58
Lāwūn, son of Rūbāl, 231
Layth-al-Dawlah Yaḥya, 65, 66, 71, 151, 153
Lu'lu', mameluke, 171, 172, 243-245
Lu'lu'ah, maid, 217, 218
Lu'lu' al-Khādim, 105
al-Luma', 238

Ma'arrah-al-Nu'mān, 165, 204, 239
Ma'arzaf, 140
al-Maghraqah, 223
al-Maghrib [Mauretania], 99, 142, 210
Maghribi dīnārs, 38
Maḥāsin ibn-Majāju, 135
Maḥmūd al-Mustarshid, 28
Maḥmūd ibn-Baldāji, 91
Maḥmūd ibn-Jum'ah, 86, 90, 91
Maḥmūd ibn-Qarāja, *see* Shihāb-al-Dīn
Maḥmūd ibn-Ṣāliḥ, 122
Mahri camels, 35
Majd-al-Dīn abu-Salāmah Murshid ibn-'Ali, 217
Majd-al-Dīn abu-Sulaymān Dāwūd ibn-Muḥammad, 206
abu-al-Majd ibn-Majāju, 135
al-Malik al-'Ādil Nūr-al-Dīn, *see* Nūr-al-Dīn ibn-Zanki
al-Malik al-'Ādil Sayf-al-Dīn, *see* Sayf-al-Dīn 'Ali ibn-al-Sallār
al-Malik al-Ṣāliḥ, *see* Ṭalā'i' ibn-Ruzzīk
Mālik ibn-al-Ḥārith al-Ashtar, 64, 65
Mālik ibn-'Ayyāḍ, 214
Malik-Shāh, Sultan Mu'izz, 77, 117, 207, 241
Mansūr ibn-Ghidafl, 53, 54
ibn-al-Marji [Muraḥḥi?], 108
Ibn-Marwān, lord of Diyār-Bakr, 117, 118
Mary (Virgin), 164
ibn-Masāl, *see* Najm-al-Dīn
Mashhad al-'Āsi, 114
Masjid abi-al-Majd ibn-Sumayyah, 122
Masjid 'Ali, 206
al-Maṣṣīṣah, 231
Mas'ūd, King, 61
Māsurra, 188
Masyād, *see* Ḥiṣn
Mawdūd, al-Isbāslār, 97, 98
al-Mawṣil, 26, 100, 102, 188, 205, 209, 223
Mayyāḥ, 76
Mazyad, 186
Mecca, 60, 189, 210, 211
Mesopotamia, 88
Mīkā'īl the Kurd, 151
al-Mu'abbad, 137
al-Mu'ayyad, the Baghdādi poet, 100
Muḍar, 53
Muḥammad, *see* Prophet
Muḥammad al-'Ajami, 174
Muḥammad al-Busti, *see* abu-'Abdallāh Muḥammad al-Busti
Muḥammad al-Sammā', 203
Muḥammad ibn-'Ali ibn-Muḥammad, 209
Muḥammad ibn-Ayyūb al-Ghisyāni, 26, 73, 107, 119, 124, 127, 129, 130, 180, 181, 187-189
Muḥammad ibn-Mis'ar, 204, 205
Muḥammad ibn-Sarāya, 120
banu-Muḥriz, 141
Mu'īn-al-Dīn Anar, 28, 56, 72, 111, 137, 164, 166, 168, 169, 182, 183, 226
Mu'izz, of Nāblus, 164
Mu'izz-al-Dawlah ibn-Buwayh, 205
ibn-Mulā'ib, see Sayf-al-Dawlah Khalaf
al-Munaytirah, 162
ibn-Munqidh, *see* Usāmah
Muqbil, al-Qā'id, 55, 56

al-Muqtafi li-Amr-Allāh, 205, 206
abu-al-Murajja Sālim ibn-Qānit, 175
Murhaf ibn-Usāmah, *see* 'Aḍud-al-Dīn
Murtafa' ibn-Faḥl, 45
abu-Musaykah al-Iyādi, 64, 65
al-Mustaẓhir, caliph, 205
al-Mu'taman ibn-abi-Ramādah, 48
abu-al-Mutawwaj Muqallad ibn-Nasr ibn-Munqidh, 216, 239
Muthkīr, 73
Muwaffaq-al-Dawlah Sham'ūn, 81–83
al-Muwayliḥ, 53, 54
Muẓaffar ibn-'Ayyāḍ, 214

Nāblus, 164, 167, 168
Naḍrah, daughter of Būzarmāt, 159
Najm-al-Dawlah abu-'Abdallāh Muḥammad, 53
Najm-al-Dawlah Mālik ibn-Sālim, 119
Najm-al-Dīn abu-Ṭālib ibn-'Ali-Kurd, 227
Najm-al-Dīn ibn-Masāl, 31, 32
Najm-al-Dīn Īlghāzi ibn-Urtuq, 67, 69, 120, 148, 149
Nasībīn [Nisibis], 223
Nāsir-al-Dawlah Kāmil ibn-Muqallad, 121
Nāsir-al-Dīn Nasr ibn-'Abbās, 43–49, 52–55, 123
Nāsir-al-Dīn Sunqur, 186
Nāsir-al-Dīn Yāqūt, 40
Nasr, *see* Nāsir-al-Dīn Nasr ibn-'Abbās
Nasr ibn-Buraykah, 152
Nile, 225
Niqūla, mameluke, 247
Numayr al-'Allārūzi, 106, 107
Nūr-al-Dīn Balak, 150
Nūr-al-Dīn ibn-Zanki, 34, 39, 42, 49, 60, 61, 184, 221, 226, 227

Orontes (al-'Āsi), 121

Philip the knight, 69
Prophet (Muḥammad), the, 77, 123, 124, 194, 197, 203, 208, 218, 255

Qāḍi-al-Quḍāh al-Shāmi, 203
al-Qadmūs, 141
Qafjāq, al-Amīr, 187–189
al-Qal'ah, *see* Castle of Ja'bar
Qal'ah-Ja'bar, *see* Castle of Ja'bar
Qara-Ḥiṣār, 227
Qarāfitah, hill, 173
banu-Qarāja, 74
abu-al-Qasam al-Khiḍr ibn-Muslim, 202, 204
Qatr-al-Nada, 55
Qaymāz, 58
Qays ibn-al-Khatīm, 77
Qunayb ibn-Mālik, 145
al-Qutayyifah, 180
Qutb-al-Dīn Khusru ibn-Talīl, 184

Ra'bān, 61
Rabī'ah, 53
Rābiyah-al-Qarāmitah, 93
Rafaniyyah, 73, 107, 117, 158
Rāfi' al-Kilābi, 74
Rāfi' ibn-Sūtakīn, 75
Rafūl, daughter of abu-al-Jaysh, 179
al-Raḥabah, 102
Rajab al-'Abd, 131
al-Raqīm, 39
al-Raqqah, 119, 128
al-Rāshid, caliph, 25
Rā'ūl, Frankish captive, 160
Rayhāniyyah, 30, 31
Riḍwān ibn-al-Walakhshi, 55–59
Riḍwān ibn-Tāj-al-Dawlah Tutush, 82, 83
Robert, lord of Ṣihyawn, 149
Roger [*rūjār*], 67, 105, 117, 148
banu-al-Ru'ām, 138
Rūbāl, 231
al-Ruha, 144
al-Rūj, 106
Rukn-al-Dīn 'Abbās, 32, 43, 44, 46–51, 53, 55, 123

Sābah ibn-Qunayb, 76
Sābiq ibn-Waththāb ibn-Maḥmūd ibn-Ṣāliḥ, 135, 136
Sa'dallāh al-Shaybāni, 136
Sadīd-al-Mulk abu-al-Ḥasan 'Ali ibn-Muqallad ibn-Nasr ibn-Munqidh, 82, 154, 216, 217
Sahl ibn-abi-Ghānim, 96
Sahri, al-Ra'īs, 107
Sa'īd-al-Dawlah, 46
Saladin, *see* Yūsuf ibn-Ayyūb
Ṣalāḥ-al-Dīn, *see* Muḥammad ibn-Ayyūb al-Ghisyāni
Sālim, bath-keeper, 165
Sālim al-'Ijāzi, 157
Ṣalkhad, 56
ibn-al-Sallār, *see* Sayf-al-Dīn 'Ali
Samāwah, 214
al-Ṣamṣām, Amīr, 249, 250

Şandūdiya, 205
Şandūq, slave, 171
Sarhank ibn-abi-Manṣūr, 63, 64, 91
Sarūj, 160
Sawmān [Shawmān ?], 72
Sayf-al-Dawlah Khalaf ibn-Mulā'ib al-Ashhabi, 80, 83, 125, 156, 157
Sayf-al-Dawlah Zanki ibn-Qarāja, 213
Sayf-al-Dīn 'Ali ibn-al-Sallār, 31–34, 38, 42–43, 45
Sayf-al-Dīn Suwār, 172, 173
Shābūrah Palace, 45
Shāhanshāh, 213
Shammās, *see* Sābiq ibn-Waththāb
Shams-al-Khawāss Āltūntāsh, 107
Sham'ūn, *see* Muwaffaq-al-Dawlah
Shārūf, 131
Shayzar, 26, 27, 67, 68, 72, 76, 85, 96–99, 105–108, 116, 121, 122, 130, 133, 135, 137, 139, 140, 143, 144, 146, 148, 150, 155, 158, 159, 163, 171, 173, 175, 177, 178, 181, 190, 192, 193, 213, 217, 221, 222, 228, 229, 234–236, 238, 248, 249
Shihāb-al-Dīn abu-al-Fatḥ al-Muẓaffar ibn-As'ad, 205
Shihāb-al-Dīn Aḥmad ibn-Şalāḥ-al-Dīn, 127, 128
Shihāb-al-Dīn Maḥmūd ibn-Būri ibn-Ţughdakīn, 127, 221, 224
Shihāb-al-Dīn Maḥmūd ibn-Qarāja, 63, 65, 66, 74–76, 84, 127, 131, 235
Shihāb-al-Dīn Maḥmūd ibn-Tāj-al-Mulūk, *see* Shihāb-al-Dīn Maḥmūd ibn-Būri
Shihāb-al-Dīn Mālik ibn-Sālim ibn-Mālik, 128, 159, 253
Shihāb-al-Dīn Mālik ibn-Shams-al-Dawlah, *see* Shihāb-al-Dīn Mālik ibn-Sālim
Shujā'-al-Dawlah Māḍi, 91
Sībawayhi, 237, 238
Sinān-al-Dawlah Shabīb ibn-Ḥamīd ibn-Ḥumayd, 153
Sinbis, 50
Sinjār, 223
Sirāj-al-Dīn abu-Ţāhir Ibrāhīm ibn-Ḥusayn, 202
Sūdānese, 30, 32, 33, 55, 59
banu-al-Şūfi, 158
Sultan Malik-Shāh, *see* Malik-Shāh
Sunqur Dirāz, 102
Sūnuj, attendant, 182
Sūq al-Suyūfiyyīn, 45
Şūr [Tyre], 166
al-Suwaydiyyah, 150
Suwayqah Amīr-al-Juyūsh, 31
Syria, 26, 48–50, 54, 55, 57, 117, 124, 149, 180, 192

Ţabarayyah, *see* Tiberias
Tadmur [Palmyra], 99
al-Tafsīr al-Kabīr, 81
Tāj-al-Dawlah Tutush, 82, 83, 177
Ţalā'i' ibn-Ruzzīk, 48–50, 52, 60
Ţalḥah, 50
Tamīrak, 102
Tancred, 94–100, 126
Ta'nīl, 184
Tarūs, son of Rūbāl, 231
Tayy, tribe, 36, 53
Tell-al-Tulūl, 98, 136
Tell-al-Turmusi, 98
Tell-Bāshir, 144
Tell-Milḥ, 84, 85
Tell-Mujāhid, 127
Tell-Şaqrūn, 235
Tell-Sikkīn, 243
Templars, 163, 164
Thābit, physician, 162
Theodoros Sophianos, 169
Theophile the Frank, 102, 157
Tiberias [Ţabarayyah], 34, 35, 166
Tirād ibn-Wahīb al-Numayri, 128
Tripoli, 78, 84, 108, 237
Ţughdakīn, Atābek, 56, 57, 120, 149, 150
al-Ţūr [Mt Sinai], 109
abu-Turāb Ḥaydarah ibn-Qatrmatar, 244
Turcopoles, 79
Turk, 89, 101, 104, 224
Turkomans, 57, 74
Turks, 51, 104, 177
Tyre, *see* Şūr

banu-Ubayy, 36
'Umar, al-Salār, 173
al-'Uqāb, the poet, 99
Usāmah ibn-Munqidh, 41, 53, 60, 74, 92, 114, 201, 242
Uswān, 60
Uzbeh, Amīr-al-Juyūsh, 102, 105

Valley of Bohemond, 67
Vizierate Palace, 31, 32, 44

Wādi-al-Qanāṭir, 248
Wādi-Ḥalbūn, 182
Wādi-ibn-al-Aḥmar, 229

Wādi-Mūsa, 53
Abu-al-Wafā' Tamīm, 217
William of Bures, 166
William Jiba, 110, 111

al-Yaḥshūr, falcon, 232–236, 241
Yaḥya, bonesetter, 144
Yaḥya ibn-Ṣāfi al-A'sar, 96
Yānis, 238
Yāqūt al-Ṭawīl, 79
Yārūq, 112
Yasmālikh, 229
Yubna, 42
Yuḥanna ibn-Buṭlān, 214–216
Yūnān, al-Ra'īs, 108, 109
Yūsuf, groom, 174, 242
Yūsuf, son of al-Ḥāfiẓ, 47
Yūsuf ibn-abi-al-Gharīb, 143
Yūsuf ibn-Ayyūb (Saladin), 195

al-Ẓāfir bi-Amr-Allāh, 31, 43–46, 54
Zahr-al-Dawlah Bakhtiyār al-Qubruṣi, 116
Zalīn, 99
al-Zammarrakal, 72, 73
Zanki, *see* 'Imad-al-Dīn Zanki
Zanki ibn-Bursuq, 102
Zarqā' al-Yamāmah, 156
Zarzūr Bādiyah, 252
Zayd the surgeon, 80
Zayn-al-Dīn 'Ali Kūjak, 186, 209
Zayn-al-Dīn Ismā'īl ibn-'Umar ibn-Bakhtiyār, 173
Zurayq, 50

www.ingramcontent.com/pod-product-compliance
Ingram Content Group UK Ltd.
Pitfield, Milton Keynes, MK11 3LW, UK
UKHW031312030225
4420UKWH00050B/1045

9 788197 662621